STONEWALL JACKSON

The Black Man's Friend

STONEWALL JACKSON

The Black Man's Friend

RICHARD G. WILLIAMS JR.

CUMBERLAND HOUSE

NASHVILLE, TENNESSEE

B JACKSON

STONEWALL JACKSON: THE BLACK MAN'S FRIEND
PUBLISHED BY CUMBERLAND HOUSE PUBLISHING, INC.
431 Harding Industrial Drive
Nashville, Tennessee 37211

All Scripture quotations are taken from the King James Version of the Holy Bible.

Cover design by Gore Studio, Nashville, Tennessee

Library of Congress Cataloging-in-Publication Data
  Williams, Richard G., 1958–
    Stonewall Jackson : the Black man's friend / Richard G. Williams, Jr.
        p.   cm.
    Includes index.
    ISBN-13: 978-1-58182-565-7 (hardcover : alk. paper)
    ISBN-10: 1-58182-565-X (hardcover : alk. paper)
    1. Jackson, Stonewall, 1824–1863—Relations with slaves. 2. Jackson, Stonewall, 1824–1863—Relations with free African Americans. 3. Jackson, Stonewall, 1824–1863—Relations with African Americans. 4. Generals—Confederate States of America—Biography. 5. Sunday school teachers—Virginia—Lexington—Biography. 6. Slaves—Virginia—Lexington—History—19th century. 7. Free African Americans—Virginia—Lexington—History—19th century. 8. African Americans—Virginia—Lexington—History—19th century. 9. Lexington (Va.)—Race relations—History—19th century. I. Title.
    E467.1.J15W49 2006
    973.7'3092—dc22   2006016586
    [B]

Printed in the United States of America

1 2 3 4 5 6 7 8 9 10—10 09 08 07 06

To Desmond Radcliff "Raddy" Jackson Sr.
(1913–2005)
and
to all who wish to understand

Take him, ye Africans, he longs for you,
Impartial Savior is his title due:
Wash'd in the fountain of redeeming blood,
You shall be sons, and kings, and priests to God.

—*Phillis Wheatley*

He was indeed the black man's friend.

—*Robert Lewis Dabney*

He was emphatically the black man's friend.

—*William Spottswood White*

His prayers were very attractive to the slaves and he was often spoken of in Lexington as the black man's friend.

—*Henry Boley*

CONTENTS

FOREWORD

OR OVER A CENTURY, it has seemed almost fashionable to relegate Gen. Thomas J. "Stonewall" Jackson to the category of oddballs. He did have quirky ideas about health and diet, but no more than countless Americans today. He was uncomfortable in general society and not an accomplished conversationalist, yet the same can be said now of people who are not branded as eccentrics.

In truth, while Jackson became a great man oblivious to his greatness, many praised his magnificent plainness, his natural shyness, his blind obedience to duty. The key to Jackson the man, however, lay in Jackson the Christian.

The faith that Jackson treasured in adulthood was a long time developing. He had grown up without memory of a father. Jackson was twenty-seven years old when, in 1851, he dedicated his life to God. Hence, he eagerly accepted God as his heavenly father, and he came to love that parent with all the adoration of a little child. Moses Hoge, the most prominent minister in Civil War Richmond, did not exaggerate when he observed: "To attempt to portray the life of Jackson while leaving out the religious element would be like undertaking to describe Switzerland without making mention of the Alps."

Jackson treated the Bible as the literal Word of God. This was especially the case with the Ten Commandments. For example, on the Sabbath he would do nothing secular (such as reading a newspaper). His life to the end was an honest belief in the power of prayer. Of Jackson's ten years as a member of the Lexington, Virginia, Presbyterian Church, one member of the congregation declared: "It would be difficult to find in the entire Church any other member who disciplined himself so strictly, obeyed what he believed to be the will of God so absolutely, prayed so fervently, or found so much happiness in his religion" as did the Virginia Military Institute professor.

Those feelings carried over into the two years of civil war in which Jackson became arguably the most esteemed soldier in the world. Yet he considered himself only the instrument of his Father. At the moment of one of his victories, Jackson turned to an aide and, with a sublime look on his face, exulted: "He who does not see the hand of God in this is blind, sir, blind!"

A sister-in-law accurately summarized Jackson's brilliant general-ship. "To serve his country, to do God's will, to make as short work as possible of the fearful struggle, to be ready for death if at any moment it should come to him—these were the uppermost ideals of his mind, and he would put aside, with an impatient expression the words of confi-dence and praise that would be lavished upon him. 'Give God the glory' would be his curt reply."

Many field commanders in American history have been God-fearing; none has ever been so God-loving.

A few writers have dismissed Jackson's views on slavery as rational-izing or overly simplistic. They overlook the complete faith inherent in the man.

Subservience to God's will overrode every fiber of Jackson's being. God in his judgment, Jackson concluded, had decreed that a race of Americans should be in bondage at that time. Man had no right to challenge the deci-sions of the Almighty. Jackson therefore accepted God's decree, even though he viewed the system of enslavement without enthusiasm. He could not change society; but at the same time, Jackson fervently believed that all of God's children, regardless of color, had an equal right to seek the kingdom of heaven. With slaves, Jackson not only followed the Golden Rule—"Do unto others as you would have them do unto you"—in 1855 he organized a Sunday-school class in Lexington solely for blacks. He be-came a spiritual teacher for scores of slaves and freedmen as well as the best friend many of them ever had.

Jackson's extraordinary relationship with African Americans in the Slave South and in the Confederacy deserves a book of its own. That is what Richard Williams has produced. Exhaustively researched, teeming with useful nuggets, and written with an undertone of faith that Jackson himself would have admired, this study clears the air of a lot of myth—accidental and otherwise. The narrative surprises and informs, memorializes and inspires, all at the same time. Williams's analyses reveal clearly that nineteenth-century religiosity, which some writers and reviewers conclude was nonsense, was in fact very much alive.

Stonewall Jackson died a year before the U.S. Congress adopted our national motto. Nevertheless, his life, as well as the lives of so many he touched, was a pursuit of a simple, earthly pilgrimage: "In God We Trust."

—James I. Robertson Jr.
Virginia Tech

INTRODUCTION

He is your friend who pushes you nearer to God.
—*Abraham Kuyper*

Friendship is a responsibility, not an opportunity.
—*Calvin Coolidge*

The past, and all of its lessons, must not be denied.
—*Essie May Washington-Williams*

I WAS FIRST INTRODUCED to Gen. Thomas J. "Stonewall" Jackson by reading a biography[1] when I was in the fourth grade—long before such books began disappearing from the shelves of our politically correct public school libraries. Oddly enough, the school at which I read this biography was formerly a black high school known as Rosenwald in racially segregated Waynesboro, Virginia. This school lies in the beautiful and historic Shenandoah Valley—the same valley where Jackson gained immortality for his unrivaled battle strategies against superior Union numbers, numbers that sometimes were four times his own.

It was 1968. Virginia's "massive resistance" against integrated schools had ended, and I was a student at Rosenwald. The school had been converted to an elementary school for fourth through sixth grades and was now being used for the instruction of both black and white students. The name of the school was changed to Wayne Hills Upper, and my teacher that year was Mrs. McKinney, a dear middle-aged black lady with the gift of teaching. I vividly remember that she always said grace before we marched to the cafeteria for lunch[2] and that she openly wept when she told the class good-bye at the end of that school year, later telling my mother she was going to retire because she could not bear the pain each year as the students she had come to know and love left for the next grade. I also remember Mrs. McKinney's love of history, which she helped to instill in me as she taught the required subject of Virginia history with great interest. It was Mrs. McKinney who first piqued my curiosity about Stonewall Jackson. She was the first African American adult with whom I had close contact, and my class was the last class she taught. My mother always thought she was one of the best teachers I ever had. So did I.

As I read of Jackson in the school library, I imagined myself as one of his "foot cavalry," bravely defending my homeland against the Yankee invaders. Having been born in 1958 in a hospital that was built upon ground that had served as the battle of Waynesboro in March 1865, I grew up with a natural admiration for my ancestors who willingly sacrificed all they possessed to defend hearth and home. My great-great-grandfather, John W. McGann, fought with the Fifty-first Virginia Infantry and defended this very land. His son, Charles L. McGann, my great-grandfather, came to own much of that battlefield that had become apple orchards and, later, a residential area known today as the Tree Streets. His home would pass to my grandmother, then to my father, and then to my brother and me. Like my father before me, I spent many hours playing and roaming the ground that held the blood of those brave soldiers.

Because I am descended from Confederate veterans on both my father's and mother's side of the family, my interest in and connection to the South's struggle has been keen since childhood. As I wrote this book, I was struck by this ironic providence—an African American teacher in recently desegregated Virginia was, in large measure, responsible for introducing me to a love of history and a lifelong study of the South's heroes. It is a peculiar providence, but given the subject matter of this book, an appropriate and fateful one.

On Father's Day in 1997, my son gave me an autographed copy of James I. Robertson's *Stonewall Jackson: The Man, the Soldier, the Legend*. As I devoured this masterpiece that summer, I acquired a renewed fascination of Jackson but became more focused on his "Colored Sunday school." Because I've taught both black and white boys in Sunday school for more than twenty-five years, I was learning about Jackson's successes not only for my benefit but for the benefit of my students. Of course, I could not help but be drawn to the intrigue surrounding what at first glance would seem to be a contradiction: the Confederacy's most feared general and his love for the souls of black men.

This intrigue raised questions. How did this orphan child from a slave-owning family on the frontier of western Virginia come to evangelize blacks with such zeal? So much zeal that he sent contributions for these efforts from the battlefield as he was winning laurels for stunning victories against the Union army. Why did he risk criminal prosecution for his ministry efforts on the behalf of blacks? What motivated Jackson? Who influenced this orphan boy along the way? How did two preachers independently come to describe Jackson as "the black man's friend"? Why were blacks in Lexington drawn to Jackson? Why did they honor and pay tribute to him long after his death and long after they had gained their freedom? Why did many of these blacks who had lived under the curse of slavery help to erect monuments and memorials to Jackson? Why did they weep at his passing? Why do some still honor him today? This book seeks to answer these questions. And all of the answers are centered on Jackson's active Christian faith—especially his faith in the providence of God. And providence seemed to play a part in the timing of the publication of this book as well. I completed the book in the fall of 2005, the 150th anniversary of the year Jackson began his black Sunday-school class. This past May 10, 2006, marked a special 100th anniversary: the placing of a memorial stained-glass window honoring Jackson in an African American church by a former member of this same Sunday-school class.

I was familiar with Jackson's Christianity even before I started my in-depth study of his relationship with the slaves and free blacks of his day. I knew the motivation that drove him to tell his wife, "I will make my army an army of the Living God," was the same motivation that led her to say, "His interest in that race was simply because they had souls to save." That motivation was the gospel of Jesus Christ.

It is impossible to understand Jackson without keeping the influence of Christ's transforming message at the forefront of one's thought, realizing it was always at the forefront of Jackson's. This influence has been noted by many. Confederate Maj. William McLaughlin[3] took note of this influence when he spoke at the unveiling ceremonies of Jackson's bronze statue at his grave site in Lexington on July 21, 1891: "His alliance with eternal realities; his foretaste of the powers of the world to come; his deep and genuine piety, his adherence to the Bible, the Church, and the

Lord's day, his keeping of his own conscience before God and men, are the outstanding traits of a spiritual prince who was greater than anything he did, and whose deeds took rise in his being."[4]

The first dollar offered for this statue was given by some of Jackson's black converts. And it is this particular set of deeds that "took rise in his being" that is the primary focus of this book: Jackson's efforts to befriend African Americans and the fruits of his labors.

I have endeavored to bring together a thorough study and reference resource of the relationship that Jackson enjoyed with his African brethren. The scores of letters, references, and accounts of Jackson's black Sunday-school class and his relationships with other Lexington blacks are scattered in numerous biographies, newspaper clippings, magazine articles, personal letters and accounts, and various other sources. Yet there has been no single source where one could get a full account and understanding of this association, an association that has become almost cryptic with the passage of time. Therefore, I hope to add, in some measure, to the study of not only Jackson but also of Southern Christians as a whole during the late nineteenth century. My love of history, of Southern culture, the power of the gospel and the positive influence it has upon lives were all motivating factors in writing this book.

Jackson's relationships with his Christian brethren crossed and intertwined so frequently it became quite impossible to fully comprehend all the connecting threads of history. I was astounded at how seemingly casual and inconsequential contacts and associations impacted history, often for generations and in many cases to this very day. Everything we say and do, everyone we meet, and everything we read truly "echoes in eternity." This was especially true of the dynamic Christian community that was part of nineteenth-century Lexington, Virginia.

As I studied Jackson's relationships, I witnessed how God providentially weaves friendships and influences in and out of our lives, how He molds men and times to accomplish His will and divine plan. These influences often come unexpectedly and through means scoffed at by secular culture. The frantic pace of modern American society often obscures what is truly important in life: relationships. As Solomon reminds us, "The words of wise men are heard in quiet more than the cry of him that ruleth among fools" (Ecclesiastes 9:17). It is in the quiet shadows of life, far removed from the frenzied pace, where God often speaks to us through the counsel and influence of friends. As George Grant observed, "Friendship is one of the most powerful, though underrated, forces in shaping the destinies of men and nations. . . . Though history is generally recorded as a series of individual achievements or corporate movements, more often than not momentous events are shaped by the hidden persuasions of interpersonal concerns. They are the first fruits of familiarity."[5]

Thomas Jackson's life is confirmation of this truth. By realizing that human relationships are often more complicated than what they may appear to be on the surface, readers may allow Jackson's example to teach us more about how God wants us to treat our fellow man—and learn from him—despite our differences and despite what others may think is proper. Jackson's example teaches us that we cannot always change the difficult circumstances and injustices we see around us, but we can change how we react to them. We can choose to ease the burdens of others. By studying Jackson's life, particularly his interaction with nineteenth-century African Americans, I have been humbled and, I hope, grown wiser. I have gained a greater appreciation for my black brethren and their struggle for freedom and justice in America—often made much more difficult and confusing by their enemies as well as by those who claim to be their friends.

This work is not intended to be an all-encompassing study of Southern slaveholders' relationships with their slaves, nor is it by any means a justification for slavery. Slavery is, in the words of Robert E. Lee, "a moral and political evil." Sufficient material on the mistreatment of slaves and free blacks in nineteenth-century America is abundant and should be studied by all who wish to fully understand America's history.

Understanding this tragic era in our past includes looking at the issue from Jackson's perspective as a representative of many nineteenth-century white Southern Christians. His second wife, Anna, offers a concise but accurate explanation of Jackson's view on the issue of slavery:

It has been said that General Jackson "fought for slavery and the Southern Confederacy with the unshaken conviction that both were to endure." This statement is true with regard to the latter, but I am very

confident that he would never have fought for the sole object of perpetuating slavery. It was for her constitutional rights that the South resisted
the North, and slavery was only comprehended among those rights. He
found the institution a responsible and troublesome one, and I have
heard him say that he would prefer to see the negroes free, but he believed that the Bible taught that slavery was sanctioned by the Creator
himself, who maketh men to differ, and instituted laws for the bond and
the free. He therefore accepted slavery, as it existed in the Southern
States, not as a thing desirable in itself, but as allowed by God for ends
which it was not his business to determine. At the same time, the negroes
had no truer friend, no greater benefactor. Those who were servants in
his own house he treated with the greatest kindness, and never was more
happy or more devoted to any work than that of teaching the colored
children in his Sunday-school.[6]

Many of the quotes and comments by Jackson and his white contemporaries appearing within these pages will seem patronizing, condescending, prejudiced, and even racist. We must resist, however, the temptation
to judge nineteenth-century men by twenty-first-century standards. That
would be unjust, unwise, and lead to false conclusions. Jackson and his
contemporaries were products of their times as we all are. Former slave
Solomon Northup attributed his "master's blindness to the evils of slavery"
to "the influences and associations that had always surrounded him."[7]

It is my prayer that this study of Jackson's relationships with
nineteenth-century blacks as well as whites will shed light on the subject
and provide some balance to the shrill voices condemning all things
Southern, particularly those associated with the Confederacy. These con-
demnations have become daily fare in much of the mainstream media.
War hero, former secretary of the navy under Ronald Reagan, and noted
author James Webb said it best when he wrote:

Even the venerable Robert E. Lee has taken some vicious hits, as dishonest or misinformed advocates among political interest groups and in aca-
demia attempt to twist yesterday's America into a fantasy that might better
serve the political issues of today. The greatest disservice on this count
has been the attempt by these revisionist politicians and academics to de-

fame the entire Confederate Army in a move that can only be termed the Nazification of the Confederacy. Often cloaked in the argument over the public display of the Confederate battle flag, the syllogism goes something like this: Slavery was evil. The soldiers of the Confederacy fought for a system that wished to preserve it. Therefore they were evil as well, and any attempt to honor their service is a veiled effort to glorify the cause of slavery.

This blatant use of the "race card" in order to inflame their political and academic constituencies is a tired, seemingly endless game that is itself perhaps the greatest legacy of the Civil War's aftermath. But in this case it dishonors hundreds of thousands of men who can defend themselves only through the voices of their descendants.[8]

Yet some voices defending Southern heritage are just as shrill and dishonoring to the worthy heritage of black Americans, each side shouting so loudly that they cannot hear the other. Both sides would be well advised to remember the apostle Paul's admonition to "speak the truth in love." More desirous of being right than being righteous, some defenders of Southern culture and heritage have done more harm than good to their cause.

One of the more reasoned voices to recently enter this fray is an unlikely one. Essie May Washington-Williams's mother was a black maid, Carrie Butler Clark, and Essie May's father was the late Strom Thurmond of South Carolina. In late 2003, after Thurmond's death in July of that year, Mrs. Washington-Williams revealed her parentage.

In 2005, she wrote an autobiography titled *Dear Senator* addressing the discrimination and prejudice she endured in the South as well as the North and of her distant and secret relationship with her father. In the closing pages of her painful memoir, she courageously defends her decision to join the United Daughters of the Confederacy (UDC):

As for the UDC, many people have raised the question of how a black person could consider joining a society that honors a past of racism. The answers are much more complex than the question. First of all, the United Daughters of the Confederacy is anything but a racist cabal of ancestors of slave owners. It is not the Simon Legree Society. The Confederacy was composed of many great Americans: Judah P. Benjamin, Robert E. Lee, Lucius Lamar, Wade Hampton. These were hardly Klansmen, just as the Civil War was hardly a battle to the death over slavery alone. There were many black slave owners as well, many free people of color who supported the Confederacy. There were also slaves who fought and died for the Confederacy. Were they forced by their masters, or were they loyal to their masters' cause? Or were there other compelling reasons that led them to fight and die in this terrible war? I wanted to join the UDC to find the answers, to learn more about this key conflict that defined America and continues to define us. I've lived my life believing that knowledge was power, and certainly empowering. I want all the knowledge I can get. And I want my children and my grandchildren to connect to all aspects of their heritage, whether patriot or politician, slave or slave owner. The past, and all of its lessons, must not be denied.[9]

Jackson once inquired of a companion, "Did you ever think, sir, what an opportunity a battlefield affords liars?"[10] The writing, telling, and interpretation of history can also be a battlefield, and as Jackson so astutely observed, "an opportunity for liars." But I believe the truth in Jackson's heart will be confirmed by his actions, comments, letters, and the testimony of his black and white contemporaries and will leave little doubt that Thomas J. "Stonewall" Jackson was, without question, the black man's friend.

—Richard G. Williams Jr.
Huckleberry Hollow, Virginia

CHRONOLOGY

1824	Born the third child of Jonathan and Julia Beckwith Neale Jackson on January 21 in Clarksburg, Virginia (now West Virginia).
1826	Jackson's father dies on March 26.
1830	Jackson's mother marries Blake B. Woodson. Thomas moves in with his stepgrandmother, Mrs. Edward Jackson, and the rest of the family, including Uncle Cummins Jackson, at Jackson's Mill near Weston, Virginia (now West Virginia)
1831	Jackson's mother dies on December 4.
1841	Jackson is appointed constable of Lewis County, Virginia (West Virginia) on June 8.
1842	Jackson is admitted to West Point on July 1.
1846	Jackson graduates from West Point seventeenth out of a class of sixty with the rank of second lieutenant of artillery.
1847	Fights in the Mexican War and is promoted to the brevet rank of major.
1848	Stationed at Fort Hamilton, Long Island, New York. Jackson makes a public profession of faith in Christ and is baptized.
1850	Transferred to various stations in Florida.
1851	Appointed professor of artillery tactics and natural philosophy at the Virginia Military Institute (VMI) in Lexington, Virginia. He reports to VMI on August 13. He becomes a member of the Lexington Presbyterian Church on November 22.
1853	Marries Elinor "Ellie" Junkin, daughter of the Reverend Dr. George Junkin, president of Washington College.
1854	Jackson's wife, Ellie, along with their infant child, die during childbirth.

1855	Jackson begins his "Colored Sabbath-school" in the autumn.
1856	Jackson tours Europe during the summer months.
1857	Jackson marries Mary Anna Morrison on July 16.
1859	Jackson leads a company of VMI cadets to Harpers Ferry and follows radical abolitionist John Brown to the gallows in Charlestown, Virginia (West Virginia)
1861–63	On April 21, 1861, Jackson leaves Lexington with 175 VMI cadets at the outbreak of the War Between the States.[1] Jackson distinguishes himself during the ensuing two years as a brilliant and courageous officer and strategist. On May 2, 1863, Jackson is mistaken for the enemy and shot by men of the Eighteenth North Carolina. Jackson's arm is amputated, and he succumbs to complications from his wound on May 10. He is laid to rest in Lexington on May 15, 1863.

Jackson's Marriages and His Descendants

Jackson married twice. On August 4, 1853, Jackson married Elinor Junkin (1825–54), daughter of George Junkin and Julia Miller Junkin. Elinor died in childbirth on October 22, 1854. Their child, a son, was stillborn. On July 16, 1857, Jackson married Mary Anna Morrison (1831–1915), daughter of Robert Hall Morrison and Mary Graham Morrison. Anna's family resided in North Carolina; her father was the retired president of Davidson College. Anna gave birth to a daughter, Mary Graham, on April 30, 1858; the baby died less than a month later. In November 1862, Anna bore a daughter, Julia Laura, the only Jackson child to survive into adulthood. She married William E. Christian in 1885; she died of typhoid fever in 1889, at the age of twenty-six. Her children were Julia Jackson Christian (1887–1991; married Edmund R. Preston) and Thomas Jonathan Jackson Christian (1888–1952; married three times). Both of Jackson's grandchildren had several children; thus there are many living descendants of Stonewall Jackson.—*From the Virginia Military Institute Archives*

STONEWALL JACKSON
The Black Man's Friend

1

Let the Oppressed Go Free

Southern Slaves and the Gospel

And ye shall know the truth, and the truth shall make you free.
—*John 8:32*

I believe [the Negro] is destined to preach a lesson of supreme trust in God and loyalty to his country, even when his country has not been at all times loyal to him.
—*Booker T. Washington*

Let us no more contend, nor blame each other, blamed enough elsewhere, but strive in offices of love, how we may lighten each other's burden, in our share of woe.
—*John Milton*

CHIMBORAZO HOSPITAL IN RICHMOND, Virginia, was a most depressing place to be in March 1865. The doctors and staff were in dire straits, as were the wounded and dying Confederate soldiers who languished there. Medical supplies were in short supply, especially morphine. The gloom of death permeated the halls and stalked the wounded. Pain was the soldiers' constant companion, and routine sicknesses and infections were often fatal. Unsanitary conditions made the situation even worse. One out of every ten Confederates brought to Chimborazo with diarrhea or dysentery died. The overall mortality rate was 20 percent, which was actually good by nineteenth-century standards. Mixed with the stench of sweat and gangrene was the scent of the day's "medicines": turpentine, camphor, castor oil, and whiskey.

My great-great-grandfather, John Meredith Crutchfield, was one of the soldiers at Chimborazo in the closing days of the War Between the States. Taken prisoner after being wounded at the battle of Piedmont the year before, he was marched to the infamous Federal prison in Indiana known as Camp Morton. There he suffered along with the rest. One prisoner described witnessing a Yankee guard take a prisoner outside when the temperature was below zero and give him a bath with a broom. "The fiendish deed was repeated a second time."[1] That prisoner subsequently died.

Transferred to Chimborazo on March 10, 1865, my great-great-grandfather died there on March 28, succumbing to his wounds and the ill treatment he had endured at Camp Morton. His widow died not knowing what became of him.[2]

Yet even in the cruel despair of war and death, God often sends hope. In the final days of the war, hope came to Chimborazo in the form of a preacher. This particular preacher was required to obtain special permission from the Confederate authorities to minister to the wounded at Chimborazo. But he sincerely wanted to help these men. He knew what it was to suffer. Permission was granted, and the preacher roamed the 150 wards of the hospital, praying with and for the wounded and dying. It was the perfect mission field for a minister of the gospel—the chance to share eternal salvation with those facing eternity, a chance to comfort the comfortless and to befriend the friendless. But there was something unusual about this preacher. He had no church, no formal education, and he was owned by a white man. The preacher's name was John Jasper. William E. Hatcher wrote of Jasper's unusual duties: "It was no idle entertainment provided by a grotesque player. He always had a message for the sorrowful. There is no extended record of his labours in the hospitals, but the simple fact is that he, a negro labourer with rude speech, was welcomed by these sufferers and heard with undying interest; no wonder they liked him. . . . Wherever he went, the Anglo-Saxon waived all racial prejudices and drank the truth in as it poured in crystal streams from his lips."[3]

John Jasper was born into slavery, the twenty-fourth child of Philip and Tina Jasper, on Independence Day in 1812. His mother was a devout Christian and prayed God would call her son to become a preacher. But as a young man, Jasper became bitter after his master cruelly separated him from his first wife. His bitterness caused him to sink into a lascivious lifestyle. He was eventually purchased by a Richmond businessman, Samuel Hardgrove, who was a deacon and a devout member of the First Baptist Church. His 1862 obituary noted him as "a great citizen, businessman and Christian." Hardgrove's concern for Jasper's spiritual welfare soon became obvious.

Hardgrove prayed earnestly for Jasper's conversion. And it was largely due to his kindness that Jasper acquired a love for the white race even though it was the white race who denied him his freedom. Jasper would often speak of Hardgrove's piety and kindness and the influence he had on his life.

In July 1839, Jasper was "stemmin' tobacco" (removing the leaves from the plant stems) in Hardgrove's warehouse. There, among scores of other slaves, the air heavy with humidity and the pungent sweet smell of tobacco, John Jasper accepted Christ as his Savior. As Jasper's tears mingled with the sweat on his face, he could not contain the joy of his salvation. He clapped his hands, alternately laughing and weeping as he, at first quietly and cautiously and then raucously, went from co-worker to co-worker, hugging, shaking hands, rejoicing in Christ. Soon the excitement caught the attention of the overseer, who reported the ruckus to Hardgrove. Hardgrove immediately sent for Jasper. After hearing the story of his redemption, the two men wept together.

In the black dialect of his day, Jasper relates what happened next: "Den Marse Sam did a thing dat nearly made me drop ter de flo'. He git out uv his chair an' walk over ter me an' give me his han', an' he say: 'John, I wish you mighty well. Your Savior is mine, an' we are bruthers in de Lord.' Wen he say dat I turn 'roun' an' put my arm agin de wall, an' put my fis' in my mouf ter keep from shoutin'."

By now Hardgrove was overcome with emotion, and, according to Jasper,

Marse Sam's face wuz rainin' tears, an' he say: "John, you needn' wurk no mo' terday. I give you holiday . . . go up ter de house an' tell your mother; go roun' ter your neighbors an' tell dem; go enywhere you wan ter an' tell de good news. It'll do you good, do dem good, an help ter honor your

Lord an' Savior." Af'er awhile Marse Sam lif' up dem kin' black eyes uv his an' say: "Keep tellin' it, John . . . wherever you go, tell it!"[4]

Though illiterate at the time of his conversion, Jasper soon learned to read and was a much sought-after preacher, especially for slave funerals. He became a leader among his people, and when the Confederate capital fell and descended into chaos in April 1865, Jasper stood in the streets of Richmond and pleaded with looters: "Richmond has fallen! We are free! But in the name of God let us act like men!"[5]

In the winter of 1867, Jasper became the first black minister to organize a church in postwar Richmond. His first church building was an abandoned Confederate horse stable on Brown's Island in the James River.

The congregation grew quickly, and after a few short years and several moves, Sixth Mount Zion Baptist Church occupied a beautiful brick edifice in what was known at that time as "Little Africa." For more than thirty years, Jasper preached and ministered to black and white alike from the pulpit of this church. Sixth Mount Zion is still at the same spot and is a vibrant ministry to this day. There is a room at the church set aside and dedicated to Jasper's memory, containing many artifacts from his years there as pastor. Jasper's influence in the life of old Richmond is impressive. The mayor of Richmond still opens city council meetings with a gavel fashioned from wood taken from Jasper's home after it was torn down.

It was Jasper's preaching style and passionate love for God that served as the principal attraction through his years at Sixth Mount Zion. He set an example of perseverance, faith, and humility and was a model of the power of Christ's forgiveness and love. Though Jasper was often treated unjustly, he never harbored any bitterness. He rose to prominence and preached to legislators, governors, and other men of renown. He once preached before the Virginia legislature and stated, "I've read in the Bible that Pharaoh was an awful liar, just like they tell me most politicians are."[6]

On many occasions, white pastors in Richmond could find their missing members at Jasper's church, their faces streaked with tears as Jasper preached a red-hot gospel message filled with love and compassion.

On Sunday, March 28, 1901, at the age of eighty-eight, he mounted his pulpit for the last time. His congregation sensed something was amiss, and many wept. Jasper himself sensed the end was near. But this battle-hardened gospel warrior who had overcome slavery, lack of education, and prejudice—and accomplished more in thirty years than what most white men in his day accomplished in a lifetime—did not shrink from the final enemy: "My chillun, my work on earth is done! I'se no mo' skeered uv death dan uv a hossfly." He preached his final sermon, walked slowly back to his home, and went to his room to rest. Late in the afternoon the ebony soldier of the cross stirred and whispered his last words: "I have finished my work. I am waiting at the River, looking across for further orders."[7]

Exactly thirty-six years to the day, my own great-great-grandfather had crossed that same eternal river from Chimborazo hospital. Perhaps John Jasper was there with him when he crossed. Perhaps the black slave preacher and white Confederate soldier were reunited on the far bank.

This tobacco-house miracle should touch the most calloused and skeptical heart—the master weeping and rejoicing at the slave's newfound faith in Christ; the slave barely able to contain his joy—the cross of Christ uniting master and slave in brotherly love. The sins of slavery covered by the love of God—"Love covereth all sins" (Proverbs 10:12)—at least for these two men.

While politicians and prejudices have been dividing black and white folks since our nation's founding, Christ has been uniting them. The account of John Jasper's conversion in a Richmond warehouse is illustrative of the gospel's life-changing impact on Southern slaves and the paradoxical position in which Christian slaves and masters often found themselves. Many times the tables were turned. Numerous other accounts also exist of slaves reaching their white slave masters with the gospel. Princeton University professor Albert J. Raboteau includes one such incident in his book, *Slave Religion:*

I went on to the barn and found my master waiting for me. . . . I began to tell him of my experiences. . . . My master sat watching and listening to me, and then he began to cry. He turned from me and said in a broken voice, "Morte I believe you are a preacher. From now on you can preach to the people here on my place. . . . But tomorrow morning, Sunday, I want you to preach to my family and my neighbors." . . . The next morning . . . I began to preach to my master and the people. My thoughts came so fast that I could hardly speak fast enough. My soul caught on fire, and soon I had them all in tears. . . . I told them that they must be born again and that their souls must be freed from the shackles of hell.[8]

Raboteau observes: "The spectacle of a slave reducing his master and his master's family and friends to tears by preaching to them of *their enslavement* to sin certainly suggests that despite the iron rule of slavery, religion could bend human relationships into some interesting shapes."[9] Interesting indeed.

Before one can comprehend the kind relations and mutual respect Thomas Jonathan Jackson enjoyed with the slaves and free blacks of his day, one must understand this "bending" influence of the gospel on Southern slaves as well as upon Jackson and the South's culture as a whole. Without the influence of Christianity, history would have been much different for the South and for the slaves. White and black, master and slave, free and bond are intricately interlaced in an esoteric mosaic of a shared Christian culture. But this culture includes, along with a very rich heritage, the contradictions and cruelties of slavery, the aftermath and wreckage of Reconstruction, dark decades of lawful discrimination, and ultimately, the mixed results of the civil rights movement. Black and white Southerners share a legacy and a history that includes a bittersweet relationship that is both antithetical and unprecedented. We share the same land, sometimes the same ancestors, and the same history, though from different perspectives. We also share the same God.

The South and the gospel of Jesus Christ have become almost synonymous in American culture. From irreverent jokes about dishonest and immoral Southern preachers that permeate late-night television to the thousands of sincere, Bible-believing Christian congregations—black and white—that dot the landscape of the old Confederacy, the South's connection with old-time religion is fixed in the cultural mindset of America, as well it should be.

Also connected with the old Confederacy is slavery. The institution of slavery was, besides a cruel and sad episode in our history, a complicated and multifaceted practice that still impacts our culture today.

Though it runs contrary to popular thought, Southerners were not alone in establishing or perpetuating the institution of slavery in America. Although most slaves were ultimately purchased by Southerners, the slave trade was established by the North. The institution would never have taken root without the profit-motivated slave-traders of New England.[10] It was Massachusetts in 1641 that passed the first statute establishing slavery in America, and Massachusetts also has the distinction of enacting the nation's first fugitive slave law. The North, no less than the South, was responsible and suffered for the evils of slavery.

As veteran New England journalists Anne Farrow, Joel Lang, and Jenifer Frank wrote in their groundbreaking book, *Complicity: How the North Promoted, Prolonged, and Profited from Slavery:* "Slavery has long been identified in the national consciousness as a Southern institution. The time to bury that myth is overdue. Slavery is a story about America, all of America. . . . Together, over the lives of millions of enslaved men and women, Northerners and Southerners shook hands and made a country."[11] In this fascinating account of the North's connection to the institution of slavery, these writers offer irrefutable evidence as to the source of the North's (especially New York City's) early wealth: "Slave cotton is, in large part, the root of New York's wealth. . . . Cotton was more than just a profitable crop. It was the national currency, the product most responsible for America's explosive growth in the decades before the Civil War. As much as it is linked to the barbaric system of slave labor that raised it, cotton created New York."[12]

The authors further noted, "By some estimates the North took 40 cents of every dollar a planter earned from cotton."[13] And that cotton had been picked by slaves.

Thomas J. Jackson's native Virginia originally resisted the establishment of the slave trade. Beginning about 1700, the General Assembly routinely approved bills that prohibited the importing of slaves, but the bills were consistently overruled by the king of England. The Crown's motive was to protect the profits of New England slave traders. In another attempt to discourage the trade, Virginia legislators steadily increased the tariff on imported slaves in hopes of making the trade less profitable.[14] Moreover, while colonial America bears the most responsibility for slavery gaining a foothold on the continent, it is intellectually dishonest to blame

Americans—North or South—solely for the establishment of slavery in this country. Even National Public Radio acknowledged as much:

> "The slave trade could not have endured for four centuries and carried nearly 12 million people out of Africa without the cooperation of a huge network of African rulers and merchants," says Dr. Robert Harms, a professor of African History at Yale University who has extensively researched the trans-Atlantic slave trade. "Most Americans think that ships would come from the United States or from Europe to Africa and the sailors would just get off and run out and grab a shipload of people and stuff them in the ship and bring them back. And I think that is a very condescending view of Africans. That view suggests that Africans were so disorganized that they could let that happen year after year after year after year," Harm says. "I think we need to see African societies as well-organized societies that participated in the slave trade, because the ruling classes often thought they had something to gain from it."[15]

Virginians grappled with the obvious contradictions contained in America's founding documents. In 1778, Virginia became the first state to outlaw the slave trade, making it the first[16] government in the modern world to criminalize slave traders. Virginia further showed its progressive inclinations regarding slavery by passing legislation in 1782 that encouraged emancipation. That legislation went so far as to require slave owners to support their emancipated slaves who might not be able to sustain themselves in a gainful occupation. The slavery question continued to come up for debate and public discourse until Thomas Jefferson's grandson, Thomas Jefferson Randolph, introduced legislation in the House of Delegates in 1832 that would have ended slavery in Virginia. He proposed an idea that had originated with his grandfather, a proposal that had been defeated by the General Assembly in 1779. Randolph suggested that every male slave born after July 4, 1840, be granted his freedom upon his twenty-first birthday. The legislation would grant the same freedom to female slaves upon their eighteenth birthday. Randolph's bill was defeated by only a "small majority." In fact, the Reverend Randolph McKim (1842–1920), a Confederate chaplain and one-time rector of Christ Church in Alexandria, wrote in *A Soldier's Recollections* that Randolph assured him in 1860 "that emancipation would certainly have been carried the ensuing year, but for the revulsion of feeling which followed the fanatical agitation of the subject by the Abolitionists of the period."[17] And although the bill was defeated, the Virginia legislature "passed a resolution postponing the consideration of the subject till public opinion had further developed."[18] An editorial in the March 6, 1832, *Richmond Whig* praised the legislature's efforts and further noted: "The great mass of Virginia herself triumphs that the slavery question has been taken up by the legislature, that her legislators are grappling with the monster, and they contemplate the distant but ardently desired result [emancipation] as the supreme good which a benevolent Providence could vouchsafe."[19]

Randolph's legislation, had it been enacted, would have eliminated slavery in the Old Dominion within one hundred years. It is quite certain that, as the nation became more progressive with the passing of time and the industrial age revolutionized agrarian economies, the timetable would have been condensed considerably. It is highly improbable that slavery would not have survived the nineteenth century, even without the War Between the States. Thus many Southerners,[20] with Thomas Jackson's Virginia leading the way, knew that slavery's days were numbered and sought to address the issue in ways that were politically feasible, given the economic realities of the times.

The era of slavery in American history is tragic. Millions of human beings were herded like cattle into seagoing vessels and subjected to months of the most horrific conditions imaginable. The Reverend Robert Walsh (1772–1852), a Church of England minister and writer, served on a British ship whose mission was to intercept slave traders off the African coast. Walsh described what he witnessed aboard slave ships:

> She had taken in, on the coast of Africa, 336 males and 226 females, making in all 562, and had been out seventeen days, during which she had thrown overboard 55. The slaves were all inclosed under grated hatchways between decks and stowed so close together that there was no possibility of their lying down or at all changing their position by night or day. . . . Over the hatchway stood a ferocious-looking fellow with a scourge of many twisted thongs in his hand, who was the slave driver of the ship,

and whenever he heard the slightest noise below, he shook it over them and seemed eager to exercise it. I was quite pleased to take this hateful badge out of his hand, and I have kept it ever since as a horrid memorial of reality, should I ever be disposed to forget the scene I witnessed. . . .

The circumstance which struck us most forcibly was how it was possible for such a number of human beings to exist, packed up and wedged together as tight as they could cram, in low cells three feet high . . . and this when the thermometer, exposed to the open sky, was standing in the shade, on our deck, at 89 degrees. . . .

The heat of the horrid places was so great and the odor so offensive that it was quite impossible to enter them, even had there been room.

It was not surprising that they should have endured much sickness and loss of life in their short passage . . . and they had thrown overboard no less than fifty-five, who had died of dysentery and other complaints in that space of time. . . . Indeed, many of the survivors were seen lying about the decks in the last stage of emaciation and in a state of filth and misery not to be looked at. Even-handed justice had visited the effects of this unholy traffic on the crew who were engaged in it. Eight or nine had died, and at that moment six were in hammocks on board in different stages of fever. . . .

In such a place the sense of misery and suffocation is so great that the Negroes, like the English in the Black Hole at Calcutta, are driven to frenzy. They had on one occasion taken a slave vessel in the river Bonny; the slaves were stowed in the narrow space between decks and chained together. They heard a horrible din and tumult among them and could not imagine from what cause it proceeded. They opened the hatches and turned them up on deck. They were manacled together in twos and threes. Their horror may be well conceived when they found a number of them in different stages of suffocation; many of them were foaming at the mouth and in the last agonies—many were dead. A living man was sometimes dragged up, and his companion was a dead body; sometimes of the three attached to the same chain, one was dying and another dead. The tumult they had heard was the frenzy of those suffocating wretches in the last stage of fury and desperation, struggling to extricate themselves. . . . Many destroyed one another in the hopes of procuring room to breathe; men strangled those next to them, and women drove nails into each other's brains. Many unfortunate creatures on other occasions took the first opportunity of leaping overboard and getting rid, in this way, of an intolerable life.[21]

As Joseph was sold by his brothers to the Egyptians, these poor souls were sold by their own race to strangely dressed white men who spoke a language they had never heard before and did not understand. They were then forced by these strangers, with whom they could not communicate, to suffer unimaginable conditions. The emotional pain, sense of loss and fear, and physical abuse experienced by the African slaves cannot be comprehended by anyone outside the experience. As English surgeon Alexander Falconbridge noted in a 1788 account of his experiences aboard a slave ship: "It is not in the power of the human imagination to picture a situation more dreadful or disgusting."[22] Torn from their homeland, families, and separated from all that was familiar and loved, these forlorn human beings were transported to a land unknown to them to be sold at an auction to the highest bidder, with potential purchasers poking and prodding them like livestock, checking their teeth, and examining muscle tone. The Africans were then carted off by their new owners to a plantation in the South, a mill on a river in the North, or a fine house where they were assigned to wait on white families or nurse white infants.

The defenders of what was and what is commendable in Southern culture cannot ignore the cruel injustices of slavery and how the institution as a whole was antithetical to the Christianity that permeates the South to this day as well as to the principles of liberty eloquently articulated in the nation's founding documents. While many nineteenth-century Southern theologians went to great lengths to propound a biblical basis for slavery, and though neither Christ nor Paul ever directly condemned slavery, one cannot reconcile the broader themes of the gospel— liberty, peace, freedom from bondage, reconciliation, and brotherly love—with the institution of slavery. Robert E. Lee offered his opinion on the compatibility of slavery and Christianity: "Their [slaves'] emancipation will sooner result from the mild and melting influence of Christianity, than the storms and tempests of fiery controversy. This influence though slow, is sure. The doctrines and miracles of our Saviour have required nearly two-thousand years to convert but a small part of the human race, and even among Christian nations, what gross errors still exist!"[23]

To argue that slavery and Christianity could peacefully coexist denies the obvious. Since man-stealing and slave-trading was specifically condemned and punishable by death in the Old Testament (see Exodus 21:16: "He that stealeth a man, and selleth him, or if he be found in his hand, he shall surely be put to death"), American slavery was destined for God's judgment from the beginning. Slavery is[24] inherently accompanied by evils and mistrust. And race-based slavery is particularly evil and sinful. Man-stealing, coupled with the haughty, prideful spirit of superiority by nineteenth-century white Americans—North as well as South— invited the judgment of God. God visited the nation with a war that took more lives than all other American wars combined—decimating a generation of white[25] Americans within four terrible years.

Yet many patriotic and prominent Southern Christians believed they were trapped by foreboding circumstances beyond their control. They were uncomfortably aware that the South's future was precarious because of slavery. Most saw the storm clouds of war on the horizon, and they heard what one slave described as "de rumblin' o' de wheels." Many would have agreed with George Washington Parke Custis, the father of Mary Custis Lee and the adopted son of George Washington, who taught his children that slavery was "a curse upon their section by the folly of their ancestors."[26]

While slavery was only one of several issues that brought about the war—economics,[27] states' rights, and cultural and religious differences between the two sections being the other issues—slavery precipitated God's judgment on the nation. The pharisaical attitude of racial superiority further kindled God's wrath. But Thomas J. Jackson was no defender of slavery. He accepted it as the mysterious providence of God and worked to lift the existence of the slaves within his sphere of influence. As James I. Robertson has noted, "Jackson neither apologized for nor spoke in favor of the practice of slavery. He probably opposed the institution. Yet in his mind the Creator had sanctioned slavery, and man had no moral right to challenge its existence. The good Christian slaveholder was one who treated his servants fairly and humanely at all times."[28]

Though cynics will scoff at the seemingly hypocritical notion of a master "who treated his servants fairly and humanely at all times," that was truly the case among many devout Christians in the South. Those who were known to mistreat their slaves were often ostracized by others in the community. In a biography of Mary Washington, the mother of the first president, author Sara Agnes Rice Pryor writes: "We have reason to believe that house servants were treated with the affectionate consideration they deserved . . . this was true of Mary Washington,—that she was kind to her servants, and considerate of their comfort. The man or woman who treated servants with severity was outlawed from the friendship and respect of his neighbors, many of whom at a later day freed their slaves and left them land to live upon."[29]

Of course, not all slaveholders treated their slaves with "affectionate consideration." Yet Thomas Jackson was among those who did what he could for his slaves, given the realities and circumstances of his time. And as previously noted, judging nineteenth-century Americans by modern standards is unjust. Just as an individual is to "grow in grace, and in the knowledge of our Lord and Saviour Jesus Christ" (2 Peter 3:18) so too should a Christian culture and nation.

As years and generations passed, the strong, proud Africans adapted well. They even came to love their new homes and developed a sincere devotion, patriotism, and attachment to their second country. One former slave returning to his home years after the war expressed his sympathies: "Dear old Virginia! A birthplace is always dear, no matter under what circumstances you were born."[30] Another great Virginian, Booker T. Washington, could even go so far as to express a sense of sarcastic humor in the predicament of African Americans: "The Negro is the only citizen of America that came by special invitation and special provision."[31] Author Stephen Mansfield eloquently expressed the slaves bonding with their new homeland:

> Yet through all the dreary decades, something unintended happened. A people cannot live in a land long without it in some way becoming theirs, without its promise and its poetry entering their hearts, no matter how much their neighbors seek to prevent it. And so it was with blacks in America, for America became theirs, too. Despite their chains and illiteracy, their hearts, too, drank in the hope and the dream of the new land and in silence they took possession by faith of an inheritance yet unfulfilled.[32]

Still, these Americans were denied their freedom. No human can be truly happy in bondage. So the slaves prayed and waited. Rebecca Grant tells of her slave mother's fervent prayers: "All de time she'd be prayin' to de Lord. She'd take us chillum to de woods to pick up firewood, and we'd turn around to see her down on her knees behind a stump a prayin'. We'd see her wipin' her eyes wid de corner of her apron, first one eye, den de other, as we come along back. Den, back in de house, down on her knees, she'd be prayin'."[33]

But who taught these Africans to pray? And to *whom* or *what* did they pray? The religion of their fathers' was not one that taught them to petition a loving God. The gods of the Africans had been deities to appease out of fear, not a god one beseeched for blessings and deliverance from bondage.

Did they discover the God of the Bible, the God of the Hebrews on their own? Or had someone introduced them to this God? This God of Joseph, the God of the Hebrews and of Moses—this God of *slaves*—this God of their white *masters*. Had not the Hebrews been held in captivity and slavery for generations? Were not the Hebrews forced to endure years of harsh, cruel treatment at the hands of the Egyptians? Had not the Hebrews been forced to labor for masters with no reward in a land that was not the land of their fathers? Is it any wonder that the African slaves felt an immediate kinship with the Hebrews and their God?

But what of their white *Christian* masters? How could the slave and the slave owner worship the same God? How could the God of the Hebrews who called upon Moses to tell Pharaoh to "let my people go" be the same God the white slave owner worshiped? Many slaves simply held on to the hope that God would eventually free them. What other choice did they have? Many truly believed they were destined for greatness out of their understanding of the miracles of the Old and New Testaments and by God's faithfulness. University of Virginia professor Ervin L. Jordan Jr. wrote of this faith in *Black Confederates and Afro-Yankees in Civil War Virginia:*

On the subject of religion Afro-Virginians widely believed they were God's chosen people and that he had promised to set them free. This "promise" was derived from the example of the Hebrews who had been held in bondage in Egypt. A slave named Aunt Aggy for twenty years had predicted the freeing of the slaves: "I allers knowed it was a-comin. I allers heerd de rumblin' o' de wheels. I allers 'spected to see white folks heaped up dead. An' de Lor', He's kept His promise, an' 'venged His people jes' as I knowed He would."[34]

Another slave later told of hearing older slaves pray for deliverance: "I've heard 'em pray for freedom. I thought it was foolishness, then, but the old time folks always believed they was to be free. It must have been something [re]'vealed unto 'em."[35]

Other historians and scholars have mentioned the "kindred spirit" that Africans felt with Hebrew slaves: "Gazing back at their lives in slavery, former slaves affirmed that they had trusted in the Lord and that the Lord had delivered them. Like the children of Israel of old, they had lived through Egypt and Exodus and the experience had constituted them a peculiar, a chosen, people. This identity was to remain—in the midst of the chaos, disappointment, and disaster of Reconstruction—a bedrock of hope for freed black Christians as it had been for them as slaves."[36]

Black preachers made the association often and with impassioned pleas to their brethren in bonds:

> We have been in the furnace of affliction, and are still, but God only means to separate the dross, and get us so that like the pure metal we may reflect the image of our Purified, who is sitting by to watch the process. I am assured that what God begins, he will bring to an end. We have need of faith, patience and perseverance, to realize the desired result. There must be no looking back to Egypt. Israel passed forty years in the wilderness, because of their unbelief. What if we cannot see right off the green fields of Canaan, Moses could not. He could not even see how to cross the Red Sea. If we would have greater freedom of body, we must free ourselves from the shackles of sin, and especially the sin of unbelief. We must snap the chain of Satan, and educate ourselves and our children.[37]

Ironically, this faith in an avenging and delivering God had been taught to the slaves by those who held them in bondage. From the very beginning, Southern slaveholders expressed an interest in the religious instruction of their slaves and the eternal destiny of their souls. While this may seem the height of hypocrisy to twenty-first-century Christians, looking at the relationship through modern lenses prevents us from grasping the complicated connection slaveholders had with an institution that was "politically unjust, economically unsound, and morally wrong."[38] Both races were trapped in a system that neither wanted: the whites by economic realities, the blacks by law. Thomas Jefferson aptly described how many white Southerners felt about slavery: "We have the wolf by the ear, and we can neither hold him, nor safely let him go. Justice is on one scale, and self-preservation in the other." But as odd as it may seem to us today, this situation did not prevent the two races from sharing beliefs about the God of the Bible. In his classic work, *The Education of the Negro Prior to 1861*, Carter G. Woodson[39] examines how this came about: "The early advocates of the education of Negroes were of three classes: first, masters who desired to increase the economic efficiency of their labor supply; second, sympathetic persons who wished to help the oppressed; and third, zealous missionaries who, believing that the message of divine love came equally to all, taught slaves the English language that they might learn the principles of the Christian religion."[40]

Thomas J. Jackson would fall into the last two categories. Woodson adds: "This charity, however, was not restricted to the narrow circle of the clergy. Believing with churchmen that the Bible is the revelation of God, many laymen contended that no man should be restrained from knowing his Maker directly. Negroes, therefore, almost worshipped the Bible, and their anxiety to read it was their greatest incentive to learn."[41]

In Woodson's words, "the accounts of the successful strivings of Negroes for enlightenment under the most adverse circumstances read like beautiful romances of a people in an heroic age."[42] Carter Woodson was a highly educated black man in 1919 when he completed this work, and he was a product of the culture he was writing about. He was educated at the University of Chicago and earned a PhD from Harvard and also studied at the Sorbonne in Paris. His stature, education, and his position freed him from any intellectual shackles that white society had placed on blacks regarding the history of slavery and the telling of its sad truth. His work is balanced, telling both sides of the story. He was no "Uncle Tom," feigning the white man's veneered version of history. At the end of his preface to *The Education of the Negro,* Woodson writes: "With the hope of vitally interesting some young master mind in this large task, the undersigned has endeavored to narrate in brief how benevolent teachers of both races strove to give the antebellum Negroes the education through which many of them gained freedom in its highest and best sense."[43]

This "freedom in its highest and best sense" included the knowledge of the gospel. For it is the freedom every heart yearns for—not just political freedom but the freedom of forgiveness and freedom from the bondage of sin, the freedom to know the Creator, the freedom to know that the God of the universe loves you, and the freedom that the truth brings to every soul who experiences it. Many of the Africans brought to this country in bondage experienced spiritual freedom in Christ: "For coming to the white man's country as a slave, was the means of making me free in Christ Jesus," exhorted "Uncle Jack," a Virginia slave preacher.[44]

Phillis Wheatley (1753–84) was the first African American to publish a book in America. She expressed this same sentiment:

> ' Twas mercy brought me from my Pagan land,
> Taught my benighted soul to understand
> That there's a God, that there's a Savior too:
> Once I redemption neither sought nor knew.[45]

This does not excuse the sin of man-stealing and the subsequent evils of slavery, yet God often uses apparent injustices to providentially bless His people: "But as for you, ye thought evil against me; but God meant it unto good, to bring to pass, as it is this day, to save much people alive" (Genesis 50:20).

Other imminent scholars of the nineteenth century readily acknowledged the success of the white Christians in their evangelization and education of the black race. John Jasper's biographer, William Eldridge Hatcher, noted:

They know little of the facts who imagine that there was estrangement between the negroes and the whites in the matter of religion. Far from it.

There was much of good fellowship between the whites and negroes in the churches, and the white ministers took notable interest in the religious welfare of the slaves. They often visited them pastorally and gladly talked with them about their salvation. . . . [I]t is worthwhile to let it be understood that it was during their bondage and under the Christian influence of Southern people, that the negroes of the South were made a Christian people. It was the best piece of missionary work ever yet done upon the face of the earth.[46]

As already mentioned, an even lesser known aspect of this unusual relationship was the reciprocal efforts of Christian blacks ministering to whites. In addition to Jasper's work among Confederate soldiers at Chimborazo Hospital, the first known incidence of a black minister officially serving white troops as an army chaplain belongs to the Confederate army. In fact, "Uncle Lewis," as he was known to a particular Tennessee regiment, may have been the first black chaplain in America. His reputation was that of a "devout servant," and due to the shortage of white chaplains, he was asked to conduct religious services. Records indicate that the army credited his efforts with bringing about several "seasons of revival" and a newspaper correspondent wrote, "He is heard with respectful attention, and for earnestness, zeal and sincerity, can be surpassed by none."[47]

The success of the missionary work among the slaves was evident by the time South Carolina seceded from the Union. When the first shot of the war was fired in April 1861, there were approximately 417,000 black Christians in the South.[48] This confirms that white Southerners had a sincere desire to see their slaves benefit from the fruits of the gospel. If the economic and political realities of their day prevented white Christians from freeing the slaves, they could nevertheless endeavor to free their souls. Thomas J. Jackson was destined to undertake such an endeavor, for he had tasted this fruit and had reaped the benefits of a free soul.

2

The Fatherless Findeth Mercy

Stonewall Jackson and the Gospel

Unquestionably the highest privilege granted to a man on earth is to be
admitted into the circle of the friends of God.

—*A. W. Tozer*

We must all measure ourselves by our friendships—apart from the
Scriptures, there is no surer measure to be had in this poor fallen world.

—*Francis A. Schaeffer*

That is one of the great lessons of history. It is simply that in the
providence of God, ordinary people are ultimately the ones who
determine the outcome of human events.

—*George Grant*

STONEWALL JACKSON'S ZEALOUS CHRISTIAN faith is as legendary as his
daring battle tactics. It was this faith and the influence of the gospel
that governed his treatment of blacks, both free and slave. James I.
Robertson noted: "In Jackson's mind slaves were children of God placed
in subordinate situations for reasons only the creator could explain.
Helping them was a missionary effort for Jackson. Their souls had to be
saved. Although Jackson could not alter their social status as slaves, he
could and did display Christian decency to those whose lot it was to be
in bondage."[1]

The path that led Jackson to the cross of Christ contained many
twists and turns. There were also many fellow travelers he met along the
way. Like Christian in John Bunyan's *Pilgrim's Progress,* Jackson would be

assisted and succored as he trod the narrow way. Many who have not studied his faith assume that Jackson did not become seriously interested in Christianity until he settled in Lexington, just prior to the outbreak of the War Between the States. Although it was in Lexington that Jackson's faith matured, his faith in Christ had taken root much earlier. And while it is true that Jackson did not formally unite with a church until he settled in Lexington, he was interested in Bible truths from his youth. Historian Roy Bird Cook observed:

> No student of the life of Jackson can fail to note his constant interest in his spiritual and his physical well-being. Earliest records show an ever-present feeling of a divine leadership which continued to be uppermost in his thoughts and through his entire life. When a boy at the mill, he was influenced by the Baptist faith. Just over the hill from his home was Broad Run Baptist church . . . to the south, in nearby Weston, the Methodists predominated the religious activities of the day. The Jackson family seems to have participated in the affairs of both churches.[2]

Though Jackson was fatherless at the age of two, orphaned by the age of seven, and brought up primarily by an uncle who had no interest in spiritual matters, Tom Jackson was exposed to sound Bible preaching when he attended Harmony Methodist Church. The church was in Weston[3] and had been organized in 1829. The captivating preacher, the Reverend John Mitchell, pastored the church, and his daughter once remarked, "Thomas Jackson, a shy, unobtrusive boy, sat with unabated interest in the long sermon, having walked three miles in order to attend."[4]

There were ample opportunities afforded those who were interested in Bible truths. Jackson had some interest in Baptist organizations as there was a Baptist church near his home. Broad Run Baptist, founded in 1808, often saw young Tom in the congregation. There was also an active Baptist society nearby, at Freeman's Creek, that had been around since 1820. Furthermore, some of Jackson's companions and associations were also conduits for God's "beginning a good work" (Philippians 1:6) in the heart and mind of the future Confederate Joshua. That good work was evident in Jackson's letters as early as 1841 when, at the age of seventeen, Jackson wrote his uncle Alfred Neale about the death of Jackson's brother, Warren: "He died in the hope of a bright immortality at the right hand of his Redeemer."[5]

Interestingly, it is likely that Jackson's early attraction to Christianity was aroused by the slaves in his own household[6] and those of nearby relatives as well as by slaves that lived in his community. Roy Bird Cook noted that "the religious inclinations of Jackson were accentuated by the intense interest in the subject manifested by some of the slaves in the household" and mentioned one slave by name.[7] "Granny Nancy Robinson" was one of the few slaves in the community who had been taught to read and to write, and her faith was well known by all who lived in the area. It is believed she "preached" on at least one occasion at a public gathering. She was a devoted student of the Scriptures, reading and talking to any who would listen. Another slave mentioned by Cook was named "Cecelia." She had direct charge of many of the younger white children in the community, and she was a "follower" of Granny Robinson. In the Jackson household, Cecelia was "housekeeper, cook and seamstress."[8] Both of these women, along with a number of other slaves, were members of the Jackson household and Jackson's extended family right up until the outbreak of the War Between the States.[9] Some of the former Jackson family slaves would, like so many others throughout the South, continue to live with their former masters and work as domestic help after the war. One such example in the Jackson household was Frances Ramsey, known as "Miss Fanny." Fanny holds the distinction of being the only non-Jackson to be buried in the Jackson's Mill cemetery. Her obituary mentioned that she "was with the Jackson family from infancy, more than 100 years and saw generation after generation grow up. She was a young girl when Gen. Stonewall Jackson was born, and helped to care for him in his infancy and youth."[10] Fanny died in 1911 at the age of 112. Another biographer, Jackson's nephew, Thomas Jackson Arnold, confirmed that the Jackson family slaves were close to the children, including young Thomas Jackson: "The family slaves, whose well-known partiality and affection for the white children was ever in evidence, and the sincerity of which was unmistakable."[11]

Jackson's affection for the family slaves was mutual. This is evidenced, in part, by the fact that he kept in touch with them while he was away at West Point.[12] How fitting, then, that Jackson would one day repay these goodly influences by teaching the way of salvation to other African Americans in his Sunday school. These slaves had sown the seeds of friendship and faith in his heart that would one day bless other slaves and free blacks.

There were other Christian influences in Jackson's youth. When Jackson was about sixteen years old, he befriended Joseph Andrew Jackson Lightburn.[13] The Lightburn family had moved from Pennsylvania in 1840 and settled on a farm about three miles from Jackson's home. The Lightburns were great lovers of books and had a large library. This acquaintance proved to be a key influence on Jackson as the two boys shared their interest in the Bible and its life-changing truths. Lightburn possessed a copy of Mason Weems's *The Life of Francis Marion*. Also known as the "Swamp Fox," Marion was a South Carolina hero of the Revolution, and the accounts of his escapades while battling the British surely fired the imagination of many boys. Jackson owned his own Bible and had become quite well versed with many of its precepts. According to those who often saw the two boys together, it was not uncommon to see them studying and discussing the two books. A 1991 interview with one of Lightburn's surviving granddaughters, Ruth Lightburn Bailey, who was one hundred at the time, shed some light on the friendship: "When they were living at home he [Lightburn] would take the grist to Jackson's Mill and when he was waiting his turn he would take a book with him and he and Tom—that was Stonewall—would sit on the river bank and grandfather would read and help Tom with his reading because grandfather had had a chance for more education than Tom at that time."[14]

She recalled that the boys sometimes attended services at Broad Run Baptist Church—a church Lightburn would later pastor (he is buried in the church's cemetery). Bailey added, "Grandfather helped Tom a lot because Tom was an orphan and grandfather furnished the books." Lightburn would eventually influence Jackson in another profound way—a way in which Jackson would be warned not to make public.

Jackson was delighted over the New Testament's assurances of hope and divine love; Francis Marion's wildly successful and heroic guerrilla tactics captivated Lightburn. Only eternity will tell how much influence one boy had on the other and how the hours spent studying the Bible and the biography together impacted each life. It is known that Lightburn, and to a lesser extent Jackson, were devout and seeking to know more about God and His influence upon history. According to James I. Robertson, it was likely that Lightburn had as much influence on awakening Jackson's religious interests as anyone. And it was Lightburn who first planted the seed in Jackson's mind that slavery was wrong and that blacks should be free and taught to read the Bible.[15] This friendship, along with the influence of Granny Robinson, would eventually lead to Jackson's very successful "Sabbath" school for blacks. And though both boys discussed their desire for military careers, both would also be loyal to the cross of Christ and spread the gospel. The two would bravely answer the call of their country and fight in the War Between the States, but they would each choose different loyalties: Jackson fighting for the Confederacy, Lightburn for the Union. Cook noted, "The one surviving the Civil War was ordained a minister in the Baptist Church and continued to fight for Christianity as he had earlier fought for the Union."[16]

Lightburn would, like his boyhood companion, rise to the rank of general and would also distinguish himself at the siege of Vicksburg and at the battle of Atlanta. He, like other ministers in the armies, became known as a "Fighting Parson."[17] Although Jackson would ultimately choose a military career, he too expressed an interest in becoming a minister of the gospel. It is a strange irony. Lightburn fought for the Union, survived the war, and later ministered to a white congregation. Jackson fought for the Confederacy, did not survive the war, but his ministry was primarily to slaves and freedmen before the war.

Jackson once said that he thought he lacked sufficient education to enter the ministry, yet the desire never left him. This fact is evident in a letter addressed to his Aunt Clementine, written from Lexington around 1852:

> The subject of becoming a herald of the Cross has often engaged my attention, and I regard it as the most noble of all professions. It is the profession of our divine Redeemer, and I should not be surprised were I to die upon a foreign field, clad in ministerial armor, fighting under the banner of Jesus. What could be more glorious? But my conviction is that I am doing good here, and that for the present I am where God would have me.

Within the last few days I have felt an unusual religious joy. I do rejoice to walk in the love of God.[18]

Considering Jackson's dynamic faith and his active efforts in spreading the gospel, had he survived the war, it is plausible that he would have become a minister. Further evidence of this is the makeup of Jackson's staff and confidantes during the war. Most were devout Christians; Jackson preferred men who feared God over those who did not. His promotion of "divine services" and his encouragement for the work of the chaplaincy in his army are further indications that his activities always contained an element of the spiritual.

Jackson's interest in Christianity as a youth was more than academic. It was obvious from the accounts and testimony of others that religion influenced his moral character. He was known to be fair, honest, and upright in all his dealings. He would unhesitatingly endeavor to right a wrong if it were in his power to do so. His cousin William E. Arnold once told of one of these "righting a wrong" incidents: "Thomas was a pupil and whilst on the way to school an overgrown rustic behaved rudely toward two of the girls. He was fired at his cowardly conduct and told him that he must apologize to them at once or he would thrash him. The big rustic, supposing that he was an overmatch for him, declined to do so, whereupon he pitched into him and gave him a severe pounding."[19]

There is no further record that Jackson ever had to repeat the lesson in gentlemanly manners to the "overgrown rustic." Arnold would later write in the *Weston Democrat*: "He was a youth of exemplary habits. . . . [H]e was one of the most matter-of-fact persons who never would give up an undertaking until he accomplished his object."[20]

Further confirmation of Jackson's principled character comes from an encounter with a Col. John Talbott as Jackson was en route to deliver a fish to Weston's gunsmith, Conrad Kester. Jackson had become quite a fisherman, living on the West Fork River that flowed by his uncle's mill. He would catch and sell what he could and use the money to purchase books. One morning, Jackson was passing by the Talbott home with a desirable three-foot pike slung over his shoulder—the fish still fresh from a morning adventure on the river. Talbott called out to him, asking him what he would take for the fish. Jackson replied, "This fish is sold,

Colonel Talbott." Talbott was not satisfied with that answer and offered Jackson a dollar for the catch. "I can't take it, Colonel Talbott; this fish is sold to Mr. Kester." Talbott raised his offer twenty-five cents, noting there was no way Kester would match that price. Jackson's sense of duty and integrity manifested itself clearly. "Colonel Talbott, I have an agreement with Mr. Kester to furnish him fish of a certain length for fifty cents each. He has taken some from me a little shorter than that; now he is going to get this big fish for fifty cents."[21] When Kester heard of the story, he too offered Jackson a dollar, but Jackson refused it for the same reason he had expressed to Talbott.

Tom Jackson's cousin Sylvanus White wrote about Jackson to a relative: "He was a great favorite of mine, one of the most sincere, upright, polite persons I ever knew. The biographies written of him as to his early life are in many respects erroneous."[22]

Another acquaintance, a former schoolmate, wrote in the *Clarksburg Telegram* in 1894: "Tom was always an uncommonly behaved lad, a gentleman from a boy up, just and kind to everyone."[23] Biographer Roy Bird Cook noted that "his strict adherence to truth, his unfailing honesty, and his courage are still proverbial in the community."[24]

At the age of seventeen, Jackson was appointed to the position of "constable"—the equivalent of a deputy sheriff. This position carried the responsibility of serving court papers, levying property for debts, etc. Jackson would hold the position for ten months. His sound moral character, inspired by his knowledge of the Bible, was again manifested on several occasions as he performed his duties. One account reports that Jackson was ordered by the court to enforce an order against a penniless widow. According to this version of the incident, Jackson paid the debt himself "and resigned his office."[25]

Both James Robertson and Roy Bird Cook relate a similar story in their biographies of Jackson, their versions probably being closer to the truth. It seems that the widow in question had been awarded a judgment by the court for a debt owed to her by a not-so-reputable preacher named Holt. Jackson was assigned to collect the sum owed, but Holt failed to meet him as he had agreed. According to Robertson, "Jackson paid the widow from his own pocket and said nothing more about the incident."[26] A few days afterward, Jackson chanced to surprise Holt near a blacksmith shop in Weston and forced him off his horse. Evidently, Holt paid up "either in cash or with the horse." Jackson may have been reminded of Solomon's words, "He that hath pity upon the poor lendeth unto the LORD; and that which he hath given will he pay him again" (Proverbs 19:17).

The biblical principles that Jackson embraced, at least intellectually as a youth, continued to serve him well. His unlikely appointment to West Point at the age of eighteen would lead the Christian reader to believe that providence was at work in Jackson's life. Though Jackson's education was not sufficient to prepare him for the rigorous academics of the U.S. Military Academy, he was astoundingly successful: "Jackson's four years at the academy consisted almost solely of study and solitary walks. Perseverance brought success. By sheer determination, Jackson rose from dead last among the plebes in 1842 to seventeenth of fifty-nine graduates in the Class of 1846."[27]

Most historians agree that if Jackson had one more year at West Point, he would have finished first in his class—not bad for a poor orphan boy from western Virginia. This feat was especially noteworthy when one considers that West Point's cadets were among the most brilliant and ambitious in the country. Jackson left the academy in 1846 a polished "officer and gentleman." He would never end his self-improvement efforts or the goal to become the best Christian gentleman possible. He would always be consumed with exactness and betterment. Jackson wrote to his sister, Laura, of these efforts in early 1848: "My studies are now principally directed to the formation of my manners and the rules of society and a more thorough knowledge of human nature."[28]

This desire to be his best was rooted in Jackson's knowledge of Scripture acquired in his youth—"Only let your conversation be as it becometh the gospel of Christ" (Philippians 1:27)—and in his studies of such notable writers regarding Christian graces, wisdom, and etiquette as Lord Chesterfield (Philip Dorner Stanhope) and George Winfred Hervey.[29] These efforts served Jackson well in war and in peace. God was preparing him for great works, and Jackson knew that God expected him to dedicate his best efforts to everything he attempted. He would never undertake a task without putting his whole being into it.

He lived out Solomon's admonition in everything he did: "Whatsoever thy hand findeth to do, do it with thy might; for there is no work, nor device, nor knowledge, nor wisdom, in the grave, whither thou goest" (Ecclesiastes 9:10). Jackson, though not assured of a relationship with Christ at this time in his life, displayed this might in his next challenge: the Mexican War.

On August 12, 1846, twenty-two-year-old Thomas Jackson raised his right hand before a justice of the peace in New Utrecht, New York, and took the oath of allegiance to the U.S. Army. He was immediately put under the command of a devout Christian, Capt. Francis Taylor. According to Jackson's widow, it was Captain (later Colonel) Taylor who was instrumental in reawakening the desire for a relationship with Jesus Christ within the soldier's heart—a desire that had first been awakened in childhood. Taylor was "an earnest Christian who labored for the spiritual welfare of his soldiers."[30] Presbyterian theologian Robert Lewis Dabney served as Jackson's adjutant during the War Between the States and noted Taylor's influence on Jackson: "All the information which can now be gathered, points to the devout Colonel Frank Taylor, commanding his regiment of artillery, as [Jackson's] first official spiritual guide. This good man was accustomed to labor as a father for the religious welfare of his young officers. . . . During the campaign of the summer, his instruction and prayers had produced so much effect as to awaken an abiding anxiety and [a] spirit of inquiry in Jackson's mind."[31]

Jackson was now a "seeker," and he "resolved to make the Bible his study."[32] His experiences in church as a boy, the example of the godly slaves he had known while still at home, and the influence of his boyhood chum Joe Lightburn were all being used by God to bring Jackson into the fold. Taylor was an Episcopalian, but Jackson, in his customary thoroughness, was earnest in determining the truth for his own conscience' sake. Jackson studied the Scriptures systematically, just as he would have set out to resolve a mathematical equation.[33] He was determined to find the truth and held no prejudices as to the superiority of one denomination over another. Since Jackson was at that time in Mexico, the Roman Catholic Church was the natural first choice for the young soldier to investigate. While in Mexico City, he was introduced to a sect of Catholic monks. He visited with them for several days and also became friends with the archbishop of Mexico. Jackson questioned, studied, and questioned some more, but finally he became convinced that "the Catholic religion was not his road to salvation."[34]

According to Dabney, Jackson's soundness in the faith and "progress towards the full light was extremely gradual," and he "remained in suspense" for two years, having "no clear persuasion of his own acceptance before God."[35] Yet there is no doubt that this period in the middle of the Mexican War was when the seeds of the gospel truly took root in Jackson's soul. During this time, letters to his sister, Laura, took on an increasingly pious tone, with more and more mentions of a real, living God who ruled in the affairs of men. It was also during this time that Jackson came to regard Sunday as sacred. From this time forward, the Lord's Day would always be revered in his life, even to the point that Jackson would pray he be allowed to die on the Sabbath—a prayer that would be answered. The day was so holy in Jackson's opinion that he would not write or mail a letter that would be in transit on a Sunday.

The Mexican War did much to shape Jackson's manhood and character. As an army lieutenant, he distinguished himself valiantly in Mexico. These experiences would prove invaluable in Jackson's service to the Confederacy. He had mastered reconnaissance, artillery tactics, logistics, and flanking movements that would one day devastate the same army from which he had learned them. His own bravery had also been confirmed in his heart—bravery that would eventually cost his enemies many sleepless nights.

The Mexican War ended in 1847, and by the late summer of 1848, Jackson's company was transferred to Fort Hamilton on Long Island, New York.[36] Once again, Francis Taylor, now a brevet lieutenant colonel, proved instrumental in keeping Jackson on the straight and narrow. Both Dabney and Anna Jackson referred to Taylor's influence "as one of the chief instruments of God in bringing him to a saving knowledge of the truth."[37] Taylor took advantage of Jackson's keen sense of duty and convinced him that every man was compelled to seek God and true religion.

While stationed at Fort Hamilton, Jackson's path crossed with another influential Christian. The Reverend Martin Philip Parks was chaplain of the garrison and also served as rector of Trinity Church in New York City. Dabney asserts that it was by the influence of Parks that Jackson finally "arrived at a comfortable hope of salvation," adding that Parks baptized Jackson.[38] Certainly Parks was very influential in encouraging Jackson in the faith he "strived to enter in," but it was not Parks who baptized Jackson. Upon visiting New York after the war, Anna Jackson discovered that the Reverend Michael Scofield of St. John's Church had baptized Jackson, noting in the church register, "On Sunday, 29th day of April, 1849, I baptized Thomas Jefferson Jackson, major in the U.S. Army. Sponsors, Colonels Dimick and Taylor.—M. Scofield."[39] As both Parks and Scofield were Episcopal ministers, it is believed that Parks introduced Jackson to Scofield, who further tutored and discipled Jackson. Though Jackson knew it was not the baptism that sealed his relationship with Christ, the public act was beneficial to the new convert. It helped confirm in his own mind that he was now recognized by a local church as belonging to Christ and had made that recognition "official,"[40] or as Anna declared, "having accepted Jesus Christ as his Saviour and Redeemer, he wished to avow his faith before men."[41] Jackson was still not convinced, however, of the rightness of the Episcopalian doctrines. Dabney explained, "He had been baptized, upon profession of his faith, by an Episcopal clergyman, but refused to be considered as committed to Episcopacy."[42]

Jackson visited other New York churches, still seeking to know as much truth as possible. The Presbyterian faith of his Scots-Irish forbears slept uneasily in his spirit, but the faith of his fathers would soon be awakened to full vigor. After leaving his post at Fort Hamilton for an unhappy stint at Fort Meade, Florida, God directed Jackson's steps to the sleepy Shenandoah Valley village of Lexington and a military school that, to this day, unmistakably bears his mark. As Jackson's friend and eventual brother-in-law Daniel Harvey Hill[43] observed: "The circumstances attending the election of Major Jackson to a chair in the Virginia Military Institute will be of interest to those who believe in the special providence of God."[44]

Hill had served with Jackson in the Mexican War and, after resigning from the army in 1849, accepted a position at Washington College in Lexington. One morning in February 1851, Hill was visiting VMI superintendent Francis H. Smith and realized Smith was having some difficulty securing someone for an open professorship. Frustrated,

Smith handed Hill an army catalog and register and asked his opinion. Smith wanted a West Pointer. Smith and Hill's shared Christian faith was the foundation for mutual trust and respect. As Hill turned the pages, his attention was immediately drawn to Thomas J. Jackson. He recalled that Jackson's spiritual mentor, Colonel Taylor, had told another officer during the Mexican War that had Jackson "been a year longer (at West Point) he would have graduated at the head of his class. He will make his mark in this war."[45] Hill was convinced, and Smith was pleased. "So strongly did Hill push his Virginia friend that Smith promptly wrote Jackson to see if he would be interested in the job."[46] The VMI board of visitors met on March 28, and "Jackson was selected by acclamation."[47] Providence had chosen a professor, and Jackson accepted the position.

A discussion of Jackson's Christian faith would not be complete without discussing the influence that the Virginia Military Institute, along with Lexington society, had on Jackson and the mark Jackson left on VMI and the picturesque community it calls home. Dabney was well aware of this bond: "The most important feature of Jackson's character was the religious; and this is the most appropriate topic for illustration at this place, because it was mainly developed at Lexington."[48] It is hardly possible to mention VMI or Lexington without thinking of Jackson. VMI's founding and the "distinctive mission for which it seemed to be providentially prepared and adapted"[49] can be traced to 1816. In a speech before the Franklin Society[50] in 1873, Col. John Thomas Lewis Preston (Jackson's brother-in-law by Jackson's first marriage) described what Lexington—this "Athens of the Old South" and "God-favored place"— was like in 1816:

> The town was in about the same limits decreed in 1777. Main Street was not compactly built up. The finest structure was the Ann Smith Academy and beyond it were corn fields. On each side of the college [Washington College] were two brick halls, two stories high. Water was from the pump and from the back spring and hawling water by sleds was quite an institution. Ice houses were unknown. The Presbyterian was the only church, with two services on Sabbath, separated by an "intervale" of one-half hour and both were well attended. A large oak grove extended from the

church gate to Wood's Creek and this was a rambling ground during the intermission.[51]

In February 1816 the state's General Assembly authorized the formation of three arsenals to warehouse and maintain the arms and munitions leftover from the War of 1812. One of these was to be established west of the Blue Ridge Mountains.[52] Twenty soldiers originally manned this arsenal. These men, though generally well behaved, sometimes caused trouble in the peaceful town of Lexington, and the pious citizenry was unhappy with the soldiers' immoral behavior. Lexingtonians were known for their devout temperament. Local historian and author Henry Boley accurately described the pious Presbyterians: "These Scotch-Irish . . . were Presbyterians 100%. They also differed from the Germans and the 'Irish Presbyterians' in that they did not countenance dancing and other worldly amusements, being exceedingly serious minded, their principal entertainment was 'attendance upon religious services.' The finest recommendation that a young man could have was that he had been a regular and orderly attendant of the Sabbath school."[53]

Boley also pointed out that the devout faith of these Presbyterians had earthly benefits: "They were the people who, wherever they were borne to the tumultuous tide of a various and constant emigration that rolled through the channels of centuries, carried with them a stout and stalwart body, a clear head, a physical courage that feared not mortal enemy, a moral courage superior to disaster, indomitable industry, a scorn of ease, a love of letters, a thirst for freedom, and who inscribed on their banners the name of the Lord God of Hosts."[54]

Even with concerns over the soldiers' behavior, the townspeople were grateful for the security of having a military outpost so close by. That part of Virginia was still something of a frontier at the time, and even though the threat of Indian attacks had become nonexistent by the 1830s, uneasiness remained about possible political factions resorting to violence. So locals concocted a plan in 1834 to "replace the soldiers with young men whose education in the customary manner was to be combined with military training and duty as the arsenal guard."[55] Legislation to that effect was enacted in 1837, and Gov. David Campbell appointed five men to the Virginia Military Institute's first board of visitors.[56] In 1838, Campbell appointed two more, one of which was John Preston.[57] Preston devised the name: *Virginia* because it was a state institution, *Military* to indicate "its characteristic feature," and *Institute* because it was to be "something different from either a college or university."[58]

VMI rises fortresslike on the hills above the Maury River,[59] overlooking some of the most beautiful scenery in the great Valley of Virginia. As a military school, VMI ranks second only to West Point in age in America, and its founders had "a keen eye for the beautiful as well as the practical." Somewhat Gothic and Spartan in appearance, it rests on soil once owned by the Walkup family. The Walkups were Irish immigrants, and they, like so many Lexington residents, were devout Presbyterians. Thus it could be said that VMI's foundations rest literally on Presbyterian footings. The Walkups' roots can be traced to Scotland, and their ancient abode, *Wauchope Hills,* is referenced in *Scottish Chiefs.* The Presbyterian connection would prove stronger than coincidence.

Although VMI was founded with no denominational ties, Christian philosophy and efforts permeated the school. Francis Henney Smith (1812–90) was chosen as the school's first commandant. Smith also taught several classes and served as the institute's "principal professor."[60] He was also a devout Christian and Episcopalian. He loved the Bible and once declined the presidency of the oldest and most prestigious school in Virginia—William and Mary in Williamsburg. Smith initiated the practice of giving not only a diploma to each graduating cadet but also a copy of the Scriptures, a practice that continues to this day.[61] His letters and correspondence are peppered with references to the various "seasons of revival" that occurred at VMI, including comments regarding his concern for the cadets' spiritual welfare.

Though Presbyterian, Preston was instrumental in the founding of VMI and also taught at the school. Local Presbyterians, however, were uncomfortable with Smith's evangelical flair and proselytizing. They complained to authorities in Richmond that Smith was running a "sectarian institution." The conflict may have its roots in an element of jealousy between the two denominations—Smith was influential in the founding of an Episcopalian church in Lexington. (After the war, Robert E. Lee worshiped and served as a vestryman in this church, which is known today as the Robert E. Lee Memorial Church.) Despite the complaints by the Presbyterian townspeople, Smith was undeterred. Under his leadership, VMI experienced several religious revivals among the cadets. The two most notable occurred in 1856 (during Jackson's tenure on campus) and 1869.

During the 1869 revival, cadets would meet in Section Room no. 10 and listen as Commandant Smith led them in prayer and Bible study. Smith's wife wrote inspirational poetry, and this was distributed among the cadets. Mary Lee was also involved in encouraging the conversion of the student body at VMI. On April 20, 1869, she sent the following correspondence to her friend Mrs. Eleanor Burwell, who was staying with the Smiths at the time:

> It gives me great pleasure, my dear friend, to send you these little tracts. If they pour comfort into one anxious heart, or enlighten one dark soul, they will have fulfilled their mission. I have put my name to some I had time to examine, as it might save you the trouble of doing so. They are all good, I believe. Those of Doddridge I know are, as his work was so useful to me when first my young heart was led to seek my God. I pray that many hearts may be touched now, as well officers as cadets, and that the impression now received, and the interest now felt may be enduring, and bring forth the fruit of righteousness.[62]

The first spiritual awakening at VMI influenced and spilled over into the Lexington community at large. "The town, the [Washington] College, and the Military Institute shared about equally in this blessed work."[63] Jackson commented on the impact of the revival in a letter to Mrs. Alfred Neale in May 1856:

> We have had a great revival of religion here. . . . [W]e have had such an outpouring of the Spirit of God in our churches here as I never remember of having seen elsewhere. . . . The Episcopal church about a week since took in nearly twenty-five, and from present appearances I suppose that about fifty will join the Presbyterian church in a few days when we are to have our communion. The Baptist church is also being blest, and I think that we may reasonably expect more than one hundred from this revival.[64]

The newspaper also reported on the revival in Jackson's church: "An extensive and deeply interesting work of grace is now in progress in the church and congregation of the Rev. Dr. White. It is confined principally to the young persons of the town and College, and is constantly spreading. There are some forty-five or fifty persons in deep and earnest concern in regard to the all important interest of eternal salvation."[65]

The impact was lasting. On April 8, 1858, the *Lexington Gazette* featured an extended piece about the daily union prayer meetings. According to the article, more than one hundred attended these prayer meetings "pervaded by a grave solemnity." This revival would also give birth to Jackson's most successful Christian ministry.

By the time Thomas J. Jackson arrived in Lexington in 1851,[66] the tight-knit community was a robust evangelical village. The town paper would refer to Lexington and surrounding Rockbridge County as "the very home of gospel blessings."[67] Five Christian congregations were clustered within the town limits. Inside one block were three churches: Lexington Presbyterian (1797), Randolph Street Methodist (1816), and the Lexington Baptist Church (1841). At the bottom of the hill, just a stone's throw from Washington College, was Grace Episcopal Church (Robert E. Lee Memorial Church). The Methodist Episcopal Church was then meeting in the county courthouse until a building was completed in 1853. Just outside the town limits stood the African Baptist Church near what was then the North River (Maury River). The congregation was composed of both slaves and freedmen and was overseen by the elders of the Presbyterian church.[68] The community was bustling with missionary and Christian endeavors: "Far from being cold and sectarian, Lexington was home to a flourishing evangelical tradition of ecumenical[69] fellowship, prayer, and revivals, and a busy center for colporteurs,[70] missionaries, and visiting agents from eastern benevolent societies and publishing houses. Local chapters of the American Bible Society, American Colonization Society, and the Sons of Temperance, attracted members from all churches."[71]

Jackson's first order of business upon arriving in Lexington[72] was to join a church. He visited all four churches. According to Dabney, "He at first attended the public worship of all their churches indiscriminately, listening with exemplary respect and attention. But after a time he discontinued this promiscuous worship."[73] God would use a most unusual and interesting Lexington resident to curtail Jackson's "promiscuous worship" and to help him find the church where he could best serve the Savior. A full understanding of Jackson's faith and his black Sunday-school class is incomplete without a sketch of this most remarkable saint.

John Blair Lyle[74] was a pillar of the Lexington Presbyterian Church. Born in 1807 into a family with a rich Christian heritage,[75] young John Lyle had been raised to love three things: Jesus Christ, His church, and books. Lyle's pastor noted, "He was a great reader of books on practical divinity, and especially the word of God."[76] A bookseller by trade, the genial and hospitable bachelor was beloved by many in Lexington. Henry Boley, a man who later owned Lyle's bookstore, aptly described his predecessor: "He was a bachelor, a bookseller, a man of middle age, well connected, but with [a] small fortune, who devoted nearly the whole of his leisure to the spiritual interests of his charge. He was constantly the friend of the afflicted, the restorer of the wayward, the counselor of the doubting, a true shepherd of the sheep and his inward Christian life was [as] elevated as his outward was active."[77]

From the VMI cadets and Washington College students to some of the most prominent leaders in Virginia, all gathered daily at Lyle's bookstore on Main Street to seek spiritual advice and to discuss the weighty issues of theology, current events, and politics. A chance visit to this bookstore would often find a group of illustrious men congregated around the counter. William Spottswood White (Jackson's pastor), Daniel Harvey Hill (future Confederate general), Francis Smith (VMI superintendent), John Preston (a prominent local attorney, founder of VMI, and confidante of Jackson's), John Letcher (Virginia's governor[78] during the War Between the States), and William H. Ruffner (the state's first superintendent of public education[79]) all visited Lyle's bookstore often, and all were influenced by the earnest, wise, and affable Lyle.

This eclectic assembly of prominent townspeople became close friends that one observer recalled as a "lively, inquisitive . . . close-knit group that loved a lilting song, a witty conversation."[80] Francis Smith once noted that among Lyle's patrons there "always existed the most pleasant and friendly relations." Another customer referred to the bookstore as "a sort of clubhouse in which assembled frequently the professional men of the town, the professors and officers of the College and Institute, and every genteel young man in the community." Though Lexington was little more than a small mountain village in 1851, God providentially assembled a high number of influential professionals there. These men demonstrated the truth observed by eighteenth-century preacher and revivalist George Whitefield: "No man is the whole of himself. His friends are the rest of him."[81] As many of them met at Lyle's bookstore—"iron sharpening iron"—in rich, vigorous conversation and debate, it is apparent God was intellectually and spiritually preparing them for what lay ahead in the next decade. Little did these men know that the gathering political storm clouds would soon separate them and end their earthly fellowship. Yet the collective influence this small select group of Christian men had on the history of Virginia is staggering to consider. Their legacy remains and haunts Lexington to the present day.

John Lyle was the type of unique man that God raises up from time to time whose influence, though obscure and unsung, is profound and lingering. An 1875 article appearing in the *Lexington Gazette and Citizen* (seventeen years after Lyle's death) pondered whether there was any name that was "more familiarly remembered and dearly cherished by the people of Lexington and vicinity, than that of John B. Lyle?"[82] Though the answer to the question in 1875 would have been a resounding "no," there are few alive today who have ever heard of Lyle, much less know anything about him. Yet had it not been for this man, it is unlikely that Jackson's famous "Colored" Sunday-school class would have ever existed. Lyle is truly an unsung hero of the faith. His influence on Jackson was such that Anna Jackson wrote: "The story of Major Jackson's life in Lexington would be lacking in one important link of the chain without the mention of his dear and honored Christian friend, Mr. John B. Lyle, to whom he was more indebted for spiritual profit than to any one else except his pastor."[83]

Lyle was not known for his business acumen. According to William Ruffner, his Uncle John was "too fond of society, too jovial, too philanthropic to care much for money, or to be an attentive business man. It made him happier to give than to take; and the size of his gifts was measured by his feelings, rather than by his ability."[84] Lyle's nephew called his uncle's establishment an "automatic bookstore"—the proprietor often left the store unlocked and unattended while he went about the community doing the Lord's work. Lyle would simply leave a slate at the store "with a request lying on the counter to the effect that if anyone wanted anything in the store he could take it, provided he would make the proper entry on the slate." Perhaps Lyle took a benevolent approach to his business because of his days studying at Washington College. While there, he joined the Graham Philanthropic Society, which was concerned with "improvement in literature." The society funded its own small library and discussed "morals, politics, literature, and other subjects."

Lyle's influence in Lexington extended beyond those who visited his bookstore. As an elder in the Lexington Presbyterian Church, he often accompanied Pastor White on preaching trips to other churches in the Valley. Lyle's part was to sing, and he was noted for his "ringing, melodious voice." White described his companion's commitment to the church: "In season and out of season, through evil report and good report, he gave a full portion of every day to the service of that church whose purity, peace and prosperity he had vowed to seek, both when he was received into its communion and when he was ordained to his office. These vows he faithfully performed, not confining himself to any one district. He was always posted as to the state of the congregation."[85]

Lyle had a burning desire to see souls brought to Christ, and speaking to others about their spiritual needs came as natural to him as breathing. White saw Lyle's winsome ways used by God in amazing ways:

> He was especially faithful and successful in finding cases of religious concern. No man was freer from "fashionable religious cant," or possessed less austerity. He could speak to any one on personal religion in a way so affable and gentle as to never give offense, and yet so pointed as to learn just what he wanted to know. I have reason to believe that he conversed and prayed with more young men when partially or deeply awakened than any man not in the ministry I ever knew, and with far more than many ministers did. Such cases he always reported to me, and many such he brought to my study. His habit was simply to bring them in and then retire, leaving me to discover their state of mind as best I could.[86]

Lyle's innate gift for influencing the young men of the area was legendary. His Christian witness caused many of them to consider the destiny of their souls and to seek Christ. This influence directly benefited Pastor White's family: "It was by him that I was first made acquainted with the case of General Jackson, and also that of two of my own sons. I have reason to regard him as, in a great degree, the spiritual father of these two sons, one of whom is now a preacher of the gospel and the other is in heaven."[87]

White's multigenerational vision and the positive impact his family had for the cause of Christ is quite remarkable, which Robert Hunter noted in his history of the Lexington Presbyterian Church:

> Dr. Henry M. White, youngest son of the Reverend William S. White, held a long and notable pastorate at Winchester. His son, in turn, Hugh W. White, graduated from Washington and Lee (1889) and Union Theological Seminary, and entered the China mission field in 1894. During his fourth decade of service in the 1920's, White feared that the Communist movement "if unchecked will undermine Christian civilization." By the end of the 1980's, it was Communism, not Christianity, that was beginning to crumble, due in no small measure to the spiritual labors of these dedicated missionaries to China.[88]

Again, the influence and friendship of one man can have historic implications. As George Grant has written, "That is one of the great lessons of history. It is simply that in the providence of God, ordinary people are ultimately the ones who determine the outcome of human events."[89] Though John Lyle may appear little more than "ordinary" in the eyes of the world, he was much more in God's divine plan.

White also noted Lyle's "generous spirit." Several calls had come to the Lexington congregation for funds to endow Union Theological Seminary. The third attempt to collect additional funds apparently caused some division among the brethren. When one member responded, "I cannot give anything, and I do not think the church ought to give anything," the patient and influential Lyle, as was his habit, spoke last and said, "I am willing to double my last subscription. I think the church ought to do the same, and that they will do it." White added, "The church doubled their second subscription."

White believed the commitment was more than Lyle could afford and questioned how he would be able to pay. Lyle responded with a smile, "By making and selling brushes of peacock feathers, which I can get from Timber Ridge. You know, that part of the county abounds in peacocks, and it will do me real good to make their tails contribute to the education of young men for the ministry." According to White, "He paid his subscription that way."

Lyle taught Sunday school at his church and led the choir. White commented: "He not only had an ear but a soul for music. His voice, both for compass and melody, was inferior to none I had ever heard. He occupied the center seat in the choir gallery, directly in front of the pulpit. The sound of his far-reaching yet melodious voice, and the sight of his broad, full face, radiant with devout emotion, kindled by the sacred truth embodied in the psalm or hymn, often led me to think that his singing was as helpful to me as my preaching could be to him."[90]

The secret of Lyle's success and the impact he had upon others was his intimate relationship with Christ. He carried the glow of God with him wherever he went and exuded the vibrant fullness and confidence of the Christian life that draws others to the Savior. White averred: "The true source of the divine life this good man led was his faith. His acceptance of every jot and tittle of the word of God, his reliance upon the scheme of salvation revealed in the gospel, were literally unqualified and unwavering. Neither the speculations of the fanciful nor the cavils of the skeptic weighed a feather with him. He habitually went from his closet to the prayer-meeting, the church, and even on visits to his friends."[91]

Thus it was easy for this man to win the confidence of the cautious Thomas J. Jackson. When Jackson arrived at Lexington in mid-August 1851, he first befriended Daniel Harvey Hill, who was largely responsible for bringing Jackson to VMI. Now Hill played another pivotal role in Jackson's life, for it is likely that Hill introduced Jackson to John Lyle.

Lyle lived at his bookstore in a furnished room at the rear of the building. This arrangement saved him the expense of maintaining a home; money that he gave to his church and to those in need.

The hotel where Jackson stayed in his initial days at Lexington was across the street from Lyle's bookstore. His own love of books and history drew him to Lyle, and Jackson "rarely passed a day without a visit to Mr. Lyle's sanctum."[92] During these visits, the conversation often turned to religion and eternal truths. Both Lyle and Jackson recognized the truth penned by Scottish preacher Thomas Chalmers: "Only three things are truly necessary in order to make life happy: the blessing of God, the benefit of books, and the benevolence of friends."[93] Jackson and Lyle both enjoyed the intellectual stimulation, and even though Jackson had no singing ability, he enjoyed the song sessions as well. It did not take long for Jackson and Lyle to become devoted and intimate friends.

According to D. H. Hill, Lyle "was instrumental in arousing a religious interest in Jackson's mind." In actuality, Jackson's religious interest was already aroused, but Lyle certainly encouraged and guided Jackson's interest in a certain direction—toward Presbyterianism. Sometime in the early autumn of 1851, Lyle introduced Jackson to William Spottswood White. Jackson made public his Christian faith, along with six others, and formally united with the Lexington Presbyterian Church on November 22.[94] As Jackson's faith developed and the influence of Lyle became more prevalent, Jackson struggled with two tenets of reformed Presbyterian theology: infant baptism and predestination. Most of Jackson's biographers acknowledge that Jackson doubted these doctrines, including the two biographers most familiar with Jackson's Christian faith: R. L. Dabney[95] and Anna Jackson.[96] Both Dabney and Anna write that Jackson eventually reconciled these doubts. She wrote, "His difficulties of doctrinal belief all vanished, and he was a most loyal and devoted member and officer."[97] Dabney gave a more detailed, if not fully convincing, account[98] of these "difficulties" and tells how Jackson, "in conversation with an intimate friend," made his concerns known. According to Dabney, this friend responded, "Major, if you have these opinions, you had better become a Methodist."[99] At Jackson's insistence, the two met with Pastor White to settle the matter. Meeting in White's study, the discussion was long and straightforward but cordial. After the matter had been fully aired, White concluded, "Major, although your doctrinal theory is not in perfect accord with ours, yet in your practical life you are so good a Presbyterian, that I think you may safely remain where you are."[100]

Dabney concluded, "It was not very long before all his difficulties gave way before his honest, persistent, and prayerful inquiries." But it was unlikely for Dabney to know with any measure of certainty that this was true, as he was not acquainted with Jackson at that time. Contradicting Dabney, Daniel Harvey Hill wrote to Dabney in July 1864, stating that Jackson "professed himself pleased with everything except predestination and infant baptism. His scruples about the latter did not last long . . . but his repugnance to predestination was *long and determined*."[101] How long and determined is uncertain. Conclusively, Jackson was troubled by some of the doctrines of the Presbyterian Church, but it is difficult to say with the same certainty that Jackson ever totally overcame his "repugnance" toward predestination. If anything, the most authoritative and unbiased statement (that of Hill's) would seem to indicate Jackson may have never fully embraced the doctrine. Hill lends further credence to this possibility in an 1894 article, published just five years after Hill's death: "I knew Stonewall Jackson from 1846 till 1863, was often thrown into intimate relations with him, had many hundreds of conversations with him, heard his opinions upon a vast variety of subjects, saw him in many different positions,—a lieutenant of artillery, a lieutenant general, a college professor, a church deacon, a Sabbath-school teacher, etc.,—and the estimate if formed of him in these different walks of life and phases of character was in many respects *different from that usually accepted*."[102]

In this article, Hill uses the exact wording he used in writing to Dabney: "He professed himself pleased with everything except predestination and infant baptism. His scruples about the latter did not last very long. In the last years of his life he was regarded as a fatalist; but his *repugnance to predestination was long and determined*." Hill does not state that Jackson's "repugnance" was ever laid to rest. One would think that Hill would have made it clear that Jackson—especially so many years after his death—had overcome his objections, as he did with infant baptism, if he had done so. His wording also suggests that Jackson's aversion to predestination persisted "in the last years of his life." Many Christians of the reformed faith have vocally claimed Jackson as one of their own and likely take issue with the idea that Jackson was anything less than 100 percent Calvinistic in his doctrine. And while that remains a possibility, Hill's comments make it clear there is room for debate on the issue of Jackson's view of predestination.[103] Regardless, it was not a divisive issue with Jackson, as he was thoroughly catholic in his acceptance of all sincere believers. In a letter written to the Southern Presbyterian General Assembly regarding chaplains for his army, Jackson made this plain: "Denominational distinctions should be kept out of view, and not touched upon. And, as a general rule, I do not think that a chaplain who would preach denominational sermons should be in the army. . . . I would like to see no question asked in the army of what denomination a chaplain belongs to; but let the question be, Does he preach the Gospel?"[104]

Despite Jackson's misgivings about predestination and whether or not those misgivings were temporary or lasting, the doctrinal issue in no way hindered his faithfulness to his church and his vibrant, active faith in a sovereign God. Pastor White described the church at the time of Jackson joining and how Jackson soon took on a position of responsibility:

> To a body of communicants numbering over two-hundred and fifty there was a mixed assembly composed of people of the town and vicinage, members of the academy of young ladies, students of Washington College, cadets of Virginia Military Institute, and a few colored people. . . . There were five trustees, twelve ruling elders, but no deacons. The duties were performed by the ruling elders and trustees jointly. This defect, however, was soon remedied by the election of a board of five deacons, of whom General Thomas J. Jackson was one.[105]

The church was blessed with "some of the most venerable and well-informed ruling elders and members" and included "two doctors of divinity and five other resident Presbyterian ministers."[106] During the War Between the States, the congregation proved to be a living testimony of Christ's admonition that "of whom much is given, much shall be required" (Luke 12:48). Though indeed blessed with an abundance of Christian manhood, many would be called upon for the ultimate sacrifice. By the end of 1864, the church had provided "106 officers and privates, of whom 28 were casualties."[107]

Beyond doctrinal questions, Lyle was instrumental in convincing Jackson of the power of prayer—a practice for which Jackson would become legendary. The two discussed prayer often, and Lyle loaned books on the subject to Jackson. Maggie Preston wrote that Lyle had

> put into Jackson's hands a little volume illustrative of the power of prayer. . . . It was the recorded experience of an humble English soldier, most of

whose life had been passed in the army, and who, on retiring from service, devoted himself to the establishment of Sunday schools among the neglected purlieus [suburb] of London, which in time grew up in Christian churches. This man's experience of the power of prayer was of the most remarkable character, very similar to that of Franke, the originator of the famous Halle Orphan Schools. I allude to this book because of the peculiar manner in which it arrested Jackson's mind; for so frequently did he afterwards revert to it, that it was evident its influence was far-reaching and lasting. Thus the simple act of the devout elder may have had a traceable bearing upon the brilliant successes and achievements of the Christian hero![108]

These achievements included Jackson's efforts on behalf of Lexington's African Americans as well as his military feats. Certainly Jackson must have taken note of the reference to Sunday schools and the part that prayer played in their success. Andrew Lytle wrote, "Ultimately a man is not judged by what he has done or what he has written but who he has influenced."[109] If that is true, John Lyle has heard the words: "Well done thou good and faithful servant." Jackson attributed his dramatic victories over astounding odds to the "divine blessings of God" in answer to prayer. Could it be that this joyful, obscure bibliophile living in the backroom of a dusty bookstore, giving away much of what he owned, was, at least in part, responsible for Jackson's astounding battlefield successes? Could it be that this "little volume" was also one of the inspirations for Jackson's black Sunday school?

Anna Jackson took special note of Lyle's tutoring of Jackson regarding the subject of prayer: "He also taught him to cherish a high sense of the value of prayer, and to expect an answer to it."[110]

Lyle was tireless in his work for the Lexington Presbytery and rarely missed attending the various committee and elders' meetings and, of course, regular worship services. While attending worship on November 2, 1856, Lyle suffered a stroke that paralyzed his left side. He was taken to the house of close friend John Preston, and he lived there for the remaining two years of his life. The day after Lyle's stroke, Jackson wrote to a relative that he believed Lyle "would soon bid farewell to this world." Lyle improved somewhat over the following weeks, though he never regained his full health. His stroke occurred during the great revival of 1856. Given Lyle's reputation for prayer and concern over spiritual matters, it is possible he carried a prayer burden during this "season of revival" that was more than his body could endure. He began a second decline in 1857, though Dr. White noted, "His powers of speech were spared him until very near the end." Lyle retained the joy of his salvation and influenced others as White noted: "His sick room was frequented by large numbers of warmly attached friends. His intercourse with such was characterized by what I must call a sanctified cheerfulness which made his room like a vestibule of heaven. Truly it was good to be there."[111]

Finally, on July 20, 1858, "a final stroke removed him to a better world." Major Preston was, at that time, acting superintendent of VMI and issued a special order praising Lyle's constant support of the institute. Though Lyle "died as he lived, the fearless, faithful servant of God," he also died a pauper. After all his debts were paid, his estate totaled $40.92.[112] Lyle did receive a decent burial, nonetheless. His dear friend, John Preston, donated space from his family plot in the Lexington Presbyterian Church cemetery[113] and paid for his tombstone, upon which is inscribed, "He was the truest friend, the bravest man, and the best Christian ever known to him who erects this stone to his memory."[114]

Jackson would never forget John Blair Lyle. Anna noted: "He was one of those whole-souled, large-hearted Christians whose lives are full of love and sunshine. His genial face and ready sympathy made him a great favorite with young and old, and he was known as the comforter of the afflicted, the restorer of the wayward, and the counselor of the doubting. Indeed, his heart was big enough to take in all who sought a place there."[115]

Henry Boley's description of Lyle is perhaps the best epitaph: "Under a warm appeal, he would plunge his hand into his pantaloons pocket, which was his money-drawer, and bring out a handful of silver change and drop it in the collection basket. He died about the time he reached the bottom of his pocket. But while his chief book account was that of profit and loss, his moral record was rich in words and deeds . . . no better friend ever watched over the weak and erring. He was indifferent to money because of his greater regard for the salvation of men."[116]

Lyle's remains rest in a borrowed grave, next to his friend John Preston. Within a few steps are many of those robust Christian gentlemen who frequented Lyle's "automatic bookstore" for fellowship, debate, and a "lilting song." Over Jackson's dust, his life-size statue keeps a close watch over those with whom he shared so many hours of camaraderie: William S. White, John Letcher, Francis Smith, William H. Ruffner, and many others whose names, though forgotten by history, are recorded in the Lamb's Book of Life.

Jackson's silent watch is aided by the land he loved, as he wrote his wife: "Here the mountains keep watch and guard around the home and the tombs of those who were dearest to me on earth." Beneath the canopy of ancient oaks, in the centuries-old Lexington cemetery, these dead in Christ patiently await the resurrection. Their headstones, worn by the ravages of time, stand as silent sentinels to the truth that friendships, though temporal, have eternal consequences.

The Christian friendship these men enjoyed, and most notably the influence John Lyle had upon Jackson, would spawn additional friendships, also with eternal consequences—especially for those in Jackson's charge.

3

He That Is Greatest Among You

Stonewall Jackson and His Slaves

Treat your friends like family and your family like friends.
—*Cotton Mather*

Not now as a servant, but above a servant, a brother beloved, specially to me, but how much more unto thee, both in the flesh, and in the Lord?
—*Philemon 1:16*

We know that we have passed from death unto life, because we love the brethren. He that loveth not his brother abideth in death.
—*1 John 3:14*

WHEN THOMAS J. JACKSON first came to Lexington in 1851, blacks accounted for approximately 40 percent of its population. Though condescending by modern standards, nineteenth-century Lexington's treatment of its black population was characterized as benevolent: "In general, a paternalistic ethos influenced both slaves and masters in Rockbridge County. This sensibility deemed masters responsible for protecting and supporting their slaves, in exchange for the slaves' labor. . . . However, the notion of inequality was always present."[1]

Even free blacks were not afforded opportunities for education and financial gain. This lack of opportunity made blacks unequal to whites, not because of some inherent or genetic defect, as many whites at that time believed, but because of their lack of status, their lack of access to the legal and political system, and their lack of prospects for self-advancement. When observing Jackson's conduct in his relationships with his slaves, the slaves of others, as well as free blacks, one has to conclude that Jackson believed blacks were capable of—and deserving of—much more than many nineteenth-century Americans were willing to grant.

The motivation for this attitude was Jackson's relationship with God. It ruled his conduct regarding his fellow man, regardless of a man's color or station in life. James I. Robertson observed, "The good Christian slaveholder was one who treated his servants fairly and humanely at all times."[2] Jackson was a serious student of the Scriptures. He was so serious that some of his contemporaries viewed him as a religious zealot. But Jackson was no fanatic. He was, in the words of one historian, "a mainstream southern evangelical."[3] As one who took the Scriptures literally, Jackson was mindful that God was concerned about how he treated his servants and fellow man. Since Jackson knew that he would one day have to answer to *his* Master, he desired to be treated mercifully, and he knew he could expect no better treatment than he exhibited: "Masters, give unto your servants that which is just and equal; knowing that ye also have a Master in heaven" (Colossians 4:1).

These thoughts must have been in Jackson's mind as he went about his day-to-day routines and interactions with blacks. And he was certainly aware that his own family, though not subject to the same cruelties as the Africans, had experienced the bondage of indentured servitude. Both of Jackson's great-grandparents had come to America "under a seven-year indenture."[4] Due to his family's history, along with Jackson's boyhood interaction and familiarity with slaves, the contemplative Jackson must have felt some kindred connection to the Africans' plight.

Jackson would also have recalled the nurture and love given him by the family slaves when he was a boy. One such slave was referred to as "Stonewall Jackson's Nurse," but during Jackson's childhood, he was known as "Uncle Mose" Jackson. He told a West Virginia reporter that when "Jackson's mother occasionally paid visits to his 'ole mistus' she would bring the infant 'Stonewall' with her and it was his duty to take charge of the future great general while the 'white folks' were at dinner."[5]

When Jackson's mother became too ill to care for her son, she sent the six-year-old Jackson, along with his sister, Laura, to live with relatives and the family slaves. When Jackson's mother was near death a year later, he and Laura went, "in the care of one of the negro men, Uncle Robinson, a trusted servant, to see their mother, then on her deathbed" arriving in time "to receive her dying blessing and prayers."[6] It was also Robinson who once helped young Tom fashion a canoe from a burned-out log.[7] Jackson no doubt felt some sense of duty to return the kindness he had received at the hands of his childhood slaves and surrogate parents.

Details about the slaves Jackson owned during his lifetime are sketchy at best. It is believed that Jackson owned a total of eight or nine[8] slaves during his time in Lexington, but not all were in the household at the same time. The 1860 census shows that Jackson owned four slaves at that time: Albert, Hetty, Cyrus, and George. Cyrus and George were sons of Hetty.[9] Another four-year-old slave girl, named Emma, was purchased by 1861. Anna Jackson noted that Emma was purchased at the behest of "an aged lady in the town" who apparently came into possession of Emma due to her "having been left an orphan."[10] The older women seemingly felt unable to care for such a young child and convinced Jackson to purchase the child to relieve her of the burden and as an act of benevolence toward the girl. Jackson was diligent in teaching Emma the child's catechism, which she did, "reciting her answers with the drop of a courtesy at each word."[11] Another slave, named Amy, though not listed in the census for some reason, was believed to be in the household in 1860.[12]

Albert was the first slave purchased by Jackson, and according to Anna, he did so at Albert's request: "Albert . . . came to him and begged that he would buy him on the condition that he might be permitted to emancipate himself by a return of the purchase-money."[13] By this arrangement, Albert was hired out "as a hotel-waiter" and did not live with the family. According to Anna, he only stayed with the family during an illness: "On one occasion, when he had a long spell of illness, and his master took him to his home to care for him as an act of humanity, for Albert had no family of his own. Every morning my husband paid him a call to see how he was getting along and what he needed."[14] Albert was also hired out to VMI for $120 a year. Records indicate that, by early 1863, Albert had paid his debt to Jackson and was a free man.

Amy was also purchased before Jackson's second marriage. She was an elderly woman, and he purchased her because she "was about to be sold for debt . . . who sought from him a deliverance from her troubles."[15] Anna wrote that his heart "was moved by her situation, and he yielded to her entreaties, and gave her a home in a good Christian family."[16] Jackson became especially attached to Amy; Professor Robertson noted that she "was closest to Jackson's heart."[17] Anna was particularly fond of her culinary abilities. And Amy received religious instruction from Jackson and, after he left Lexington when the war began, from Margaret Junkin Preston. Jackson was grateful for his former sister-in-law's attention to Amy and expressed his appreciation in a letter to her in October 1861: "I am under special obligations for the religious instruction that you have given Amy, and hope that it may be in your power to continue it."[18] Such sentiment reveals that he was motivated by more than mere duty or facade; he had a genuine concern for the spiritual welfare of those in his charge.

During his absence and while Anna was with relatives in North Carolina, Jackson instructed Maggie Preston to check on Amy and Emma regularly and to ensure that they were suitably clothed. At this point, Amy and Emma boarded with a free black woman, Winnie Buck. Jackson included money in his correspondence, "paying all her expenses of board, medical attendance, and comforts."[19] In the autumn of 1861, Amy became ill and died. Maggie Preston conveyed that news to Jackson, offering as a comfort that Amy was now with her Savior:

She died last night at midnight without any fear, and, as I believe, with a simple reliance on Jesus for salvation. It was only the death of a poor slave—a most insignificant thing in men's eyes—and yet may we not hope that there was joy in heaven over another ransomed soul—one in whom the Saviour saw the result of "his travail" and was "satisfied." . . . She told me that she wanted to thank you for the money, and to let you know about her. She expressed entire resignation to God's will and trust in Christ alone. . . . I knew that it would be your wish that she should have a well-ordered burial, so Dr. White attended, and my servants tell me that it is many a day since so large a colored funeral has been in Lexington. . . . I am sure your true Christian feeling will appreciate all that I have told you of the humble faith of this saved soul, gathered from your own household. The cup of cold water you have ministered to this poor disciple may avail more in the Master's eye than all the brilliant deeds with which you may glorify your country's battle-fields. So differently do man and his Maker judge![20]

Amy was in heaven due in large measure to Jackson's efforts and gospel witness. His heart was touched by the news of her passing. He replied: "My Dear Maggie. . . . More than once your kind and touching letter respecting the sainted Amy brought tears to my eyes. . . . I am very grateful to you for your Christian kindness to her. I am much gratified that you gave her a decent burial, and that so many followed her remains to the grave."[21]

Such thoughts reveal again the complicated relationship in which master and slave found themselves. Drawn together by what became familial connections over time, black and white Southerners in nineteenth-century America were captive to a strange dichotomy. Many slaves discreetly resented being owned by another and longed for their freedom. At the same time, they could not help growing emotionally close to their masters and even loving them and their families. Whites, on the other hand, though prejudiced and discriminatory in their practical interactions with blacks, often grew to respect and love their slaves. Sharing the day-to-day burdens, the toils of life, sicknesses, and the deaths of children and loved ones along with the joys of a shared existence constrained slave and master in mutual attachment. The injustice of slavery coexisted peacefully with feelings of affection and compassion in many Southern homes. This was especially true in regard to the Jackson household.

When Jackson married Anna, her father gave him five or six slaves as a wedding present. Jackson kept three—Hetty and her two sons, George and Cyrus—and sold the others. Hetty had a long connection to the Morrison family. She had been Anna's nursemaid, and the tenderness between the two was instinctive; Anna commented, "There had always existed between us a bond of mutual interest and attachment."[22] So attached to her was Hetty that she asked to move to Virginia when Anna left North Carolina. Hetty was known for her passionate spirit. Anna described her as an "energetic, impulsive, quick-tempered woman, with some fine traits, but inclined to self-assertion."[23] She attributed Hetty's "self-assertion" in part to the fact she was quite a bit older than her and her husband. This spirit is best illustrated by an incident that took place during the war. Hetty was en route to North Carolina, where Anna was staying with family. As she was changing trains, she noticed a man picking up her trunk, which "contained all her valuables." Not sure of his intent or honesty, she yelled out in a self-assured voice, "Put down that trunk; that's General Jackson's trunk!"[24]

Hetty became especially devoted to Jackson, and the two shared a love for gardening. Anna once wrote to her husband, "There is a very long row of celery: this is due to Hetty, and I told her that as she has succeeded so well I wouldn't touch its culture."[25]

At the time Jackson died in 1863, Hetty was serving as nurse to the Jackson's infant child. Upon learning of his death, she "was a sincere mourner . . . her tears flowing freely." Anna wrote that Hetty had spoken mournfully of Jackson's death, stating, "She had lost her best friend."[26]

After the war, Hetty left Anna to live independently. Though Anna kept in contact, her departure saddened her former master: "I would gladly have kept and supported her for the rest of her life, but she was allured by her freedom to seek greater independence and gain, severing a tie which had been one of mutual attachment and confidence."[27] But there was no bitterness in the parting. Anna reported, "The sturdy old woman lived to be over ninety years of age, and it is hoped that the prayers and example of her master proved a benediction to her during all the remaining years of her life."[28]

Hetty's two boys, Cyrus and George, were between the ages of twelve and sixteen when they joined the household. They apparently inherited their mother's spirited constitution. Jackson observed, "If these two boys were left to themselves they would be sure to go back to barbarism."[29] He had no intention of leaving the boys to themselves and was "unwearying in his efforts to elevate them."[30]

One method Jackson used to "elevate" his slaves was strict observance of family devotions. All of the household servants were required to attend family worship and prayers. Morning devotions were at seven, and everyone was required to be prompt. Though Virginia law prohibited it, Cyrus and George were taught to read, and both were required to attend not only family worship but also Sunday school and church services.

Jackson's concern over the spiritual condition and religious training of his slaves is further evidenced in one of his letters, referenced by Anna:

> The following extracts from letters to a gentleman in Lexington will show that he [Jackson] took time to attend both to the temporal and spiritual interests of his servants, even in the midst of absorbing military occupations: "I desire, if practicable, that my boys [Cyrus and George] shall have the opportunity of attending the colored Sabbath-School in Lexington, if it is still in operation. I am glad to hear that they are both well. . . . Should you not need George, please hire him out to some suitable person, with the condition that, if in or near town, he be required to attend Sabbath-school; and wherever he may be, let him be required to attend church at suitable times, as I am very desirous that the spiritual interests of my servants shall be attended to."[31]

Other services that Jackson's servants would have been present at, and received instruction, were the evening family worship times conducted in the Jackson household. During the Sunday-evening worship services in his home, Jackson also welcomed other neighborhood blacks to attend. These "community prayer meetings" took place weekly and were held in the family dining room. The services won the confidence and hearts of many Lexington blacks, and "it was in his home that Jackson had the most intimate and wide range of experiences with slaves and free blacks in Lexington."[32]

In the evenings, passersby could see through the soft glow of candle and lantern light of the Jackson home the pious man of the house, his wife, and several inquisitive faces. With Bible open, the Major (as he was known to many of the townspeople) read the Scriptures and did his best to explain and share the wisdom and love of God. One might also hear the slaves singing familiar hymns with Jackson (who was always off-key) and Anna. Laughter and conversation flowed freely. And the attending blacks were there because they wanted to be. Jackson was approachable and hospitable, opening his home up to those seeking spiritual guidance. His sincerity reciprocated their admiration.

A remnant of this admiration can still be found among African Americans who have connections to Lexington. A 1988 local newspaper article[33] noted that Desmond R. Jackson and his daughter, Margaret Jenkins, proudly and confidently claimed to be direct descendants of one of Jackson's slaves. But the story is not without controversy. Some historians believe the relationship has been exaggerated through the years and its authenticity cannot be confirmed. I phoned Jackson on September 13, 2004, to get his family's side of the story. Our conversation went something like this:

"Hello, is Mr. Jackson there?"

"Which Jackson?"

"Mr. Desmond Jackson."

"Whatcha want with him?"

"Well, the curator at the Jackson House told me I might be able to interview—"

"Oh, yeah, Stonewall. Yeah, yeah. I'm here. What can I do for you?"

So went my first contact with Desmond R. Jackson. "Raddy," as he preferred to be called, was more than happy to talk to me and invited me to his Lexington home.

I drove over and pulled up to the two-story brick dwelling in an older part of Lexington the next afternoon. The home has been in the Jackson family since 1923.

It was rather warm and sunny, and on the porch sat an elderly black man. He greeted me warmly and shook my hand when I stepped onto his porch. Jackson had quite a firm grip for a ninety-one-year-old man. He also had a warm smile and a very hospitable spirit, giving me the grand tour of the old home place, sharing family artifacts and pictures with me as he reminisced about his long life in Lexington. He said that he had worked at Washington and Lee University for forty-three years and worked at Lee Chapel on Sundays. He claimed that many years ago he helped move one of the Lee family bodies from the crypt in the basement of Lee Chapel. Though he does not recall all of the details, Jackson said that the family had the body moved to North Carolina.[34] He also showed me a chair with Washington and Lee's seal painted on the backrest. The school had given it to him upon his retirement, along with a card that he carried in his wallet conferring upon him "life membership" at Washington and Lee University.

Jackson related a number of stories and legends about old Lexington, most of them long forgotten. He was quick to add that he still drove, still mowed his own grass, and still worked part time at the local newspaper, the *Lexington Gazette.* When I asked what he did at the *Gazette,* he smiled and said, "Sit mostly." He told me that he was born just a couple of blocks away from where we sat. The structure is no longer there; the site is now an alley. Jackson's great-grandfather owned the house where the younger Jackson was born, and he wondered where a black man in those days got the money to purchase real estate, establish a business, and "walk around with a big ole' gold chain" in his pocket.

As the afternoon passed, Raddy reminisced about his life in Lexington and was grateful for the good life he had lived in the small historic mountain village. He recalled that his mother would go to VMI to do the hair of Gen. George C. Marshall's wife. He also mentioned that he had done housework for Virginia Senator Willis Robertson, father of televangelist Pat Robertson, recalling, "Pat used to sit on my knee." Jackson told me of the time, as a young boy, he developed pneumonia and spent some time in the original Stonewall Jackson Memorial Hospital, which was situated in Stonewall Jackson's Lexington home (which has since been restored to its current state and use). Raddy lamented, "The black people back in that time had more in Lexington than they got now, ten times more." He was saddened by the fact that so many young blacks had left Lexington and "gone to the big city." He thought many of them would have been better off staying in Lexington and establishing businesses, as his great-grandfather James "Deacon" Jackson had done. James Jackson owned and operated a barbershop in Lexington for many years. Subsequent generations—including Desmond Jackson's grandfather, father, and his brother, Ormond—also worked at the barbershop. For a number of years, four generations worked at the barbershop at the same time. James Jackson's obituary notes that he lived above his barbershop when he died—a fact that Desmond Jackson and Margaret Jenkins confirmed. His obituary further reported that James was "as much as four score years of age" and gave additional details about his life:

A skillful barber he commanded from the beginning a large patronage. His shop was afterwards an institution in Lexington, and enjoyed the patronage of the many honored names in the community. He recalled with pride that he was "Gen. Lee's barber," covering a period of nearly two generations. Always pleasant and courteous, skillful, and industrious in his occupation, upright in his life, and correct in his conduct, he was a worthy citizen, and a successful man in business. . . . He was a communicant of the Baptist church and for many years held the office of deacon of that congregation, an office held at the time of his death. His shop remains under the name of his son, Thomas Jackson, and the latter's sons. He left a widow, the wife of his youth.[35]

Henry Boley confirmed that James was Lee's barber: "James Jackson, 'Deacon,' as he was affectionately known, had been General Lee's barber and told interesting stories of his service to 'de Gen'l.'"[36] Boley added that some of the older townspeople still remembered the barbershop's slogan: "It was good enough for General Lee, it is good enough for you."[37]

The shop is part of the controversy surrounding James Jackson and his connection to Stonewall Jackson. Family and local tradition contends that James Jackson married one of Jackson's slaves. Some accounts, including the 1988 News-Gazette article, report that Amy—the slave to whom Thomas J. Jackson was closest—was James's wife. But the family disputes this. In a four-page, handwritten account of the family's history, Margaret Jenkins contended that, according to family records (and census records would seem to substantiate this claim[38]), James married an Indian woman named Kysanna, also known as "Kissy" or "Kizzy." In those days, the census sometimes referred to Indians as "mulattos" and "persons of color." The Jackson family speculates that James was Amy Jackson's son, but census records and other documentation cast doubt on this. Megan Haley Newman observed: "Local Lexington tradition maintains that Amy was the mother or the first wife of a prominent free black deacon and barber in Lexington named James Jackson. While this connection is possible, given that little information is known about where Amy spent her youth, it is not probable in that James Jackson was born in Campbell County between 1845 and 1850 and moved to Lexington from Lynchburg in 1863, two years after Amy died."[39]

Due to the vagueness in census records regarding "persons of color," as well as scarce genealogical documentation for nineteenth-century blacks, it is possible that Kysanna was part African American. It is also possible that she had some connection with Thomas J. Jackson or Anna.

During my visit with Desmond Jackson, he showed me two very old oak chairs in his home that he claimed came from the Jacksons' kitchen. He told me they had been given to his mother by a Lexington resident. Though oral family histories lack documentation, there is often an element of truth in stories passed down over generations. One thing is certain: James and Kysanna Jackson had a son whom they named Thomas Jackson.[40] This fact is not in dispute; both family and census records confirm this. A newspaper clipping of an obituary from Washington and Lee's special collections[41] indicates that James Jackson was born a free man in Campbell County and moved to Lexington in the summer of 1863. If the dates are accurate, this would have been after Stonewall Jackson's death, and any direct connection to the Confederate general would be unlikely. Yet Margaret Jenkins raised the question as to why James took the name of Jackson—coincidence or was there some connection to Thomas J. Jackson that is undocumented?

The fact that James and Kysanna named their son Thomas also raises questions about a connection to Stonewall Jackson's household through his slaves. And local and family tradition maintains that James's barbershop received financial backing from Stonewall Jackson or his widow.

Regarding the barbershop, James Jackson actually operated two barbershops. According to Margaret Jenkins, the original shop was in the Lexington Hotel on Main Street. The second shop, which remained in operation longer, was on Nelson Street. Jenkins and her father have long wondered: "Where did a black man come up with enough money in those days to purchase real-estate and establish a successful business?"

Though it would have been difficult, it was not unusual for free blacks, before and after the war, to acquire and operate successful business enterprises. Jenkins and her father both believe, based on oral family history passed down from generation to generation, that General Jackson or his widow funded the establishment of the barbershop. Even though census data and the timing of Jackson's death make this claim questionable, the fact that census records involving "persons of color" were often incomplete and inaccurate leaves a possibility that there could be some basis of fact for the claims of James Jackson's descendants. Regardless, the belief that Thomas J. or Anna Jackson provided funds for the barbershop remains a source of pride for his descendants. Margaret Jenkins wrote a poem about the family's association with General Jackson. It is published here, for the first time, by permission:

I Come From
Margaret Jenkins

I come from the house on the hill
My ancestors were great barbers
Three generations to be exact
An' guess who was their most famous customers
Robert E. Lee and Ole Jack.

Thomas Stonewall Jackson
The man who lived on the hill
In the house that stands today
And my grandfathers that is one block away.

I'm excited about my family
And the fact they are Jackson, too
For it is my mother's side of the family
That I know this to be true.

So many things happened
Back in the years of 1852
From then on they lived the good life
Free men to walk the streets
Property owners that no man of
Color could ever reach.

But what good fortune was given to them?
It had to be the man on the hill.

Who bravely helped my fathers?
To own their own land too

Three generations of ownership
That no one tried to undo
Could it have been from this great General too?

I often think of this great man
Some hundred years ago
An' sometime I like to ask myself
Am I part of this man too?

When I left Raddy that afternoon, he asked me to come back and see him again, saying, "I get awful lonely sometimes." I had made a new friend. Some of his last words to me that day are part of Lexington's legacy and a testimony to the Christian influence that shaped the early days of this extraordinary Shenandoah Valley town: "You know, like I say, it might be, but I don't know of any place any better that the whites and coloreds get along like they do here [in Lexington] of all the places I've been in the world." Maybe not in this world, but certainly in the next.

My cell phone rang on December 7, 2005, and I heard Margaret Jenkins's subdued voice. I knew instantly what she was going to say. Raddy was gone. He had died the day before. Jenkins said that her father had not felt well that Tuesday morning and had gone to the emergency room at the Stonewall Jackson Hospital in Lexington. Not able to find any problems, doctors sent him home. When it came time for him to go to work at the *News-Gazette* that afternoon, she begged him not to go but to stay home and rest. Raddy Jackson was old school; he had worked at the *Gazette* for seventy years and was faithful to his part-time job there. Loyalty meant something to Raddy. He drove to work and soon after suffered a heart attack and died on the job.

The day of his funeral that Friday at the Randolph Street United Methodist Church in Lexington was cold. Snow and ice blanketed the ground and crunched underfoot as the mourners carefully made their way to the entrance of the church. Bent but dignified elderly black men and women slowly climbed the stone steps to the church door. You could see in their faces that they knew a legend had passed and an era was over.

As old friends greeted one another with sad smiles and gloved hands, their frosty breath mingled in front of the historic church. Like human lives, the vapors lingered for a moment and then were gone. Being close to Christmas, the church, as well as the surrounding homes and businesses, were decorated for the season. The streets were bustling with activity, and "Merry Christmas" was a frequent refrain as shoppers greeted one another. All around us, friends and tight-knit families throughout the Shenandoah Valley were reuniting for the holidays, renewing friendships and family ties. It seemed odd that this family was gathering to say good-bye at this normally joyous time of year.

The preacher eulogized Raddy as "a great legend in this community." But to those of us who knew him, he was more than a legend: he was an inspiration. He was born on June 14, 1913, five years before Robert E. Lee's oldest daughter, Mary Custis Lee, passed away at the age of eighty-three. He probably knew as much about historic Lexington as any person alive today. It had been his home his whole life as well as four generations before him. He had, at one time, worked three jobs to support his family. In addition to his job at the *News-Gazette,* he had worked at People's National Bank in Lexington for forty-four years and at Washington and Lee University (including the Lee Chapel on Sundays) for forty-three years. One of his daughters related how she had once called the *News-Gazette* and asked, "Is Raddy there?" The employee on the other end of the phone replied, "Sure he's here, what would we do without him?!"

He was an active supporter of youth in his community, refereeing high-school football and basketball games for the Lylburn Downing School as well as other schools in the surrounding area. Raddy left behind four children, ten grandchildren, and thirteen great-grandchildren. The preacher noted that "he insisted in them [his children] knowing God's word." Desmond Radcliff Jackson Jr. was laid to rest in Evergreen Cemetery in Lexington, where many other noted Lexington blacks have been interred also.

I had the honor of knowing Raddy Jackson for a little more than a year, but I am better for that privileged experience and brief friendship. As I left Lexington the day of the funeral, I realized that Raddy Jackson has a lot to teach us.

Fortunately, Lexington never experienced the degree of racial strife that many other parts of the South did. That is not to suggest that blacks did not suffer discrimination in Lexington. But the prevailing civility or the ability to, in the words of Raddy Jackson, "get along" that was present in the Valley during the days of segregation and the civil rights movement was a direct result of the Christian ethos that still permeates the area. This is the fruit of seeds sown by Thomas J. Jackson's efforts among Lexington blacks some 150 years earlier. The inspiration for those efforts came from an unlikely source.

4

Except Some Man Should Guide Me

*Stonewall Jackson and His
Black Sunday-School Class*

A friend loveth at all times, and a brother is born for adversity.
—*Proverbs 17:17*

The iniquity of slavery can never be obliterated without "the mind of
Christ" . . . the man of Galilee took the slave by one hand, and the
owner by the other, set them face to face and said, "You are brothers."
—*Richard Ellsworth Day*

Once you learn to read you will forever be free.
—*Frederick Douglass*

ONE CAN ONLY IMAGINE what it might have been like the first day of Jackson's now famous "Colored Sabbath-School." At a quarter before three in the afternoon on the Lord's Day in the autumn of 1855, church bells in Lexington called all to worship. The lecture room[1] set aside for this new missionary endeavor of the Presbyterian church was bustling with excitement and chatter. Fifteen minutes later, precisely at three o'clock, VMI professor Thomas J. Jackson walked into the lecture room, closing and locking the door behind him. Slipping the key into the pocket of his crisp blue military coat, Jackson turned and approached the lectern. He called his class to order and straightened his notes as he slowly, confidently looked across the room of black faces—slave and free, male and female, young and old. He wanted to bow his head and petition heaven for God's blessing on the humble assembly, but he could not take his eyes off the attentive faces, many nodding and smiling appreciatively, others looking sad and empty. Jackson choked back emotion as his mind was suddenly flooded with boyhood memories in a misty haze of fondness coupled with longing and sorrow. The words of his pious boyhood chum Joe Lightburn ring in his conscience: "They should be free and taught to read so they could read the Bible." The words echo and linger as the Holy Spirit pricked Jackson's heart. He heard Granny Robinson, the black mammy of the Jackson household, quoting Scripture as she rocked a white baby on her lap, intermittently humming an old hymn of the church to quiet the child. The irony of the moment touched Jackson in a profound way. The providence of God has come full circle in Jackson's life. As he was struck by the realization of what God has wrought, Jackson's piercing blue eyes moistened with tears. He gazed upon the eager pupils looking to him for spiritual guidance and their soul's salvation. He recognized many of them. Some have given him donations from their meager earnings for the Rockbridge Bible Society and the printing of Christian literature—literature they cannot read. He owed them a debt: they deserve to know God's word. Jackson gripped the lectern harder as he struggled to control his emotions. The Spirit of God brought a verse from the book of Psalms to his mind: "I looked on my right hand, and beheld, but there was no man that would know me: refuge failed me; no man cared for my soul" (Psalm 142:4). Ah, but there was a man who cared for these souls, and that man was Thomas J. Jackson. God had prepared him for this day. John Lyle was, at that moment, on his knees praying for his dear friend and the souls in his charge—Jackson could feel it. He resolved in his heart that he would not disappoint these needy souls. He would not fail in the charge laid at his feet by the divine destiny of almighty God. He would give the gospel to the poor, and he would do so with zeal and determination. Jackson composed himself, squared his shoulders, and with trembling voice resolutely implored the gathering, "Let us pray."

The history of Jackson's black Sunday-school class or "Colored Sabbath School," as it was officially known, has been the subject of discussions and articles since its humble beginning in the Lexington Presbyterian Church[2] some 150 years ago. Yet the subject usually receives scant mention compared to Jackson's battlefield accomplishments. Though Jackson's ministry efforts are the best known and yielded the greatest long-term fruits, the often repeated myth that Jackson's was the first such Presbyterian Sabbath school for slaves in Lexington is not supported by historical fact. That honor likely belongs to another. In 1845, Dr. William H. Ruffner,[3] a Presbyterian minister and educator, with the aid of the Reverend Beverly Tucker Lacy,[4] founded the original school for slaves and free blacks at the church. One source claims that there "were as many as one hundred black pupils from the spring of 1845 until the end of the college year in summer."[5] Francis H. Smith, superintendent at Virginia Military Institute and also a devout Christian, likewise taught a black Sunday-school class as early as 1843 at Lexington's Grace Episcopal Church. This is the same year that slave baptisms first appear in church records. Smith stated in a letter to L. H. Young in March 1855 that he had conducted a Sabbath school for "a large class of colored persons."[6] And even as early as the 1830s in Lexington, Dr. Alfred Leyburn taught the basics of Christianity to the area's black populace.[7] The Reverend George A. Baxter served as pastor of Lexington Presbyterian Church from 1829 to 1831 and expressed the general sentiment of his congregation: "We believe that the duty of giving religious instruction to the coloured people, is a most solemn duty,—a duty which has been too long neglected,—to which our eyes are just beginning to be opened,—and which cannot be neglected any longer, without bringing great guilt, both upon the country and the church. . . . We believe that God has never destroyed a nation in which was found a pious and faithful church."[8]

William H. Ruffner was a zealous clergyman, as was his father, Henry Ruffner, who served as president of Washington College from 1836 to 1848. Originally trained for the ministry, the younger Ruffner left his mark on Old Virginia, eventually becoming the state's first superintendent of public education in 1870, for which he is known as the "father of Virginia's free school system"—a title Ruffner would find somewhat dubious today, given our modern government schools' plaguelike attitude toward anything remotely Christian.

Interest in the original black Sunday schools diminished until Jackson revived the idea in the autumn of 1855,[9] the same year the town experienced a dramatic spiritual awakening and revival. It is likely that Jackson's efforts were encouraged by the spiritual atmosphere among believers at that time. Worth mentioning is the fact that Ruffner's father published one of the most convincing arguments for the abolition of slavery up to that time. Entitled *Address to the People,* Ruffner appealed to the economic interests rather than the moral objections of Virginians for ending slavery. For example, he pointed out that though Virginia and other Southern states were rich in farmland and natural resources, statistics showed that "farm laborers in the free states produced 40 percent more income per capita than those in slave states."[10] He cited other economic statistics in a powerful argument demonstrating that slavery was not economically sound and was hurting the state's economy. Ruffner recognized what Booker T. Washington later observed:

> Ever since I have been old enough to think for myself, I have entertained the idea that, notwithstanding the cruel wrongs inflicted upon us, the black man got nearly as much out of slavery as the white man did. The hurtful influences of the institution were not by any means confined to the Negro. This was fully illustrated by the life upon our own plantation. The whole machinery of slavery was so constructed as to cause labour, as a rule, to be looked upon as a badge of degradation, of inferiority. Hence labour was something that both races on the slave plantation sought to escape. The slave system on our place, in large measure, took the spirit of self-reliance and self help out of the white people. My old master had many boys and girls, but not one, so far as I know, ever mastered a single trade or special line of productive industry.[11]

One of the basic tenets of free-market economics is that forced labor is inefficient—human beings simply do not produce to their full potential without the promise of reward. And as Washington pointed out, relying on others promotes sloth and a condescending attitude toward manual labor and industry. Ruffner suggested there was only one reason that farm production in free states surpassed that in slave states: "The only cause that can be assigned is that where slavery prevails, commerce and navigation cannot flourish." Though Ruffner offered yet another proposal for the gradual emancipation of the slaves, beginning in the western counties, Eastern newspapers labeled his essay "abolitionist." That label, though inaccurate, doomed its appeal. Although there is no record of Jackson ever referring to Ruffner's pamphlet, the connection the two shared with Lexington makes it plausible that Jackson was influenced by Ruffner's opinions. Jackson's conduct and efforts among the town's slave population certainly indicates he was at least sympathetic to Ruffner's ideas. Even Virginia's wartime governor, John Letcher, was persuaded to endorse Ruffner's petition for emancipation.[12] Undoubtedly, in Jackson's conversations with Letcher and the younger Ruffner (nephew to John B. Lyle) in Lyle's bookstore, the subject of abolition would have been raised and discussed. Given the presence of these individuals and the gathering storm clouds on the horizon, the elder Ruffner's pamphlet and his arguments would have been central to any debate on the abolition of slavery.

When reflecting on the efforts of Jackson and other Southern Christians to reach slaves and free blacks with the good news of the gospel, it is necessary to understand that many modern scholars view their motives with cynicism. A superficial study of the subject could easily conclude that teaching the slaves simple gospel messages was nothing more than an effort to make them more obedient and submissive. Admittedly, there are ample Bible verses that admonish obedience to authority that the spiritually shallow used to accomplish this task while at the same time ignoring the slaves' spiritual needs.

Yet a serious and objective look at the facts shows that, although this element was present in the motives of some, most sincere Southern Christians had a heartfelt desire to see blacks turn to Christ and embrace the eternal truths of the Bible. The Presbyterian Synod of Texas issued a statement that reflected the attitude of many Southern Christians: "We recognize the hand of God in placing this benighted race in our midst, and heartily accept the duty of pointing them to Christ."[13] Stonewall Jackson House graduate fellow E. Lynn Pearson's observation confirms this attitude: "The religious world-view of Stonewall Jackson and his antebellum peers was greatly influenced by the contemporary evangelical vision to build Christ's kingdom on earth, and the Southern belief that bringing salvation to slaves was part and parcel of that mission. Lexington's Christians took great pride in their acceptance of Christ's call to stewardship."[14]

Historians often look to a single pivotal event when analyzing antebellum efforts to evangelize Southern blacks: Nat Turner's slave insurrection. This slave revolt struck fear in the hearts of many Virginians.

Moreover, Turner had been taught to read the Bible and was a slave preacher. Believing he was on a mission inspired by God, on August 21, 1831—a Sunday night—following a church service, Turner and six followers murdered Turner's master, Joseph Travis, and his wife and infant child in Southampton County. Before the night was over, more than fifty additional slaves joined Turner, and together they killed more than fifty-five whites in the surrounding countryside. Eventually caught, tried, and convicted, Turner and nineteen disciples were hanged. Sadly, overzealous militiamen murdered more than twenty innocent blacks.

Nat Turner's revolt gave rise to two developments in Virginia: one regarding the law and another on how the church looked at evangelizing blacks. The general assembly established laws during the session of 1831–32 dictating tighter restrictions on the instruction of slaves and free blacks. Fearful that the attempt to evangelize blacks had contributed in part to Turner's rampage, the legislature enacted the following statute:

Code of Virginia, Ch. 198—Offences against Public Policy. (Item) 35. Every Assemblage of negroes for the purpose of religious worship, when such worship is conducted by a negro, and every assemblage of negroes for the purpose of instruction in reading or writing, or in the night time for any purpose, shall be an unlawful assembly. Any justice may issue warrant to any officer or other person, requiring him to enter any place where such assemblage may be, and seize any negro therein; and he, or any other justice, may order such negro to be punished with stripes. (Item) 36. If a white person assemble with negroes for the purpose of instructing them to read or write, or if he associate with them in an unlawful assembly, he shall be confined in jail not exceeding six months and fined not exceeding one hundred dollars; and any justice may require him to enter into a recognizance with sufficient security, to appear before the circuit, county, or cooperation court, of the county, or corporation where the offense was committed, to answer, therefore, and in the meantime to keep the peace and be of good behavior.[15]

Concerns arose within the Christian community as well. Since Turner had been a slave preacher and read the Bible, many Southern churchmen were convinced that his crimes were a direct result of efforts to teach slaves to read and to reach them with the gospel. But it is a myth to think that only those in Southern states feared what might occur if blacks were literate. As black historian Carter Woodson noted:

> The reactionary movement, however, was not confined to the South. The increased migration of fugitives and free Negroes to the asylum of Northern States, caused certain communities of that section to feel that they were about to be overrun by undesirable persons who could not be easily assimilated. The subsequent anti-abolition riots in the North made it difficult for friends of the Negroes to raise funds to educate them. Free persons of color were not allowed to open schools in some places, teachers of Negroes were driven from their stations, and colored schoolhouses were burned.[16]

Even so, the Nat Turner incident had the opposite effect on many missionary-minded Southerners. Woodson further explained that some whites ignored the law, choosing to answer to a "higher calling":

> Many of these opportunities were made possible by the desire to teach slaves religion. . . . White men who diffused such information ran the gauntlet of mobs, but like a Baptist preacher of South Carolina who was threatened with expulsion from his church, if he did not desist, they worked on and overcame the local prejudice. When preachers themselves dared not undertake this task it was often done by their children, whose benevolent work was winked at as an indulgence to the clerical profession. . . . Many southerners braved the terrors of public opinion and taught their Negroes to read the Scriptures. To this extent General Coxe of Fluvanna County, Virginia, taught about one hundred of his adult slaves. While serving as a professor of the Military Institute at Lexington, Stonewall Jackson taught a class of Negroes in a Sunday-school.[17]

In 1832, the Presbyterian Synod of Virginia became concerned about the neglect of religious instruction for slaves brought about by the recently passed law. Statements were issued encouraging local churches to fill the need. A committee was formed at the Lexington church to discuss the matter and propose remedies. Elder Sidney Baxter, who headed the committee, noted: "There should be a regular course of instruction given them. The only means of doing this is to authorize some of the lay members of the congregation to conduct meetings for their benefit, as recommended by the Synod."[18]

All members who owned slaves were also encouraged to "give them religious instruction along with family members." Members were also admonished to "promote the attendance of their servants at the meetings of the church." These efforts continued with sporadic "support and neglect" until Jackson arrived in Lexington and started his class.

Edward D. Smith noted the impact of the Nat Turner rebellion on Southern Christian attitudes in *Climbing Jacob's Ladder: The Rise of Black Churches in Eastern American Cities*:

> As the reaction against Christianized blacks developed [after Nat Turner's rebellion], a number of southern churchmen began a quiet campaign to bring about the Christianization of even more blacks. This campaign was begun partially as a reaction to the growing abolitionist movement in the North, which denounced slave-owners as anti-Christian. . . . Some churchmen hoped to prove that when placed solely under white control, religious instruction could be used to make slaves more obedient, docile, and well behaved.[19]

It is with this sentiment of making slaves "more obedient, docile, and well behaved" with the influence of Christianity that many cynics charge Jackson and others. While this attitude indeed existed among some Southern believers and unbelievers alike, it is incorrect to interpret such control as Jackson's motive. First, Jackson expressed concern over blacks' lack of religious instruction long before Turner's uprising and Jackson's coming to Lexington. When Jackson was seventeen years old, he and his friend Thaddeus Moore were sent by Jackson's Uncle Cummins to Parkersburg to pick up a piece of machinery for the mill. Moore kept a journal of their trip. They passed a farm owned by a Mr. Adams while a slave funeral was in progress. Moore recorded: "They carried the coffin across the road from the cabin and buried him in the field. It was a nice black coffin and the grave was deep. . . . Thom seemed to be very sorry for the race and thought they should be free and have a chance, and said that Joe Lightburn said they should be taught to read so they could read the Bible, and he thought so too. I told him it would be better not to make known such views."[20]

This is one indication that, at a young age, Tom Jackson and his conscience answered to a higher Judge than many around him and that his heart held a special sensitivity for the plight of blacks despite the unpopularity and risk involved with such opinions. It also illustrates that Jackson's mind had dwelled on the need for slaves to be taught to read so that they might discover the truths of God's Word and experience true freedom, not just to make them "more obedient." Biographer Roy Bird Cook observed: "Thomas was addicted to spells of contemplation. Sitting by the side of the millrace or at the end of the dam, he would be seen in a book or engaged in silent meditation."[21] God was preparing Jackson's heart, mind, and attitudes for the work that lay ahead of him, a work that would yield a bountiful harvest for generations.

Young Thomas Jackson also had an early experience in teaching blacks to read. He once taught a slave boy to read in exchange for a supply of pine knots to burn for light so Jackson could study at night. But after the slave learned to write, he forged a pass and fled to Canada.[22]

Second, according to several accounts, Jackson persisted in teaching blacks despite scorn and even the threat of prosecution for violating the law. One local stated that Jackson was subjected to "taunts and scorns for the sake of those poor people that nobody cared for."[23] While hard evidence of Jackson's actually teaching black students in his Sunday-school class to read is not to be found, there is sufficient circumstantial evidence to convict him. One historian goes so far as to say that Jackson's Sunday school operated in a "school-like atmosphere" and that "evidence strongly suggests that the teachers taught reading before the war."[24] Jackson did instruct Anna, in direct violation of state law, to teach their slaves to read. Referring to Hetty's two sons, Anna wrote, "At his request I taught them to read, and he required them to attend family worship, Sunday-school, and church."[25] Also, the ultimate successes of some of Jackson's pupils indicate that literacy was, at the very least, an unmentioned goal of the classes. Certainly Jackson never forgot that education had rescued him from poverty in western Virginia. Had Jackson not received a West Point education, he never would have attained his station in life. What education had done for him, he was convinced would do for his black brethren, intellectually as well as spiritually.

Further evidence of Jackson's teaching his black students to read abounds. He himself was an avid reader. By 1861 his library consisted of 122 books, primarily histories and biographies.[26] It would be difficult for even the most skeptical cynic to believe that an avid reader and lover of God's Word involved in the evangelization of illiterates would not want to share the gift of reading with those most in need, particularly since he had already realized that need and shared his thoughts with at least one other person. Furthermore, it is known that Jackson awarded his most faithful students with New Testaments and Bibles. It would be illogical to conclude that he would give such awards to those who could not read and that he would not endeavor to teach basic literacy skills so they could use their Bibles. It is also illogical to believe that if he were instructing blacks to read, that he would exert great efforts to make this known publicly, since it was illegal. This could explain the scarcity of hard documentation. Jackson was no doubt aware of Solomon's admonition: "A prudent man concealeth knowledge" (Proverbs 12:23).[27] If Jackson were teaching his black Sunday-school students to read, he was doing it for their benefit and the glory of God, not public accolades.

But there are public accounts that Jackson was involved in this literary effort and that, at least on one occasion, he was threatened with criminal prosecution. In 1858, two Lexington attorneys—Samuel McDowell Reid[28] and William McLaughlin[29]—approached Jackson in front of the Lexington courthouse to discuss the illegality of his class. The following account[30] of the incident was given by another attorney and participant in the confrontation, James D. Davidson:

> In the Spring of 1858,[31] T. J. Jackson, then a Professor in the Virginia Military Institute at Lexington, Va.,—now our Stonewall Jackson—was organizing a negro Sunday School in the town of Lexington.
>
> At that time such a school was regarded by our laws as an "unlawful assembly." On Saturday evening of May 1st, 1858, I left my office, and on my way home met Maj. Jackson on the pavement in front of the Court House in company with Colonel S. McD. Reid, then Clerk of our Courts,

and Wm. McLaughlin, Esq., now Judge of our Circuit Court. They were conversing on the subject of his Sunday school.

Colonel Reid said to him, "I have examined the Statute and conferred with the Commonwealth's attorney. Your Sunday School is an 'unlawful assembly.'"

This seemed to fret him much. Mr. McLaughlin then said to him that he had also examined the question, and that his school was against the letter of the law. This fretted him still more. I then said to him, "Major, whilst I lament that we have such a statute in our Code, I am satisfied that your Sunday school is an 'unlawful assembly,' and probably the Grand Jury will take it up and test it."

This threw him off his guard, and he replied with warmth: "Sir, if you were, as you should be, a Christian man, you would not think or say so." Thus also thrown off my guard, I replied tartly, in words not now remembered; when he turned upon his heel and walked to his house on the opposite side of the street.

I passed on home, and had not gone half way when I began to rebuke myself for my rudeness to Maj. Jackson, and determined to return and apologize to him.

Reaching home, I found my wife and relative, Maj. Dorman, sitting together. I told them what had occurred, and requested my wife to give me an early supper, that I might return and make my apology.

I returned to my office after dusk taking with me a negro boy to bear my apology in writing to Maj. Jackson.

I had commenced writing it, and when half written I heard a tap at my office door, when Major Jackson stepped in, saying, "Mr. Davidson, I am afraid I wounded your feelings this evening. I have called to apologize to you." "No Major," I replied, "no apology from you to me. I am now writing my apology to you."

He remained for more than half an hour conversing with me, and when he left he said in these words: "Mr. Davidson, these are the things that bring men together and make them know each other the better."

The half-written note of apology I now find amongst my papers. This incident speaks for itself, and reveals some, at least, of the features of that great and good man.

J. D. Davidson

The following is the text of Davidson's unfinished note of apology: "Maj. Jackson—Dear Sir: As I shall not have an opportunity of meeting you again before Monday, I will not rest content until I shall have tendered you a becoming apology for the hasty, and I fear uncourteous reply made by me to you in conversation this evening—."

Perhaps both men recalled the words of John Randolph:

> Reprove not, in their wrath, excited men;
> good counsel comes all out of season then:
> but when their fury is appeased and past,
> they will perceive their faults, and mend at last.[32]

The two friends mended their differences; there is no record of any legal action ever being taken against Jackson. It is interesting to observe that Jackson made no effort to deny the accusations, leading one to conclude he was, in fact, in violation of the law. Furthermore, the law also prohibited meeting with blacks "in the night time for *any* purpose . . . or if he *associate* with them in an unlawful assembly"—thus making Jackson's evening family worship sessions with neighborhood blacks illegal as well.

The incident with Davidson, McLaughlin, and Reid reveals the depth of Jackson's commitment and his conviction that he was involved in a good work and one that the Creator sanctioned, regardless of what the Virginia legislature had decreed. It also reveals his willingness to take considerable personal risk for the sake of his black students and the promotion of the gospel. Jackson was at this time a prominent citizen, but his position did not deter him from doing what he believed to be right. Despite the criticism and threats, a good many townspeople appreciated his efforts to spread the gospel among the area's blacks. Efforts to increase and encourage attendance were very public. A *Lexington Gazette* article[33] from November 8, 1860, made an open plea to slave owners to encourage their "servants" to attend "the colored Sunday school" to be "instructed." Though the article was published anonymously by "Veritas" and does not mention Jackson by name, it is safe to assume that the plea came from someone associated with Jackson's class because it refers to the "Presbyterian school," numbered current attendance at "between seventy and eighty," and mentioned the well-known fact of Jackson's sending monthly reports to the slaves' owners.

There are other lesser-known evidences revealing Jackson's concerns for the souls of blacks. Due to the limited seating in the Presbyterian sanctuary, many blacks were unable to attend regular Sunday-morning worship services. William Spottswood White mentions the problem in his biography: "To obviate this, my first effort was to preach to them on Sabbath afternoon. For a time many attended and seemed interested; but the practical exclusion from our house of worship had turned them to the Baptist and Methodist churches."[34]

Evidently, this situation disturbed Jackson. It was 1858, and Jackson had been teaching his class for two years. He had a successful track record and had become personally involved in many of his students' lives. He prayed for them on a regular basis, and they admired, respected, and loved him. Jackson knew this and had a genuine concern for their spiritual well-being. At least one African American had been given a responsibility beyond just attending church services. Congregational minutes from November 17, 1856, note that the black sexton of the church was "required to attend at the door of the church and invite strangers and citizens" to come in to worship.[35] Certainly, if a black man could invite others to the services, there should be room for black Christians as well. Having "colored people" excluded from morning worship and White's fine preaching could not continue. By now, Jackson was a deacon. His opinions and stature were respected throughout the community, but this was especially true within the fellowship of Lexington Presbyterian Church. Pastor White had the utmost confidence in him, and Jackson knew this. Although he was not known to use his position or strength of character for selfish designs, when Jackson saw something that needed attention, especially in the spiritual realm, he was bold about accomplishing the task at hand. So when the deacons of the church met on January 2, 1858, he personally appealed, on behalf of his black brethren, to the church elders: "We believe there is a strong disposition among the colored population to worship with us, and we earnestly solicit the session to consider the necessity of affording them accommodations."[36]

Jackson's plea convinced the church to expand. The church elders approved an expansion of the sanctuary in August and increased "seating capacity by adding 37 pews downstairs and 16 to the gallery." The architect's report noted that the "colored people" would enter the sanctuary through a side entrance "by means of a stairway."[37] According to White, after the extra pews were added, the "additional room was soon filled, every pew was taken, and the size of the congregation greatly increased."[38] Jackson had once again proved that he was, indeed, "the black man's friend." His influence on behalf of his black brethren is further evidenced in session notes on July 7, 1859. The carefully handwritten minutes show that a motion was made that "ordered that the Pastor pay over to the Superintendent of the Coloured Sabbath School, so much of the recent contribution in behalf of the Sabbath Schools, as may be needed by that School not exceeding 15[.]00 and balance to the Superintendent of the White Sabbath School."[39] Even during the bitter years of Reconstruction, "the mild and melting influence of Christianity" held sway among Lexington's Christian population, and most blacks and whites remained on peaceable terms, especially in the Lexington Presbyterian Church. On one occasion, a black woman named Catherine Terry was being disciplined by the Colored Baptist Church of Lexington for "questionable conduct." She presented her case to the Lexington Presbyterian Session in 1871, and upon further investigation, the elders concluded that the charges "were not sustained by the facts." She was admitted as a member in December and was the only black member of the church at that time.[40]

Prior to starting the black Sunday-school class, Jackson was teaching a white boys Sunday-school class in February 1852. So Jackson actually taught two classes every Sunday. Some of these boys would later fight under his command; at least two of them would die.[41] Confederate Capt. Thomas S. Doyle described his experience in one of Jackson's classes:

Certainly, he seemed devoted to his work, and he did it in such a fashion that his pupils found it pleasant. . . . His voice was remarkably soft in tone, his utterances quick, and, while he talked he looked straight into (not at or about) the eyes of the person he was especially addressing. There was nothing of fierceness or sternness in his gaze, but an unwavering steadiness, such as I have never seen equaled. As a matter of course, he was punctual in his attendance on his class. So far as I can remember, he was never absent from Sunday school a single time during the three years that I belonged to his class. He always wore his uniform, and every button of his coat was buttoned, no matter how warm the weather . . . we held him up to ourselves as an ideal of what a real soldier should be.[42]

By the time Jackson began teaching the black Sunday-school class, he had taken on the additional responsibility of teaching a class for Washington College students and VMI cadets. And by 1855, Lexington Presbyterian Church's membership rolls included 307 whites and 11 blacks.

The actual origin of Jackson's black Sunday-school class has been the subject of some debate. Since the church kept no official records of his class, the information comes from letters and articles. One source claims that Jackson started the class when he roomed at the home of his first wife, Ellie Junkin. Another writer, the Reverend J. William Jones, suggested that Jackson's desire to start the class developed out of his family worship services. Jackson required his household servants to be present for daily prayer and Bible reading. According to Jones,

He also had a special meeting with them every Sunday afternoon in order to teach them the Scriptures. He made this exercise so interesting to them that other negroes of the town craved the privilege of attending and he soon had his room full to overflowing of eager pupils. This suggested to him the idea of organizing a negro Sunday-school, which he did for several years before the war, and to which he devoted all of the energies of his mind and all the zeal of his large, Christian heart.[43]

Other biographers dispute these claims, including James I. Robertson. He asserts that Jackson's motivation was simply the destitute condition of religious interest among Lexington-area blacks, citing one of Jackson's co-workers in the class as saying, "A sense of duty impelled him to make an effort to redeem them from the slavery of sin."[44] While Jones contended that the Sunday-school class resulted from slaves attending family worship in the Jacksons' home, R. L. Dabney declared the opposite to be true.[45] Dabney wrote that Jackson's Sunday-school prayers "were so attractive to them" that many requested they be allowed to "be admitted on Sabbath nights, along with his own servants, to his evening domestic worship."[46] As previously noted, state law specifically forbade gatherings of blacks "in the night time for any purpose" as "an unlawful assembly." According to Dabney, Jackson received permission for these assemblies from Pastor White and the slaves' masters.

Regardless of whether Jones or Dabney is correct, there is little doubt Jackson was sincere in his missionary attitude toward those who needed the gospel—regardless of the color of their skin. When asked by John Preston how he would respond if God were to call him to be "a missionary in darkest Africa," Jackson responded, "I'd go without my hat."[47]

Still other historians have suggested that Jackson's class grew out of his work with the Rockbridge Bible Society.[48] Jackson had attended the first meeting of the society and, according to James I. Robertson, "was among the first enlistees, and became one of thirteen members of the Board of Managers."[49] He was faithful in attending the society's regular meetings and contributed financially to its work.

Pastor William S. White recounted an incident that lends credence to the view that this work with the Rockbridge Bible Society was the genesis of Jackson's black Sunday-school class:

> On one occasion Gen. Thomas J. Jackson was appointed one of the collectors for the Bible Society. When he returned his list it was discovered that, at the end, copied by the clerk of the session, was a considerable number of names written in pencil, to each of which a very small amount was attached. Moreover, the session, recognizing very few of the names, asked who these were. Jackson's characteristic reply was, "They are the militia; as the Bible Society is not a Presbyterian but a Christian cause, I deemed it best to go beyond the limits of our own church." They were the names chiefly of free negros.[50]

Robert Lewis Dabney added these comments about Jackson's fundraising among Lexington's blacks: "The free blacks of the quarters, all of whom he had visited in their humble dwellings, and encouraged to give a pittance of their earnings to print Bibles. He argued that these small sums were better spent thus than in drink or tobacco; that the giving of them would elevate their self-respect, and enhance their own interest in the Holy Book; and that they being indebted to it as well as others, should be taught to help in diffusing it."[51]

Notable is the fact that Jackson wanted blacks to "elevate their self-respect"—exactly the opposite stereotype of the slave owners in the South. He did not want blacks to think less of themselves but rather more of themselves as children of God. He did not look down on them as unable or unworthy to give and participate in the advancement of the gospel. This is one of the reasons that mutual respect for Jackson grew out of this relationship: he expected from them what others did not. Furthermore, he believed what many other whites at that time did not—that blacks were capable of greater things. That attitude garnered respect.

One can picture the devout and zealous Presbyterian deacon knocking respectfully and confidently at the door of a free black's shanty, hat in hand, perhaps becoming a little doubtful about soliciting funds from such impoverished members of society. After noticing the poor condition of the humble home, somewhat ashamed, Jackson may have considered turning and walking away before the door opened. Imagine Jackson describing the work of the Bible society to these illiterate blacks: the publication of tracts and books for Sabbath schools and education for the ministry. He would be soliciting donations for reading materials from those who could not read. He would be looking into sad faces of people who could not enjoy the benefits of reading. Did God convict him of the inequity of their plight? Yes, these blacks gave, some sacrificially, to an endeavor they had little hope of benefiting from in any meaningful way. One wonders what thoughts came to Jackson as he looked into the eyes of poor black men as they handed him a few coins for the work of the gospel. It is not unlikely that his heart was touched and convicted of the ironic injustice of such a selfless act. Or was it the simple and profound beauty of such a sacrificial gift? As Jackson went from house to house, his heart was continually touched by the need. He was reminded of his own orphaned childhood, void of any real educational opportunities that once prompted him to write a relative, "My mother and father died when I was very young and I had to work for my living and education both."[52] Perhaps as he made out his report, writing each name and donation, God impressed upon his heart and mind the call of reaching these blacks with the gospel, teaching them to read so that they could benefit from the blessings of the printed word, as his youthful friend Joe Lightburn had suggested.

Another reliable, though patronizing, firsthand account of the origin of Jackson's class is a widely circulated article written by Margaret Junkin Preston and originally printed in the *Sunday School Times*, December 3, 1887.[53] Margaret Preston was Jackson's sister-in-law from his first marriage. A writer of some renown, she was also known as the "Poetess of the Confederacy."

She wrote, "Two persons were conversing together as to what could be done for the better religious instruction of the Negroes around them." One of these persons was, of course, Jackson. Preston refers to the other as "the young lady."[54] Most historians believe the young lady referred to was Preston herself. She claims it was this "young lady" who was the inspiration of the class, quoting her as saying: "Major, I have a great notion to announce among the servants of our neighbors that I will have a Bible class for them in my father's study every Sunday afternoon. I think I have somewhat of a gift for simplifying Bible teaching, and I believe I can interest these people enough to bring as many together as I could teach. What do you think of my plan?" According to Preston, he replied: "Since you propose the thing, I think I can hit upon a better plan; which is that, instead of collecting merely the servants of your neighbors in your father's study, we should get up, in our church lecture room, a regular Sunday school, for the servants at large."[55]

Preston then reminded Jackson of the past attempts and failures of such an endeavor. He was characteristically undeterred: "But it shall succeed if I undertake it, because I make it a point to weigh all circumstances before I act; and if the thing is feasible, and I am right, then I make it succeed if that is possible."

Jackson had obviously been giving the idea some consideration as he already had a plan in mind. He continued: "Now this is the plan I would adopt: So that no fault could be found in my action, I will go around to the principal householders in the town, and ask their permission to gather their servants into an afternoon Sunday school. Then, after I have so gathered them, for two or three Sundays, I will undertake them myself."[56]

Jackson immediately set upon visiting Lexington's slaveholders, seeking their permission. Many were members of other churches, but "there was not a single objection made to the plan proposed."

He emphasized the need for responsibility and faithfulness to his pupils on the first day of his class, telling them that their masters "are not going to make you come to the school" and that "they can't make Christians of you unless you are willing to be taught yourselves."[57] Jackson then instructed those willing to commit to faithful attendance to come forward and give him their names. Immediately, they came, "men and women, gray-headed, some of them, half-grown girls and boys, and toddling children, began to proclaim their names."[58]

The sight must have moved Jackson. At the end of the forty-five-minute session, there were fifty names on the roll. The success and reputation of the school spread quickly through Lexington and the surrounding countryside. Jackson solicited the assistance of other "young ladies and gentlemen" in the church. Excitement over the new, revitalized ministry grew, as did attendance, and this despite Jackson's rigid rules and discipline. If pupils were not in the church lecture room by the time class started, precisely at 3:00 p.m. on Sunday afternoon, the door was locked. What happened after that is best described in Jackson's own words. In a June 7, 1858, letter to John Lyle Campbell—a friend, a professor at Washington College, and a fellow member and elder of the Lexington Presbyterian Church—Jackson succinctly described his class. This letter[59] was written just prior to Campbell's departure for a Sunday school convention in Richmond for delegates from Sunday schools all over Virginia. Campbell was, at that time, serving as superintendent of the Lexington Presbyterian Church Sunday school. The letter was penned almost two years after the school's beginnings and within a month or so of the confrontation at the courthouse:

In compliance with your request I proceed to give you a statement respecting the condition of the Lexington Colored Sabbath School. But in doing so, I feel it unnecessary to say more than a few words, as you are already acquainted with its leading features. The school is usually opened by singing part of a hymn, which should be announced the previous Sabbath. This is followed by reading one or more verses from the Bible, with explanations & applications; this is succeeded by prayer. After this each class is instructed by its teacher from the Bible, catechism and hymn book. At the close of the school which is near forty five minutes from the opening, there is a public examination on two verses of the child catechism, published by our Board. These verses should be announced the previous Sabbath. After the close of the examination, the school is dismissed, the remaining part of the opening hymn having been sung immediately after the examination.

The system of reward you are acquainted with, and the premiums so far have been near a dozen Testaments and one Bible. The day of their presentation is the first Sabbath of each month. Several scholars are studying the shorter catechism at the present time. Each teacher keeps a class book in which is noted each scholar's department in school. The lesson should be taught one Sabbath, with a view to examination & mark on the next. Each teacher at the close of the month give me a circular (blanks having been furnished) exhibiting for each scholar the manner in which the lesson has been prepared, the conduct in school, no. of lates, absences, &c. From these circulars, I make a monthly entry in the record book, which contains not only the no. of lates & absences, but also the names of the teachers, scholars, owners, persons with whom the scholars are living, the lates & absences of teachers, and a weekly record of the proceedings of the school. By reference to the record book, I find 91 to be the no. of scholars there reported.

Praying that the S. school convention may be a great blessing to the cause & to yourself I remain your attached friend.

T. J. Jackson

Prof. J. L. Campbell

By admitting in writing that he was giving out Bibles and testaments, Jackson once again demonstrated he feared not what others, including the authorities, would think. By his stating, "Several scholars are studying the shorter catechism at the present time," he effectively acknowledged that his black students were being instructed in reading materials. At the very least, Jackson was on questionable grounds when it came to complying with the state's prohibition against "every assemblage of negroes for the purpose of instruction in reading or writing." Washington and Lee history professor Theodore C. DeLaney Jr. further points out that Preston wrote, "The instruction was *almost* wholly oral, as only a few of the older servants had been taught to read."[60] By not elaborating, DeLaney notes that Preston "left open the possibility of a legal problem."[61] The "catechism" referred to and used by Jackson was *Brown's Child's Catechism*. Preston was one of the teachers referred to in Jackson's letter. Other teachers[62] were "recruited from among the educated ladies and gentlemen in town"[63] and included, among others, John Preston and Anna Jackson. Mrs. Jackson had once suggested that he concentrate his Sunday-school efforts on white children, but Jackson disagreed and informed her that he believed "it was more important and useful to put the strong hand of the Gospel under the ignorant African race, to lift them up."[64] Anna came to love the class as Jackson did, writing, "I have always felt thankful that his wishes guided me in this matter, for it was a privilege to witness his great interest and zeal in the work, and never did his face beam with more intelligence and earnestness than when he was telling the colored children of his Sabbath-school the story of the cross."[65]

Jackson kept close watch on his students' progress. If he noticed someone missing, "He would invariably visit the master or mistress to make inquiries as to the reason of their non-attendance."[66] Jackson was not a detached instructor, just doing his duty. He took a personal interest in each student and "cultivated the acquaintance of every scholar in the school" from the oldest to the youngest. The monthly reports that he submitted regarding progress and attendance were not only for his records. Pastor William White noted: "He issued monthly reports to the owners of the slaves. These reports he delivered in person, calling each month at every house where one of his pupils lived. When necessary he conferred with the family about all matters connected with the behavior or misbehavior of the pupils. Under his management this school became one of the most interesting and useful institutions in the church."[67]

Margaret Preston made specific mention that she was moved by the "courtesy of their politeness" whenever Jackson chanced meeting one of his students on the streets of Lexington, and "none of them did he ever pass without lifting his cap to them; and not a child passed him without giving him a pull at his frizzly forelock, or curtsying till her apron touched the ground."[68] When duty ultimately called Jackson away from Lexington, "His pupils parted with him we cannot say with how many tears."[69]

When Jackson left Lexington, he took with him the remembrance of those tears. Even in the excitement, accolades, and responsibility of the war, he could not forget his ministry back home and the precious souls whom God had put in his charge. Anna Jackson relates an often repeated story that illustrates his concern for his scholars and the ministry:

A day or two after the battle of [First] Manassas, and before the news of the victory had reached Lexington in authentic form, the post-office was thronged with people, awaiting with intense interest the opening of the mail. Soon a letter was handed to the Rev. Dr. White, who immediately recognized the well known superscription of his deacon soldier, and exclaimed to the eager and expectant group around him: "Now we shall know the facts." Upon opening it the bulletin read thus: "My dear pastor, in my tent last night, after a fatiguing day's service, I remembered that I had failed to send you my contribution for our colored Sunday-school. Enclosed you will find my check for that object, which please acknowledge at your earliest convenience, and oblige yours faithfully, T. J. Jackson."[70]

J. William Jones's account of the incident adds that the check enclosed was "for fifty dollars with which to buy books for his colored Sunday-school."[71] Jones added: "He had no time or inclination to write of the great victory and the imperishable laurels he was winning; but he found time to remember his noble work among God's poor, and to contribute further to the good of the negro children whose true friend and benefactor he had always been. And he was accustomed to say that one of the very greatest privations to him which the war brought, was that he was taken away from his loved work in the colored Sunday-school."[72]

Another, lesser-known account of Jackson's preoccupation with his class during the war comes from an article by G. W. Cable appearing in the *Century*. In an article titled "The Gentler Side of Two Great Southerners,"[73] Cable recounts a postwar conversation he had with George H. Moffett. Moffett attended Washington College and fought in the Eleventh Virginia Cavalry. He told Cable that his acquaintance with Jackson "was only such as a boy of sixteen would have with a man of mature years. Our only point of intimate contact lay in the fact that I taught a class in the now famous colored Sunday-school which he had organized in connection with the Presbyterian church of the town. But I believe this Sunday-school of negro children of which he was superintendent lay closer to his heart than any other object on earth except his home and family."

Moffett recounted how he and Jackson discussed the Sunday school on a chance meeting in early August 1862: "I found General Jackson, his cap drawn down over his forehead, riding alone and apparently buried in deep meditation of his strategic plans. I rode by with a silent salute, but he recognized me, called to me to halt, and, riding up by my side, began to talk about the colored Sunday-school in Lexington. It was a great gratification to him, he said, that the school was being kept up in his absence. So we parted, and he rode on to bloody victory."

Even in the heat of battle, Jackson's thoughts turned to his gospel work in Lexington. A few weeks later, during the battle of Second Manassas, he made one more comment about his class to Moffett: "There was hard fighting everywhere. He conversed for a few moments with Major Patrick, and then turned and spoke to me. He said that certain of our men on an eminence above the road were needlessly exposed, and bade me ride to them and call them in. I had started to obey, when he suddenly stopped me with—'Oh! I had a letter a few days ago from Doctor White, and he tells me that our Sunday-school is still kept up.'"

Moffett had once written of Jackson's sincere concern for his students; observing "his voice seemed to tremble as he prayed for a special blessing on his little charge—the negro children of the town whom he had gathered together in a Sunday school."[74]

Margaret Preston suggested that perhaps Jackson's greatest rewards would come from his work among his black students: "We have sometimes wondered if the Major was not doing a grander work, in the eyes of God, in leading his little battalion of colored people into the paths of peace, than when, at the head of the enthusiastic army, he was making a name which has since echoed over the world."[75]

The positive and long-term influence Jackson's efforts had on Lexington blacks, and even on a wider scale, is remarkable. There is no doubt that his class had an extensive impact for the gospel among black Southerners: "Three negro churches were formed in the town, and multitudes of the pupils became members of these churches. In many instances, young men went abroad from the school for further instruction, and became preachers to their own people."[76] Two of these Lexington churches—Randolph Street Methodist Church and First Baptist Church—still play a prominent role in the spiritual life of Lexington blacks today. Washington and Lee history professor Theodore C. DeLaney Jr. points out, "To some extent these institutions had their origins in Jackson's Sabbath school." While DeLaney laments that Jackson's school "existed as a paternalistic institution that conveyed values which whites hoped to instill in black participants," he also commented that the churches born of Jackson's efforts "provided freedom and the promises and dreams of the future."

Historian Megan Haley Newman further noted the impact of Jackson's labors: "It is evident that several former members of the Sunday-school organized by Jackson, as well as their children, became prominent and successful members of their communities, and that their affiliation with Jackson's Sunday-School became a point of particular pride or note."[77]

One such example is Dwight Oliver Wendell Holmes (1877–1963). He was the son of the Reverend John Alexander Holmes and served as president of Morgan State College and was the first black member of the Maryland state board of education.[78] Holmes related to his colleagues that his father had attended Jackson's Sunday-school class.[79] Another member of Jackson's class was Daniel Henry McDowell. Before the war, he was the property of Col. Samuel McDowell Moore[80] of Lexington. Daniel McDowell was, for a number of years, the doorman at the prestigious National Press Club in Washington, D.C. Two articles on file at Washington and Lee's Leyburn Library go into some detail about McDowell's life, both during the war and after it. At his death in June 1931, one article headlined: "Daniel H. McDowell, Colored Member of Jackson's Sunday School, Buried with honors by National Press Club at Washington, D.C."[81] Affectionately known as "Old Mac," he had "catered to the epicurean appetites of politicians and Presidents" and was revered for his "rare talents as servant and philosopher."[82] McDowell was eighty-eight years old at the time of his death and was buried at Lincoln Cemetery.

The news article added, "Mac was born into slavery in Lexington, Va. He studied his Bible under 'Stonewall' Jackson, when both were young and Jackson was a Sunday school teacher. When Jackson went to war, so did Mac." McDowell witnessed the VMI cadets performance at the battle of New Market and "never tired of the telling." He had worked at the Press Club the last twenty years of his life and "his friends ranged from newspaperman to President, but Mac knew no class distinction."[83]

Another article titled "Daniel Henry McDowell, Colored, Formerly of Lexington, Tells His Story" contains additional details about his life. It states that McDowell "partook of religion" in Jackson's Sunday-school class "which he attended with 'humilitude.'" Two years before he died, he said he was "aimin' to proceed through those pearly gates standin' erect." He then stood up "in the shining parlor of his home in Tenth Street, southeast, Washington and demonstrated how he purposed to enter heaven."[84]

So appreciated were McDowell's polished etiquette and Southern ways that "renowned statesman quarreled for his attention. From congress' mighty orators—Silver Dick Bland, Fire Alarm Foraker, John G. Carlisle, John G. Spooner and others 'too numerical to mention'—he gathered a vocabulary which is the delight of ears white and black."[85]

McDowell told how he followed the VMI cadets to New Market at the urging of Colonel Moore's daughter, "Miss Sally," in order to watch over a boy "in his thirteenth year." McDowell declared:

[I] progressed to the extent of forty miles, which appeared to irritate the Yankees, suh, to a belligerency it is difficult to comprehend. Yes, suh. The ground was willfully agitated with cannon balls, and one of these took occasion to explode in the vicinity I was occupyin'.

There are folks who could be plunged deep in ponderin' on what I did, but to me it came natural as the homeward wingin' of a bluejay. In other words, suh, I run. Yes, suh, I was practically the first to retreat that evening. There was a certain amount of white folks runnin', but it was inconsiderable as to quality. I hastened, suh.[86]

McDowell never lost his admiration for his Sunday-school teacher. The writer of the article took note of McDowell's high regard for Jackson: "On the wall in Daniel Henry McDowell's parlor is a picture of Stonewall Jackson, who Daniel Henry takes pleasure in assuring you, was Presbyterian 'of such religious qualities that the Baptists and the Methodists couldn't find nothing on him to take hold of.'"[87]

McDowell's confidence in Jackson's Bible knowledge was steadfast, and he stated, "General Jackson was a rounded-out man on all points of contact with the Bible." He recalled with fondness his days in Jackson's

Sunday-school class: "He . . . held Sunday school for colored of all manner of ages every Sunday afternoon at three. I had the distinction of bein' a bell ringer. It was a honor bestowed upon me by General Jackson because of my ability in stature and strict attendin' to a faithful dischargin' of promptitutde. I was the biggest boy in the class."[88]

Even at eighty-six, McDowell could recall the details of his responsibilities: "I would establish myself at the door and intone the bell which was a warnin' that the general was about to hold forth. I was instructed, suh, to whang the bell seven times and fell from grace just once as I was filled with a zeal for which there was no accountin' except it come from on high."[89] McDowell's "zeal" in ringing the bell brought a rebuke from his teacher: "'Daniel,' says the general on that occasion, 'there is no occasion for arousin' the whole state of Virginia with that bell. Seven intonatins is sufficing.'" McDowell offered a rather humorous defense: "You see, suh, . . . I was carryin' out instructions to seven times seven accordin' to Leviticus. The general was mollified, but likewise set considerable store by discipline."[90]

McDowell was also pleased of his spiritual gift regarding funerals and "outstanding talents at 'solacin' the departin' and sustainin' the bereaved." He was particularly proud of his involvement at Robert E. Lee's funeral. McDowell requested that Sally Moore speak to Lee's daughter Mildred about the possibility of McDowell's leading Lee's horse, Traveller, during the funeral procession. The request was granted. "For two hours Traveler and me, we stood outside the church whilst the services were proceedin' within, and nothin' more exasperatin' than a slight trompin' on my foot by Traveler, who was understandin' but unused to funerals, come to pass."[91]

Other Lexington blacks were also very public about their appreciation for Jackson's efforts: "The first contribution made to the fund which has placed at his grave the beautiful statue, which is the work of Edward Valentine, and is a veritable Stonewall Jackson in bronze, was made by the negro Baptist Church at Lexington, Virginia., whose pastor had been a pupil at the negro Sunday school."[92]

J. William Jones tells of another incident that illustrates the special relationship that existed between Jackson and his students. When Union Gen. David Hunter's army marched through Lexington, some townspeople were careful to remove and hide a Confederate flag that flew over Jackson's grave. When a local woman visited Jackson's grave to place some flowers during the Federal occupation, she noticed a tiny Confederate flag upon the grave "with a familiar hymn pinned to it." Jones explained, "Upon inquiry she found that a colored boy, who had belonged to Jackson's Sunday-school, had procured the flag, gotten some one to copy a stanza of a favorite hymn which Jackson had taught him, and had gone in the night to plant the flag on the grave of his loved teacher."[93]

This young boy, in a most poignant manner, wanted to express his love and respect for his teacher and his faith. He had done so anonymously and without fanfare, yet God pulled back the veil, revealing the selfless act to posterity: "thy Father which seeth in secret himself shall reward thee openly" (Matthew 6:4). Envisioning a young black boy stealing into the cemetery alone, under cover of darkness, to honor the Confederate general is a touching reminder that Jackson's Christian labors among Lexington blacks had engendered their deep gratitude. Lexington blacks were keenly aware that Jackson's class was the only opportunity they had for any formal education until after the War Between the States.[94] Jackson was sorely missed by not only the Confederacy but by his students, for whom he had so diligently labored. By twenty-first-century standards, this heartfelt affection between white and black Lexingtonians may seem like nostalgic nonsense. Despite such cynicism, these feelings are well substantiated in numerous accounts and reports. When a company of Washington College students departed Lexington to fight for the Confederacy, both white and black citizens turned out for tearful farewells:

> You could almost hear the heart-strings of mothers and sisters snap as they pressed sons and brothers in farewell embraces. In surrendering their boys to the services of Virginia, they were making sacrifices, such as their heroic ancestors were accustomed to make on the hills and among the mosshags of Scotland, for God and Presbytery. It was a willing sacrifice. And no less, yet more demonstrative than theirs, was the grief of the black mammies, who came to say good-by to the "chillun," now grown to be young masters, and press them to their warm hearts.[95]

Jackson's brother-in-law, John Thomas Lewis Preston, took over Jackson's class while Jackson was away and after Jackson's death. By 1872, Preston was being assisted by James J. White, the oldest son of Pastor William Spottswood White and professor of Greek and Latin language and literature at Washington and Lee. James White was a former captain in the Confederate service who had organized and commanded the legendary Liberty Hall Volunteers, which was composed of students from Washington College, at least one-fourth of whom were studying for the ministry.

PRESTON IS one of the most fascinating and most overlooked influences both in Jackson's life and regarding the Colored Sunday-school. He was Jackson's "most intimate colleague at the Institute."[96] As already noted in regard to John B. Lyle, Preston was a brilliant man educated at Washington College, the University of Virginia, and Yale University. He was born into an affluent Virginia family on April 28, 1811, "descended from the aristocracy of both the Valley and Tidewater Virginia,"[97] and is credited with founding the Virginia Military Institute.

He prepared for his rigorous education by attending a Richmond boy's academy where he became friends with Edgar Allan Poe.[98] Preston's grandfather, Edmund Randolph, was the nation's first attorney general. As a young man, Preston traveled abroad extensively before returning to Lexington to build a successful law practice as well as several successful businesses, making him one of the wealthiest men in town. Jackson invested in some of these businesses, and the two became close friends. They also worked together closely on their church duties, with Jackson serving as a deacon and Preston an elder. So committed was Preston to his duties as ruling elder that local tradition holds he "never missed a session meeting during his fifty-year tenure."[99] Author and historian W. G. Bean commented on this close relationship: "Ties of family—Jackson's first wife and Preston's second wife were daughters of Dr. George Junkin, President of Washington College—and of friendship had bound Jackson and Preston closely together."[100] The combined influence of their "ties of friendship" still echoes through generations of Virginians.

During the war, when Jackson was assigned to hold Harpers Ferry, Preston served as Jackson's assistant adjutant general. He eventually rose to the rank of colonel and was with Jackson through the 1862 Valley campaign. Preston struck an imposing figure: "A handsome man, six feet tall, clean-shaven, with piercing blue eyes, prematurely grey hair, and a ruddy complexion, Preston was no effete."[101]

A dedicated Christian, brilliant lawyer, successful businessman, accomplished teacher, and an influential leader in his community, Preston's interests were as broad as his influence. He was an avid hunter and dog-breeder and was interested in progressive farming methods.[102] He was very much of the old-school South—one who saw himself as a patriarch. He expected and received "instant and unquestioning obedience"[103] from his family. Preston was also a skilled writer and a masterful debater, skills honed in the prestigious and legendary Franklin Society of which he was one of the founding members. He was universally considered "a power in the town, a power in the church, a power in the lecture-room, a power in his house" and "indifferent to praise or censure in the maintenance of what he thought right"[104]—a trait he shared with Jackson.

Preston was known for having a penchant for the dramatic. On December 2, 1859, a largely military crowd in Charlestown looked on with vindication as the radical abolitionist John Brown was hanged. The only noise heard was the creaking of the wooden gallows and strained hemp as Brown's "struggles continued, growing feebler and feebler at each abortive attempt to breathe." When Brown's body mercifully stilled at last, slowly "swayed to and fro by the wind," there was a long, pained silence. Preston, present with the VMI cadets, cracked the icy air with his booming voice, uttering the words, "So perish all such enemies of Virginia! All such enemies of the Union! All such foes of the human race!" He later wrote of the incident, "So I felt, and so I said, with solemnity and without one shade of animosity, as I turned to break the silence, to those around me."[105]

Preston married Sally Caruthers—his childhood sweetheart—when he was twenty-one years old. By the time Sally was forty-four years old, she was carrying their ninth child. Sadly, Sally and the child died in childbirth on a cold January day in 1856. The chill from that bleak day lingered for years as her death left a great void in his life.

Though grief-stricken at the loss, Preston desperately wanted his home reestablished with a wife and a mother for his seven children (a daughter had died of pneumonia in 1842). He turned to one of Sally's closest friends, Margaret "Maggie" Junkin, sister of Jackson's first wife, Ellie, who had also died during childbirth. God may have been knitting the Preston's and Jackson's lives and experiences together in tragedy as well as in service. Both were devout Christians and members of the same church, both taught at VMI, both would serve the Confederacy, both would bind their destinies to their black brethren, and both had experienced the simultaneous pain and loss of a wife and child.

Preston and Margaret were wed in August 1857. The couple would be a Lexington institution for more than thirty years. Maggie was a great helpmeet to her husband after he took the reins of the black Sunday school, assisting with organization and teaching. His concerns for his black pupils were akin to Jackson's. Church records indicate that, for more than twenty years, Preston gave "religious instruction to the colored race, a delicate and difficult task, in which he met with a success that was quite disproportionate to the probabilities."[106] He continued to labor faithfully among Lexington's blacks for more than two decades after Jackson's death.[107]

Preston wrote a number of articles for the *Southern Presbyterian Review*. One 1885 article addressed "Religious Education of the Colored People of the South," in which he offered his opinions gained through his work with the "Colored Sabbath School" in Lexington. Though the condescending views expressed in this essay were typical of nineteenth-century whites, Preston also articulated opinions that countered some of the more prejudiced notions of many of his contemporaries. He opined: "Every particular of American civilization possessed by the white man is shared by the black. . . . He uses the same speech, dresses after the same fashion, lives under the same laws, and accepts the same religion, the same code of morals, and the same organization of domestic and social life."[108]

He added, "[The black] is an American, nothing but an American, and a Southerner." Preston then related, "I will add, in order to show that I am acquainted with the general subject upon which I am writing, that I am the senior superintendent of a colored Sabbath-school, which, for the character of the instruction, discipline, and progress of the pupils, will compare favorably with any white school with which I am acquainted."[109]

Preston also refers to blacks' "eagerness for education" and their "passionate attachment to their churches."[110] He closes his dissertation by accepting the providence of God regarding blacks while at the same time acknowledging past mistakes and future duties:

> The history of the black race in the United States has never been under the control of man. It is a subject too large for his grasp, too far reaching for his forecast. Whatever have been the purposes and agencies of men in connection with it, God's overruling hand has ever made itself manifest, in establishing his purposes. With all our mistakes before us, we can but look up humbly to his providence. Let us follow what seems to be the path of duty, even walking amid uncertainties. If the race is to deteriorate, let it not be because we have withheld our aid; and if they survive and are aggrandized, we will have been co-workers with God in his wide providences for good to his creatures.[111]

"Walking amid uncertainties" became routine for Preston. During the war, his oldest son, Frank lost an arm at the shoulder during the battle of Winchester. A younger son, Willie, a favorite of Jackson's, joined the Liberty Hall Volunteers just before the battle of Second Manassas. Willie was always a welcome guest at Jackson's headquarters and was almost like a son to him. Jackson intended to make Willie an aide-de-camp, but it was not to be. During the final moments of the battle, Pvt. William C. Preston of the Fourth Virginia, "whose manners were so gentle, kindly, and different, and his beardless, blue-eyed, boyish face so manly and handsome,"[112] was mortally wounded. Jackson and his staff were devastated. The next morning, just before he died, Preston handed a note to Pastor White's son, Capt. Hugh White. The note was intended for Willie's father, but he never received the message; Captain White was killed just a few hours later.[113] Jackson wrote Margaret Preston a touching condolence note, remembering again his labors with the Sunday school in Lexington: "My Dear Maggie, I deeply sympathize with you all in the death of dear Willie. He was in my first Sabbath school class, where I became attached to him when he was a little boy."[114] The Sunday-school teacher who had once pointed the young man to the Savior was now the general who had to accept the fact that the young man was now safe with that same Savior.

Just four months after Willie's death, another of Preston's sons,[115]

Randolph, a VMI cadet, contracted typhoid fever and died at the Preston home in Lexington. Margaret Preston wrote of this time in their lives: "Few parents have as noble boys to lose and yet their father bows to the stroke with entireness of Christian resignation."[116]

Eventually, it would be Margaret who would have to bow to death's cruel calling with "Christian resignation." In the late 1880s, John Preston's health declined. By the spring of 1890, he was gravely ill and gave detailed instructions regarding his funeral, down to the Scripture passages he wanted read. Preston died during the night of July 15 surrounded by his wife and children. At the time of his death, he was the oldest member of the Lexington Presbyterian Church and the oldest native of Lexington.[117] Preston left no doubt as to what he wanted to be remembered for—his tombstone is inscribed with the following words:

JOHN T. L. PRESTON

APRIL 25 1811–JULY 15 1890

AN OFFICER OF THE COMMONWEALTH

OF THE CONFEDERATE STATES

AND OF THE CHURCH OF CHRIST

HE FOUGHT A GOOD FIGHT

HE FINISHED HIS COURSE

HE KEPT THE FAITH

LAUS DEO ["PRAISE GOD"]

There are a number of other sidebars associated with Jackson's class. One involves Jefferson Shields, also known as "Uncle" Jefferson or "Jeff" Shields. One of Shields's claims, among others, was that he was the first member of Jackson's Sunday-school class: "I was General Jackson's first scholar. Somebody ought to write a history of Jackson's Christian life, for he was the greatest Christian that ever lived. Jackson had a class of boys, about eighteen. Jackson kept me from swearing, and I had to go to the Presbyterian Church because I admired him so much."[118]

Shields stated he was "indebted to General Jackson for his early religious training"[119] and recalled that Jackson routinely called his name in prayer: "When he prayed, he would say, 'Remember Jeff.'"[120] Boley, in his classic work *Lexington in Old Virginia,* includes a sketch of Shields in his chapter, "Colored Personalities": "Uncle Jeff, ebony in color, with his snow white beard, twinkling eye, high silk hat, and Prince Albert coat, was a sight as familiar on the street as the postoffice."[121]

Shields was a faithful member and trustee of the First Baptist Church (African) of Lexington for more than fifty years and is considered, along with James Deacon Jackson, to be one of the church's founding fathers. He became a favorite of Confederate veterans' groups, attending many reunions and special events after the war. While in attendance at a re-union of the survivors of the Stonewall Brigade in Staunton, Uncle Jeff was voted in as a member of the brigade and authorized to wear one of the brigade's badges.[122] According to Boley, Shields was proud to attend these meetings and display the badges and ribbons the old Confederates gave him; "Uncle Jeff attended all Confederate reunions in many parts of the South, where he was always the recipient of much attention, about which he talked freely. . . . After each reunion he had a fresh supply of medals and when he would proudly open his coat to display them he looked like the Kaiser on parade."[123]

Numerous articles and books have reported that Shields served as General Jackson's "body servant" or cook during the war. Shields's claims were accepted at face value by many Lexingtonians and veterans. But there are no Civil War–era records or accounts of Jackson, nor any of his staff, mentioning Jefferson Shields. That does not necessarily prove that Shields never cooked a meal for Jackson's staff or for some members of Jackson's army, but it casts doubt on the veracity of Shields's assertions that he served Jackson regularly. Shields also professed to have cooked for the Stonewall Brigade and Jeb Stuart. Likewise, while there is nothing to dispute this, there are no dependable historical records to prove it either. An article on file at the Stonewall Jackson House describes an encounter with Jeff Shields in 1906:

> I once had the good fortune to come in contact with a negro character who was very prominent in Virginia. His name was Jeff Shields. He lived in Lexington, and had been the body servant of General Stonewall Jack-son through his war time experiences.
>
> The Confederate veterans had made a pet and a hero of him. He used

to attend all of their public meetings. They would pin badges, medals, and decorations on him and place him at the head of their processions with a beautiful flag. . . . I believe, if he had been born in Central Africa, he would have been a king.[124]

It would be easy to speculate that the veterans exploited Shields's desire for fame, but one could also conclude that it was Shields who actually gained the upper hand from this relationship, because his fame "assured him a comfortable income to the end of his earthly pilgrimage."[125] So comfortable, in fact, that he purchased a lot on what is now Davidson Street in Lexington and built a handsome brick home that still stands.[126] Shields lived there with his wife,[127] the former Mary McNutt, until his death in 1918 at the age of eighty-nine. Today, he and his wife rest in Evergreen Cemetery in Lexington.

Other African Americans associated with Jackson's class left a much more powerful legacy than Shields. One such legacy continues to this day in a small African American church in Roanoke, Virginia.

5

By Their Fruits Ye Shall Know Them

*Stonewall Jackson and
Lylburn L. Downing*

Real friendship is shown in times of trouble; prosperity is full of friends.

—*Abraham Kuyper*

Ultimately, a man is not judged by what he has done or what he has written, but who he has influenced.

—*Andrew Nelson Lytle*

We are fortunate that the former slaves were not silent about their religious faith and that they left their testimony as a legacy for their children and for any who wish to understand.

—*Albert J. Raboteau*

STONEWALL JACKSON'S STRATEGY AT Chancellorsville and the Confederacy's subsequent victory is a textbook study in daring generalship. Jackson's flanking movement, using just twenty-eight thousand men, around Union Gen. Joseph Hooker's army of seventy thousand is probably the greatest underdog victory in modern warfare. Initially Jackson's proposal shocked even Lee, himself no stranger to bold moves.

Sometime around 5:30 p.m., on May 2, 1863, when all of Jackson's men were in place, he confidently and quietly responded to Gen. Robert E. Rodes's inquiry of his command's readiness, "You can go forward then."[1] The Confederate troops tore through the thick woods with excited anticipation and hearts pounding, knowing they were going to catch Hooker's army by surprise. When the attack began, the Federals

123

were totally off guard, many of them eating supper, joking, talking, and anticipating a quiet evening. James I. Robertson described their first clue that something was amiss: "The first hint the Federals had of anything unusual came when deer, wild turkeys, and rabbits—all startled by the onrushing Confederates—raced through the Union camps. Northern soldiers gave no thought to the cause behind the stampede; some men gaily chased the critters past tents and campfires."[2]

Then, total pandemonium struck. The all too familiar, bone-chilling, hellish scream of the Rebel yell echoed through the woods and into the camp. The sound made the blood of the Yankee soldiers run cold. There was no time to react with any orderly defensive action. One of Jackson's artillery officers, Maj. David G. McIntosh, described the scene:

> The surprise was complete. A bolt from the sky would not have startled [the Federals] half as much as the musket shots in the thickets . . . and then a solid wall of gray, forcing their way through the timber and bearing down upon them like an irresistible avalanche. There was no stemming such a tide. . . . The shock was too great; the sense of utter helplessness was too apparent. The resistance offered was speedily beaten down. There was nothing left but to lay down their arms and surrender or flee. They threw them away, and fled. Arms, knapsacks, clothing, equipage, everything, was thrown aside and left behind. . . . Men lost their heads in terror, and the roads and woods on both sides [of the turnpike] were filled with men, horses and cattle, in one mad flight.[3]

A Union soldier, observing his comrades fleeing in wide-eyed panic, said his former unit resembled "close-packed ranks rushing like legions of the damned."

The rout would make the already legendary Stonewall Jackson all the more renowned for generations to come. Jackson was overjoyed and encouraged his men to make the victory complete, exhorting them, "Press on! Press on!"

The Confederate army's delight over the resounding success would be short lived. The hours passed as the Southerners continued to press Hooker's troops. But at nine o'clock, Jackson wanted more. He believed it was imperative that the Union army be totally destroyed. He wanted his men to fight until there was no one left to fight. Jackson decided to reconnoiter on his own. He ventured beyond the skirmish lines with members of his staff. There, in the shadowy and deceptive moonlight, men from the Eighteenth North Carolina Infantry mistook the general and his entourage for the enemy and fired. Jackson was hit by three .57-caliber bullets, one striking him in the left shoulder, one in the left forearm, and a third passing through his right palm. The magnificent victory at Chancellorsville would cost the South dearly.

Eight days later, on Sunday, May 10, 1863, as his grief-stricken servant Jim Lewis looked on, Thomas Jonathan Jackson, with calm repose, uttered his final words: "Let us cross over the river and rest under the shade of the trees." The Christian warrior rested from his labors, laid down his cross and sword, and was gathered to his loved ones and brethren on the other side of the river. Jackson died on the Sabbath, just as he had always wished.

This dying statement contains perhaps the best-known last words of any figure in history. Much lesser known is the fact that these immortal words, along with Jackson himself, would one day be linked with the son of slaves and an African American church in a most unusual yet appropriate way. Jackson had sown the seeds of this bond years before his death. And this relationship continues to yield fruit more than 140 years after his death.

As Jim Lewis was grieving over Jackson's death in the violent and bloody aftermath of Chancellorsville, another life was bringing joy to a family in the peaceful village of Lexington. Lylburn (also spelled Lilburn and Lilbourn) Downing and his bride, Ellen, had become Christians through the ministry of Jackson's class. A year earlier, on May 3, 1862, Ellen gave birth to a son, named Lylburn after his father. Although he was born into slavery, young Lylburn would one day express gratitude to the Confederate general who had taught his parents the Word of God.

Lylburn Liggins Downing attended Jackson's Sunday-school class as a boy just as his parents had done. The younger Downing would sit under the tutelage of John Preston. Both of Downing's parents were faithful in class attendance during and after Jackson's involvement. Downing would later say that his participation in the Sunday-school class led him into the ministry. Though Downing never knew Jackson, he admired the Confederate general through the memory and testimony of his parents. Raised in a Christian home, he often heard his parents speak of their respect and affection for Jackson and how Jackson was a spiritual inspiration to them both and how they had come to Christ through Jackson's efforts. Downing also knew that Jackson had risked fine and imprisonment, in addition to ridicule by some in the community, to teach not only his parents but other slaves and free blacks in the Lexington area. This knowledge led the younger Downing to admire and respect Jackson as well. An article[4] appearing in the May 10, 1936, edition of the *Richmond Times-Dispatch* further describes his admiration for Jackson:

> The little colored boy was much impressed with the accounts of the life and work of the great soldier and teacher. As he grew older and studied the life of this hero of his own community he came to regard Stonewall Jackson not only as one of the greatest military geniuses of all time, but also as one of the best friends the Negro race had ever known.
>
> He frequently visited Jackson's grave in Lexington and continually lamented the fact that the place was marked only by a simple stone. Early in his life he became filled with a burning desire to erect a monument more worthy of the illustrious benefactor of the colored people of the town.

The article goes on to explain that this desire "never left him" and was "rekindled when, as a student at Lincoln University, one day he read . . . a book on Jackson's life." Though this account does not mention which biography this was, it does mention that Downing was particularly moved by the story of Jackson's sending a check for "the expenses of his Sunday school for colored children"[5] though Jackson was embroiled in the aftermath of the battle of First Manassas. After completing his studies, Downing visited Jackson's grave again and was pleased to finally see the bronze monument of Jackson's likeness adorning his final resting place. Though pleased, "The urge to make some personal expression of his admiration and gratitude persisted." The newspaper article noted that Downing wanted to have a "Stonewall Jackson Arch" built at the Lylburn Downing School[6] in Lexington, which had been named in

Downing's honor. His "urge to make some personal expression of his admiration" for Jackson eventually led him to pay a most remarkable tribute to this Confederate warrior and fellow soldier of the cross.

Lylburn L. Downing was among the first black children to attend a public school in Lexington. He showed an early penchant for learning and at first aspired to be a medical doctor, "but after his conversion he felt called to preach the Gospel."[7] Perhaps Downing was interested in the medical profession due to his father's thirty-year association as a "trained nurse" for VMI.[8] Of course, Downing's father was also involved in spreading the gospel among the area's black population and, according to numerous sources, was a strong influence on his son. The elder Downing was instrumental in the efforts to erect a new building to replace the original sanctuary occupied by the Lexington African Baptist Church. His father's example must have inspired young Lylburn to make one of the first contributions for the new building.[9] Each day, Downing's father and other former slaves gathered to dig the foundation. By night, the women would hold lanterns so the men could see to work.[10] This church is today a very familiar landmark in the Lexington skyline and is often featured in postcards and prints of historic Lexington.

Young Lylburn Downing's faith was obvious to all as "he was obedient to the heavenly vision, abandoned his own preconceived ideas of what he wanted to do in life, and with singleness of purpose consecrated himself to the ministry."[11] That "singleness of purpose" led Downing to enter Lincoln University in Pennsylvania, where he consistently ranked at the head of his class. During his early college years, he worked at a hotel to help pay his expenses; then the school awarded him a scholarship in recognition of his high grade average. Downing also did Sunday-school work when he returned to Virginia for summer and holiday vacations and served as a bookseller for the American Tract Society. His passion for the gospel and his oratory skills in proclaiming the good news became evident. In his sophomore year, Downing won the school's gold medal for an original oration. In 1888, he married Lottie Jackson Clinton, the daughter of a minister. The next year he graduated with honors and then entered Lincoln Theological Seminary. While at the seminary, he taught Latin, and upon his graduation in 1894, he was offered a position on the faculty. He declined the offer in order to pursue his true passion: to preach the gospel and pastor a church. Downing would eventually earn three degrees from Lincoln—a bachelor of arts, a bachelor of sacred theology, and in 1906 he was awarded a doctor of divinity.[12]

After graduating from theological studies in 1895, Downing struck out for Roanoke, Virginia, where he began shepherding a small mission of seven people. From this humble group, he founded the Fifth Avenue Presbyterian Church, where for forty-two years he continued his faithful stewardship of that church, until his death in 1937. He also maintained the tradition of the Sabbath or Sunday-school class he came to love as a young boy. Not forgetting the tremendous impact Sunday school had upon his family, Downing wished to influence the next generation of black children with the gospel. He was also active in civic affairs, serving as the city's first probation officer and "in that capacity [served] in the care and protection of delinquents of his race." According to at least one source, Downing "supervised a home for delinquent blacks."[13] He became the only African American member of the city's Republican Party committee. Downing was held in such esteem that he was chosen as "a collaborator of history in preparing a record of what Roanoke soldiers accomplished in the great World War."[14]

A number of years after Downing had settled in Roanoke and a new church was built, he was able to fulfill his childhood dream of honoring Stonewall Jackson—the man he credited for his family's Christian heritage. A 1992 one-hundredth anniversary history published by the church states: "An influence in his life was General Thomas 'Stonewall' Jackson who taught a 'Negro Sunday School Class,' among whom were Reverend Downing's parents."[15] Downing decided to raise funds for a commemorative stained-glass window to honor his hero. Though ridiculed by some, Downing refused to be discouraged. The window,[16] finally installed in 1906,[17] honored Jackson for his dedicated literary and gospel work among slaves and free blacks in the Lexington area. The dedication of the window made national news, and Downing received letters of commendation from as far away as England. The ceremony was attended by church members and the local Confederate veteran's camp. Many members of the press were also on hand for the unveiling as well as a number of prominent local citizens. Also in attendance was Jefferson Shields, who was the keynote speaker for the event.

Thomas J. Jackson (left) sat for this portrait in 1855, while he was living in Lexington and one year before he began his black Sunday school class. His wife, Mary Anna Morrison (below), violated the law by teaching two of their slaves to read.

At his uncle's farm, known as Jackson's Mill (below left), Thomas Jackson interacted with the family slaves and was exposed to their Christian faith. Beginning in 1858 at his Lexington home (below right), Jackson had "the most intimate and wide range of experience with slaves and free blacks" during Sunday-evening worship services.

This Lexington building on Main Street (upper left) once housed John Lyle's "automatic bookstore." A postcard (upper right) of the Lexington Presbyterian Church and Lecture Room, c. 1900, reads: "Stonewall Jackson's Church, Lexington, Va. In which he served as Deacon for a number of years and where he conducted a Colored Sunday School." The Lecture Room (below) where he taught was demolished in 1906.

Adalbert J. Volck sketched a prayer meeting in Jackson's camp, which was the basis for an 1866 etching by J. C. Buttre (above). Most historians believe that the African American pictured kneeling to Jackson's right is Jim Lewis.

John T. L. Preston (below) was one of the founders of the Virginia Military Institute, brother-in-law to Jackson, and continued Jackson's class after the general's death.

Francis Henney Smith (above) served as VMI's first superintendent (1839–89). He also taught a black Sunday school class at the Episcopalian church in 1843.

The 1891 statue of Jackson over his grave in the Jackson Memorial Cemetery was privately funded. The first contribution came from Lexington's "negro Baptist Church" whose pastor had been a member of Jackson's black Sunday school.

The photograph below was taken in the Jackson family barbershop around 1925. Standing in the left front is Walter Jackson, Raddy Jackson's father. Standing farther back on the left is Ormond Jackson, Raddy's brother. And standing to the right is Thomas Jackson, Raddy's grandfather and son of James "Deacon" Jackson, the original proprietor of the barbershop.

This Nelson Street building in Lexington (above) formerly housed the Jackson family barbershop.

Desmond Radcliff "Raddy" Jackson (left) and Jefferson Shields (right)

The 1927 photograph (above) of Sunday-school children posed in front of the original Fifth Avenue Presbyterian Church in Roanoke, Virginia, shows the Reverend Lylburn Liggins Downing standing at the far right, and one of his sons, Dr. Gardner P. Downing, standing at the far left.

Lylburn Downing's parents were members of the general's Sunday-school class, and he later attended the same Sunday-school class. Downing commissioned and designed the Jackson Memorial stained-glass window.

In the front row, fifth from the right, is Ralph Shepperson, a beneficiary of the legacy of Jackson's Sunday-school class.

The photograph at the top of the facing page shows a class of Sunday-school children inside the church in the 1930s. The Reverend Downing stands at the back on the left. One of his sons, Dr. Ellwood D. Downing, stands on the right in a white suit. Gladys Watson stands at the right, wearing a necklace, in line with the first row of children. Her brother, Ralph Shepperson, is on the second row at the far right. On the back wall, the Jackson Memorial stained-glass window can be seen in its original state with the two side windows that were later destroyed in a fire.

The present-day building of the Fifth Avenue Presbyterian Church in Roanoke, Virginia.

To the left is the Jackson Memorial window as it is today. Below are brother and sister, Ralph Shepperson and Gladys Watson, who are still members of Roanoke's Fifth Avenue Presbyterian Church.

The window was Downing's own design, and he had carefully sketched it out in pen for the artist to work from. The *Richmond Times-Dispatch* gives the best description of the original window:

> The scene, in richly blended colors on the glass, is based on the dying words of Jackson: "Let us cross over the river and rest in the shade of the trees," the words being inscribed on a scroll beneath the picture. It is the view of the Shenandoah Valley of Virginia with the Blue Ridge Mountains in the distance. There is a meandering stream, widening as it courses its way to the sea. On the left bank is seen a typical Virginia log cabin, in the door which stands a farmer's wife with milk and delicacies for the sick, suggesting the hospitality for which Virginia is known. Near the cabins are tents, before which guns are stacked, and soldiers in various camp occupations.
>
> In the foreground is an officer's tent with the flaps closed and the famous "white signal," a handkerchief, hanging on the outside to proclaim that the occupant is at prayer and is not to be disturbed. Platoons appear to be vigilantly scanning the roads, fields and hillsides. Across the river is a grove of shade trees whose foliage invites the weary-worn traveler and soldier to refreshing repose, emblematic to that "blissful rest promised to the people of God."[18]

Tragically, most of the church was destroyed by fire in 1959 and parts of the original window were lost. What remained suffered extensive smoke damage. Fortunately, the remaining window was cleaned and restored. Many older church members who remember the fire believe it was a miracle that the most important part of the window survived. Very few people today know that there were originally two smaller windows to the left and right of the centerpiece. "The two smaller windows which support the Stonewall Jackson Window are also memorials; one to Col. John Preston, for years superintendent of the Sunday school which the pastor attended during his boyhood, and the other to Dr. James I. Brownson [a renowned Presbyterian minister known for his positive influence on generations of Lincoln University students] and his wife of Washington, Pennsylvania, by whose prayers, counsel and financial aid the pastor was assisted through college."[19]

The two smaller windows were badly damaged, and according to church member Ralph Shepperson, those pieces were "thrown in the trash" after the fire. Evidently, part of the original window that remains was damaged beyond repair, encompassing the part of the window described as the "officer's tent with the flaps closed and the famous 'white signal,' a handkerchief, hanging on the outside."

Thomas Jackson and Lylburn Downing were connected by providence; they served the same God and honored each other through their service to their fellow man. In a June 14, 1960, letter[20] to Nathan G. Carder, one of Downing's sons—Dr. L. C. Downing[21]—gave an account of his father's faith and affection for General Jackson and leaves no doubt as to the eternal influence Jackson had on his black Sunday-school students and their descendants and the high esteem in which they held him:

In Re: Stonewall Jackson, Sunday School Teacher

Dear Mr. Carder:

In reply to yours of June 10th, may I state that my grandfather, Lylburn Downing and his wife, my grandmother, attended a Sunday School in Lexington, Virginia founded by and taught by Stonewall Jackson. My grandparents were slaves at that time.

When Jackson was called to the Confederate colors, the wife of General Preston took over the instruction of his Sunday School.

Upon one occasion, when a messenger brought a communication from General Jackson, friends crowded around expecting to learn something of the progress of the war. To their great surprise, it contained only some money for the operation of his Sunday school. After the Civil War ended, Col. Preston himself took over Jackson's Sunday School for Negroes.

It was through this influence of this unique Sunday School that my father, Lylburn L. Downing, received the inspiration to aspire as a lad to the Christian ministry. My father attended Lincoln University (Pa.) from which Institution he graduated with honors, also the gold medal for Public Speaking. My father taught at Lincoln briefly, then entered its Theological Seminary from which he received his S.T.B.

In 1906, Rev. L. L. Downing, then pastor of the 5th Ave. Presbyterian Church in Roanoke, Virginia, solicited monies for, had executed and installed a Memorial window in the front of his church, the main window memorializing Stonewall Jackson and the windows flanking on either side, memorializing Col. Preston and Col. Bronson, both V.M.I. professors. At the bottom of the window memorializing Stonewall Jackson were his famous last words, "Let us cross over the river and rest in the shade of the trees." The window itself pictured an army camp with tents and a stream, across which were shade trees.

It might be of interest to know that the High School for Negroes in Lexington is named for this man of God, who received his inspiration from Stonewall Jackson's Sunday School. There is a street here in Roanoke also named for Rev. Downing.

Sometime ago, I sent some data concerning the Stonewall Jackson Memorial Window to Mr. Jay W. Johns, President, Stonewall Jackson Memorial. Mr. Johns now lives in Charlottesville, Virginia.

He and the Memorial may have some helpful data which should be available to you.

I shall make an effort to locate the news item, which you referred to and if I can locate the same, shall be glad to send a clipping to you.

A quite recent clipping is being enclosed.

> Yours very truly,
> L. C. Downing, M.D.

The reference to "Colonel Bronson" is a mistake. The name is sufficiently close to James I. *Brownson,* mentioned in the *Richmond Times-Dispatch* article, to explain the error by L. C. Downing. No reference or record of a Colonel Bronson could be found in any sources, including VMI's archives. Regardless, Downing certainly left a sure legacy for his children and for those "who wish to understand."

Earlier, on February 6, 1960, Downing had written to Jay W. Johns, president of the Stonewall Jackson Memorial, Inc.[22] This communication[23] also reveals the high regard with which the Downing family held Jackson:

Dear Mr. Johns:

I, too, recall the pleasure of meeting you some time ago and regret we have not had the opportunity of subsequent contact. The Stonewall Jackson Memorial, please be assured, is very close to my heart.

The Fifth Ave. Presbyterian Church was not totally destroyed. There was only minor damage done to the Jackson window.

At a recent meeting of the Congregation, I made a vigorous appeal for the repair and restoration of the building "as was." We had Insurance coverage to accomplish same, so that procedure was with in our means, however, I was snowed in by the avalanche of votes from the majority group, who wish to raze the still standing portion and to build from "scratch." I still feel this decision was unfortunate.

I have no way of knowing whether or not the Jackson window will be replaced.

A prominent White lady of our city has forwarded a request (so I understand) for the Jackson window, should it not be used in the reconstruction.

My brother, Dr. E. D. Downing, is presently in Puerto Rico on a Religious Mission. He will return shortly and I believe he has a picture of the Jackson window, if this can be located, we shall gladly send it along to you.

Wishing the Stonewall Jackson Memorial complete success, I am,

Sincerely yours,

L. C. Downing, M.D.

Fortunately, Downing's "vigorous appeal" to preserve the window and install it in the new building won the day.

In addition to L. C. Downing, who wrote these two letters, Downing's other children included Ellwood D. Downing, a dentist in Roanoke, Lewis K. Downing, dean of the College of Applied Science at Howard University, Gardner P. Downing, also a dentist in Roanoke, and Letitia Downing, who married Bert Andrew Rose and became a teacher and dean of women at a black college in Nashville, Tennessee. The Downing's youngest child, William, died at the age of seven. The Downing family was among some of the most distinguished and accomplished in Roanoke's early history.

In 1927, the city of Lexington named the "Negro High School" in honor of Rev. Downing, and today, students pass his portrait every day in the halls of Lylburn L. Downing Middle School. Downing never forgot his fond memories of Lexington and was known as "a generous supporter of the Stonewall Jackson Memorial Hospital,"[24] consistently sending donations to support the facility.

Today, Fifth Avenue Presbyterian Church proudly displays the window honoring Stonewall Jackson. In June 2003, I had the honor of meeting and interviewing two of Jackson's "spiritual descendants"—Ralph Shepperson and Gladys Watson. They are brother and sister and still attend Bible studies together as well as regular church services. Their father and mother, along with the rest of their family, began attending Fifth Avenue in 1923. Ralph and Gladys both grew up attending Sunday school and worship services there and both have vivid memories of Lylburn L. Downing. They were eager to share their memories of him, the memorial window, and their church.

According to Gladys, Jackson's noted biographer James I. Robertson makes an annual pilgrimage to the church and usually brings a crowd with him. She informed me that he would be coming to the church on June 17 with three busloads. He would explain the history of the church and the window to the tour group and then he would head over to the historic Hotel Roanoke for supper. Gladys was going too. She smiled and, with a mischievous twinkle in her eye, said, "We call him 'Bud.'"

Gladys and Ralph both remember Lylburn L. Downing as a strict disciplinarian. According to Ralph, despite Downing's love for children, he did not tolerate any "foolishness." Gladys recalled, "If someone came in the auditorium during a class or service and the children turned to see who it was, Rev. Downing would tell the children, 'Turn around here, I'll let you know if a bear or wild animal is coming in to get you.'" Ralph also remembers Downing as one who demanded respect for the house of God and worship services: "He didn't allow no gum chewing, very orderly. Dr. Downing didn't put up with any foolishness or an usher would come and remove you from the services."

Downing was not all discipline though. He expressed his love and concern for the children of the church in many ways. Ralph remembers coming to church often and seeing a lot of "strange faces." These were usually boys who had been in trouble with the law, and as Roanoke's first probation officer for delinquents, Downing would bring these troubled youths to church to hear the gospel and to be taught the Word of God in Sunday school, just as Thomas J. Jackson had done for Downing's parents. Downing soon began a junior church with the services being conducted by youths and supervised by one of the church elders.

After publicly affirming his faith in Christ at age twelve, Ralph went before the church elders, answered a catechism, and became a member of Fifth Avenue. Two years later, when Ralph was fourteen years old, Lylburn Downing died of a heart attack at the age of seventy-four. He recalled Downing's funeral and how the church was filled to overflowing, with several hundred more people standing outside the church. Downing's body had lay in state at the church the day of the funeral, opposite the window honoring Jackson. One of his obituaries noted that Downing had "an extraordinary career that epitomized the American ideal of success, marked by service, achievement, and unselfish contributions to the welfare of fellow citizens," and the *Norfolk Journal and Guide,* an African American newspaper, called Downing a "pioneer of Virginia" and his life "both inspiring and appealing."[25]

Ralph had vivid memories of another traumatic event in the history of Fifth Avenue. He was on the trustee board when the church burned in 1959 and was instrumental in seeing that the famous window was saved and restored. He concluded by saying, "I don't know what's going to happen after I'm gone."

The window, honoring one of the South's best-known icons, is a surreal testimony to what Christ can do in our hearts despite political and racial differences. It reminds us that Jackson, though himself a slave owner, saw no contradiction in reaching African Americans with the gospel of Christ. As the pastor of Fifth Avenue Presbyterian, Bill Reinhold, said in a June 19, 2005, sermon, "Thomas Jackson, like Jesus, was willing to cross real boundaries for the sake of the Gospel."[26] Jackson's efforts to elevate blacks through religion, literacy, and opportunity, though seemingly patronizing by today's standards, were progressive for the times in which he lived. But Jackson's efforts were not progressive in a political sense; his actions transcended the political. He was motivated by his love of God and his love of his fellow man, without regard for race. Reinhold noted, "Jackson treated his students and their parents with respect wherever he saw them—in class or on the street. So much so that in Lexington after the Civil War, blacks still spoke of the way Jackson would tip his hat when meeting anyone—white or black."[27]

Lylburn Downing recognized this, and his gratitude to God for Jackson's Christian graces, along with his desire to let the world know, was more important to him than the whispers he may have heard about the "appropriateness" of such a memorial in an African American church. Downing's actions also transcended the political. Pastor Reinhold noted that Lylburn Downing "like the Samaritan woman at the well was willing to recognize the truth of what he had been taught through the work of someone who did not share his own background—but who had affirmed the dignity and worth of his parents. This pastor grew up hearing of how Deacon Jackson's faith had compelled him to share it with others and in his own turn, Rev. Downing became an evangelist of the true worship of God."[28] And while Reinhold believes that Jackson fought "at least in part to keep alive an oppressive system,"[29] he also acknowledges that Jackson took great personal risk to "teach black children to read when it was both unpopular and illegal to do so."[30]

The words of the Reverend Vernie Bolden, pastor of Fifth Avenue Presbyterian in the early 1990s, himself the grandson of a slave, give the best perspective on the window: "It represents an ideal of what could be and what should be, instead of the reality of what is."[31]

What could be and what should be—Thomas J. Jackson and Lylburn Downing would agree.

6

A Brother Beloved

Stonewall Jackson and Jim Lewis

True friends trust each other.

—*A. W. Tozer*

I never knew a piouser gentleman.

—*Jim Lewis*

Faithful, brave, big-hearted Jim, God bless him!

—*Hunter McGuire*

U NLIKE THE CLAIMS OF Jefferson Shields, Jim Lewis's service as Jackson's personal servant during the war has been well documented and established by numerous accounts of those who knew Lewis and served with Jackson. Lewis became Jackson's personal servant after the general arrived at Winchester, and he is believed to have been born in the same year as Jackson: 1824. Some historians suggest that Lewis was a freed black, and some references lend weight to this viewpoint. Yet James I. Robertson points out that Jackson paid a Lexington resident by the name of "W. C. Lewis" monies "for hire." William C. Lewis was, for thirty years, a ruling elder at Lexington Presbyterian Church and would serve as one of Jackson's pall bearers. Although no known reference exists, it is possible that Jim Lewis at least attended Jackson's black Sunday-school class, given the fact that records indicate he was the property of church member W. C. Lewis. Another payment was made a year later in the amount of $150 for the "hire of Jim."[1] This suggests that Lewis was, in fact, a slave owned by W. C. Lewis and was "leased" to Jackson during the war.

Lewis probably knew as much or more about Jackson's personal habits and Christian practices during the war than anyone else, but little is known about Jim Lewis. Robertson acknowledged this sad fact about the mysterious character known simply to all as "Jim," noting, "Of the people intimately associated with the general, less is known of this figure than any other person."[2] One thing is known about Lewis: he and Jackson were close.

Henry Kyd Douglas of Jackson's staff provided a description of Lewis in his book *I Rode with Stonewall:* "The faithful fellow has become historical by reason of his association with General Jackson, to whom his devotion was a kind of superstition. He became important and was aware of it and never denied an anecdote told of him, however incredible, if the General was in it. He was a handsome mulatto, in the prime of life, well-made and with excellent manners, but perhaps altogether true only to the General."[3] Douglas goes on to describe other, less flattering characteristics of Lewis, suggesting he was "fond of liquor" and "somewhat addicted to cards."[4] This is highly unlikely, because Jackson had little patience for drunkenness and did not tolerate any behavior that he considered immoral within the close ranks of his command, much less someone so intimate with him personally.

Robertson noted, "Jackson handpicked men who possessed high moral character, strict punctuality, and exactitude to duty."[5] These traits would certainly have been applicable to Lewis, and Robertson added that Congressman Alexander Boteler believed Lewis and Jackson shared similar views regarding conduct:

The servant [Jim Lewis] and "Old Sorrel" [Jackson's horse] being about the same color—each having the hue of gingerbread without any of its spiciness—their respective characters were in a concatenation accordingly. For they were equally obedient, patient, easy-going and reliable; not given to devious courses nor designing tricks; more serviceable than showy and, altogether, as sober-sided a pair of subordinates as any Presbyterian elder with plain tastes and a practical turn, need desire to have about him. Both man and horse seemed to understand their master thoroughly and rarely failed to come up fully to all his requirements.[6]

Another staff officer, James Power Smith, wrote that Lewis, like Jackson, encouraged others to attend church and did so by practical example: "Over in Clarke County, Jim [Lewis] on Superior, at the head of a troop of our servants, affected the style of a general and staff, and went off, with hat in his hand, to some church for the colored people. I remember the general himself and the staff coming out of their tents to see the colored contingent go off in great style."[7] Jackson was doubtless pleased to see Lewis leading others in the straight and narrow.

Lewis had a worthy mentor. There is ample evidence that he was intimate with Jackson and familiar with many of his personal habits, including prayer. On one occasion, a local citizen sent someone to invite Jackson to breakfast at the normal hour in the morning. When the messenger arrived at Jackson's tent, Lewis replied: "Sh! You don't spec' to find the general here at this hour, do you? He left here 'bout midnight, and I spec' by this time he's whippin' Banks in the Valley."[8]

Lewis would allow no disrespect when Jackson was praying; he knew the general meant business with God, and he demanded everyone understood the seriousness of Jackson's petitions. Once, when Jackson entered his tent to pray, Lewis held on to Little Sorrel's reins and raised his hand to the chattering crowd preparing to break camp. With a look of displeasure and a loud whisper, Lewis admonished the staff and soldiers, "Hush, the general is praying." There was immediate silence. Jackson emerged fifteen minutes later, ready to do battle for the Lord.[9]

This intimacy sometimes included Lewis tucking Jackson into bed. Hunter Holmes McGuire[10] wrote that Jackson was "the most difficult man to arouse I ever saw. I have seen his servant [Lewis] pull his boots off and remove his clothes without waking him up."[11] Jackson also trusted Lewis—a courtesy he extended sparingly. Though Jackson often kept his battle plans secret from even his closest staff members, Lewis was usually the first to know something was afoot, stating that he "could always tell when a battle was near at hand by seeing the general get up a great many times in the night to pray."

Henry Kyd Douglas wrote that when Lewis observed Jackson getting up in the middle of the night to pray, Lewis said, "I begin to cook rations and pack up for there will be hell to pay in the morning."[12] Anna Jackson wrote a similar account of Lewis's familiarity with Jackson's prayer habits: "The general is a great man for praying, night and morning—all times. But when I see him get up several times in the night besides, to go off and pray, then I know there is going to be something to pay; and I go straight and pack his haversack, because I know he will call for it in the morning."[13]

Lewis frequently ran errands, and Jackson depended on his servant to keep him supplied in personal stores and food stuffs, often leaving Lewis in charge of the wagons.[14] One such errand involved Lewis's bringing a letter from Lexington to Jackson. The letter was from "Cy" (Jackson's slave Cyrus, Hetty's son), "asking permission to take unto himself a wife."[15] Jackson's trust of Lewis extended to his accepting Lewis's advice on certain matters. Once when Jackson called for Lewis to bring Little Sorrel to him, Lewis protested, reminding Jackson that the horse had been ridden hard all day in battle. According to Anna, "an amusing war of words passed between them; but Jim had it in the power to gain the victory, and brought out another horse, which the general mounted."[16] This exchange reveals the special relationship between the two men. Jackson rarely disputed with anyone; he made up his mind, issued orders, and expected obedience. The fact that he, who was infamous for his exacting expectations regarding orders, would tolerate a disagreement from a servant, especially when it came to something as important as to what mount he would use in a battle, indicates that these two men were much more than just master and servant. Lewis trusted Jackson and was confident enough of his relationship that he could challenge Jackson, and Jackson obviously trusted Lewis's opinion. There was even a hint of jealousy among some staff members over the favored treatment that Lewis received from the general. John Preston once complained in a letter to his wife, "Now that Jim Lewis is going home on furlough, I cannot refrain from scribbling again. White people here have no chance of getting a furlough; it is only our colored friends who can escape for a time the evils of war."[17]

Lewis's habit of rising early fit Jackson's requirements perfectly; there are no accounts that Lewis ever disappointed Jackson in this regard. Anna again confirms this trait with her version of the late invitation to breakfast related earlier on page 139: "But when the good lady sent to summon him to breakfast, his famous body servant, Jim, met the messenger with a look of astonishment and said: 'Lor', you surely didn't spec' to find the Ginerul here at dis hour, did you? You don't know him den. Why he left here at one o'clock dis mornin', and I spec' to he is whippin' de Yankees in de Valley agin by now.'"[18]

On one occasion, Jackson instructed his staff before retiring for the evening, "Now gentlemen, Jim will have breakfast for you punctually at dawn. I expect you to be up, to eat immediately and be in the saddle with me. We must burn no more daylight." Jackson was up at "early dawn" (which to him meant between 3:00 and 4:00 a.m.), dressed and ready to eat. Lewis always had a hot breakfast waiting when the general arrived at the camp table. The only other staff member to show was the Reverend Maj. Robert L. Dabney, somewhat disheveled and still not fully awake. Jackson was furious. He ordered Lewis to put away the breakfast, and with Dabney still objecting, Jackson mounted Little Sorrel and rode off. Dabney watched in disbelief as Lewis dutifully packed the breakfast away and poured the piping hot coffee out on the ground.[19] Another account of this incident states that as Lewis was pouring the coffee out, Alexander Swift "Sandie" Pendleton[20] showed up and insisted upon having breakfast served him. Though Lewis was "devoted to Sandie," he was more devoted to Jackson and ignored Pendleton's demand.[21] Biographer Frank E. Vandiver wrote that as Jackson rode out of sight, Lewis shook his head and "with a low whistle for emphasis" said, "My stars! But the General is mad dis time; most like lighten strike him."[22] The wasted food did not bother Lewis—he had already eaten.

Lewis's reputation for grand culinary abilities was well known. Pendleton described one meal: "At the head of the table, boiled turkey; at the foot, bacon & cabbage, vegetables such as tomatoes, mashed potatoes, & apple butter with plenty of nice bread and butter. . . . Jim Lewis did that in very good style."[23]

Jackson was particular about who he had on staff. While he favored men of a pious nature, he also required skill in their duties. Lewis did not disappoint Jackson in this regard.

Naturally, Lewis was devoted to Jackson and to many of the soldiers serving with him. The admiration was mutual. The attachment to

Pendleton is illustrated by the incident of Pendleton's wounding and subsequent death at the battle of Fisher's Hill on September 22, 1864. He had been shot through the abdomen trying to establish "a line of resistance at Toms Brook, a village south of Fisher's Hill." Upon examining Pendleton, McGuire informed the young man that the wound was mortal. Though McGuire volunteered to stay behind enemy lines at Woodstock with Pendleton, the wounded soldier insisted that McGuire attend to other duties. Though left behind, Pendleton was cared for by locals, and Union surgeons also offered their assistance. But their efforts were in vain. Pendleton succumbed to his wounds in the evening of September 23, just five days before his twenty-fourth birthday. The young man that Sandie's father, William Nelson Pendleton, called "a child of God, a servant of Jesus, a partaker of the Holy Ghost" and "a joy to his sisters, a treasure to his wife, an ornament to society, and a Christian soldier,"[24] joined Stonewall Jackson on the far bank of eternity's river.

Hunter McGuire, having left Pendleton in Woodstock, was not aware of his passing. Conflicting reports filtered back to Lexington. W.G. Bean wrote, "One message was from Hunter McGuire, who had 'charged' Jim [Lewis] to tell . . . 'how and when' Sandie had been wounded and that McGuire could not believe that Sandie was dead."[25] Bean also noted that Henry Kyd Douglas sent a "strange letter" by Jim suggesting there were hopes for recovery. The family was devastated. So too was Jim Lewis. Bean observed that, after Pendleton's death, Lewis was "borne down with grief and inconsolate."[26] Douglas also mentioned Lewis's grief regarding the passing of Jackson and Pendleton: "When the General died Jim's honest grief was almost inconsolable. He then attached himself to Pendleton, but when he fell also Jim seemed to break down. He grew sad and went home on a short furlough, saying he would come back and join some one of the 'old staff,' Jackson's own. But he was taken ill and died in Lexington and lies buried in that historic town."[27]

Ten years after the war, "An Appeal to Stonewall Jackson's Old Command" for erecting a monument to Jim Lewis appeared in the *Lexington Gazette and Citizen:*

Let us not forget that James Lewis, General Jackson's faithful body servant, lies in a neglected grave in the Colored Cemetery at Lexington without a stone to record his deathless devotion to the General. Jim was with the General until his death, followed his body through Richmond and to Lexington, and then served the gallant Colonel Sandy Pendleton till his glorious death at Toms Brook. The writer met him bringing the Col's horse and baggage home bowed down with grief, inconsolable, but in apparently good health. We tried to cheer him up, but could only get for an answer, "Major de dear ole General's gone, and Mars Sandy and its Jim's time next," and sadly he went on his way to carry out Mars Sandy's last requests; and in a few days afterwards we passed his corpse going to the cemetery. He was faithful among the faithless in his devotion to and care of General Jackson, and deserves a monument at our hands, officers of the corps, and all who remember him will be received at the Gazette office.[28]

James Robertson wrote that Lewis's death was "in part presumably from grief."[29] Lewis was buried in a Lexington cemetery that was, at that time, segregated for blacks. Jackson's slave Amy was also buried there. Up until 1880 the cemetery was within a plot of land that was surrounded by what today are Marble Lane, Washington Street, and Lewis Street. In 1880, Lexington established a new cemetery for African Americans,[30] known as Evergreen Cemetery and still exists. Supposedly, the remains of all who were interred in the original cemetery were moved to Evergreen. Unfortunately, there is considerable doubt this actually occurred.[31] The original cemetery where Lewis was buried was divided into building lots and sold in 1946. Today, houses stand on ground that very likely still holds the mortal remains of many of Lexington's nineteenth-century blacks, including Amy Jackson and Jim Lewis. The latter's grave is no longer just "neglected" as it was in 1875, it is not even known to exist—a shameful legacy to consider, not just for Lewis's sake, but for all those buried in the original "colored cemetery."

Lewis expressed his attachment to others in the immortal Stonewall Brigade. When Pvt. William "Willie" C. Preston was killed at Second Manassas, Lewis overheard Hunter McGuire report Preston's death to Jackson. Lewis was overcome with sorrow, and he "rolled on the ground groaning, in his agony of grief."[32] Willie Preston was to Lewis as he was to Jackson—like a son—and he grieved as a father. According to biographer Frank Vandiver, Jim "knew and loved Willy as his own." Jackson too almost lost control of his emotions, and according to McGuire, "His eyes were all aglow. He gripped me by the shoulder till it hurt me, and in a savage, threatening manner asked why I had left the boy."[33] The earthly ties that bound these men were not easily broken. Even with death occurring around them every day, the loss of a friend and brother in Christ who was so young, so close, and so beloved was almost unbearable. They would not have to bear their grief for long. Death and their shared Christian faith soon reunited them all.

After Jackson's accidental wounding, his friend Jim Lewis was one of his constant companions and comforters as he faced his final enemy. Jackson was shot at about 9:00 p.m. on the evening of May 2, 1863. By 2:00 a.m., May 3, Jackson was in the capable hands of Dr. McGuire. Just twenty-seven years old at the time, McGuire was one of the most talented and respected surgeons in the Confederacy. Jackson and McGuire had become close personal friends in the two years they knew each other. Now, McGuire's friend's life was dependent on the young surgeon's skills. After examining the wounds, McGuire determined that it would be impossible to save the left arm; amputation was the only option. He wrote of his conversation with Jackson: "At 2 o'clock, Sunday morning, Surgeons Black, Walls and Coleman being present, I informed him that chloroform would be given him, and his wounds examined. I told him that amputation would probably be required, and asked if it was found necessary whether it should be done at once. He replied promptly: 'Yes, certainly. Dr. McGuire, do for me whatever you think best.'"[34]

Late that Sunday afternoon, it was determined that Jackson had to be moved from the temporary tent hospital to a safer location. Federal troops were close, and Jackson's position was perilous. He would make the twenty-seven mile trip by ambulance to Guiney Station. Jim Lewis was given the important responsibility of following behind "with horses, headquarters supplies, and Jackson's personal belongings."[35] Lewis would have witnessed the same heart-rending scenes as McGuire: "At Spotsylvania and along the whole route, men and women rushed to the ambulance, bringing all the food delicacies they had, and with tearful eyes blessed him & prayed for his recovery."[36] Lewis was praying too.

Upon arriving at the estate of Thomas Coleman Chandler at Guiney Station, corps chaplain Beverly Tucker Lacy requested that the wounded

Jackson and his staff be permitted to use a small frame cottage that was normally used as an office. The Chandlers were more than happy to be of service. Jackson's room was prepared, a fire was built in the fireplace, and Jackson was brought in and made as comfortable as possible. After having some bread and tea, he went to sleep immediately.

McGuire promptly limited access to Jackson. The only ones allowed in the general's room were himself, Joseph Graham Morrison,[37] staff member James Power Smith, and Jim Lewis. Retiring for the evening, McGuire, Morrison, and Smith all rested in the upper room of the cottage. Lewis slept closest to Jackson, in the room next to the wounded general. McGuire knew he could trust Lewis to listen for any sound and watch for any movement coming from Jackson's room. His recovery seemed promising through Wednesday. Although Jackson did not have much of an appetite, Lewis fetched an occasional glass of cold milk from the Chandler home for him. As James I. Robertson has written, things seemed to be going well. Jackson was in the good hands of those who loved him: "Vital signs looked good into Wednesday night. McGuire felt safe in leaving Jackson in the affectionate care of Jim Lewis. . . . Lewis sat quietly and watched Jackson fall asleep."[38]

But Jackson's condition suddenly worsened. His moaning awakened Lewis, and he and Lacy rushed to his bedside. Jackson, being a believer in water treatments, requested that a wet towel be applied to his left side where he was experiencing severe pain. Lewis soaked a towel in cold spring water and tenderly applied the cool, wet compresses to the general's side. There was no relief, and the pain grew worse. Lewis was becoming worried and tried for some time to get Jackson's permission to awaken McGuire. But Jackson knew that McGuire was exhausted and needed rest. He delayed waking his doctor as long as he could stand the pain. Finally, at daybreak, Jackson asked Lewis to fetch McGuire. McGuire was startled from a deep sleep by Lewis' solemn words, "The General wants you."[39] Lewis watched apprehensively as McGuire examined his patient. McGuire's eyes and furrowed brow betrayed his fears. McGuire had seen many men die. He had come to recognize the early warning signs immediately, instinctively. Lewis and McGuire's eyes met, and Jim knew the situation had grown more serious. His friend was fighting for his life. "The tall, young surgeon stood up and stared for a moment out the window. He was convinced that dreaded pneumonia had developed."[40]

Beverly Tucker Lacy was sent by McGuire to request the assistance of Jubal A. Early's chief surgeon, Samuel B. Morrison. Before returning, Lacy paid a visit to Robert E. Lee, informing him of Jackson's worsening condition. Lee told Lacy that he was convinced that God would spare Jackson "at such time when his country so much needed him." Lee and Jackson were immeasurably close in their respect and admiration for each other, but Lee could not risk visiting his dear friend and comrade in arms for fear of losing control of his emotions. Douglas Southall Freeman noted that Lee "could not trust his emotions" if exposed to the sad sight of his critically ill friend. Lee did what he could—he prayed, as did the whole Confederacy.

Soon, Anna arrived along with daughter Julia and their slave Hetty. Upon seeing her beloved husband, she said, "He looked like a dying man." By Thursday, Jackson was becoming delirious, intermittently shouting orders to imaginary subordinates. With Friday's sunrise, Jackson seemed somewhat better, telling Anna, "I do not believe I shall die at this time." Though a total of eight physicians attended him, Jackson's faith was in God. He told his wife, "I am persuaded the Almighty has yet a work for me to perform." The momentous struggle for life wore on: the fervent prayers of Southerners; the emotional weeping of Anna, Hetty, and Jim; the intense physiological battle being waged by Jackson's body; and the combined talents of his doctors. McGuire noted, "All that human skill could devise was done to stay the hand of death."

But that hand was tightening its grip. Saturday, May 9, dawned with Jackson having endured a mostly sleepless night. Anna informed him that the doctors had told her he would not recover. Jackson, though his wife and his doctors discouraged him, insisted upon seeing Lacy. Jackson told the chaplain there should be a stricter observance of the Sabbath among his army. Lacy promised he would do all he could to honor the general's request: "His last care and effort for the church of Christ being to secure the sanctification of the Lord's Day."[41]

Saturday night saw Jackson's condition turn grave. Anna, along with her brother Joseph, spent the early part of the night singing some of Jackson's favorite hymns and psalms.

By Sunday morning, Jackson's body was racked with fever, and he was exhausted—the final condition before death. Through tears, Anna told him, "Before this day closes, you will be with the blessed Savior in His glory." Jackson confirmed the news with his doctors and responded simply, "Very good, very good. It is all right."[42] Later, Jackson's six-month-old daughter, Julia, was brought in to see him, along with Hetty. Jackson called out: "Little darling! Sweet one!" Lovingly stroking her head, he then "closed his eyes as if in prayer."[43] After a few moments of sleep, Jackson awoke to see his young adjutant, Sandie Pendleton, standing by his bedside. The general wanted to know who was preaching at headquarters. After telling him that Lacy was doing the preaching, the boyish Pendleton, barely able to keep his emotions under control, said: "The whole army is praying for you general." Jackson replied, "Thank God. They are very kind." No longer able to contain his grief, Pendleton stepped outside, sobbing uncontrollably. He would later tell Anna, "God knows I would have died for him."[44]

Shortly after morning worship, Lacy again spoke with General Lee. Lee requested, "When a suitable occasion offers, tell him that I prayed for him last night, as I never prayed, I believe, for myself."[45] Lee, like Pendleton, could no longer contain his grief. As their conversation ended, Lacy noted that Lee "turned away in overpowering emotion." It is hard for even the strongest of men to say good-bye to a dear friend. McGuire chronicled Jackson's final moments and last words:

> About half-past one, he was told that he had but two hours to live, and he answered again, feebly, but firmly, "Very good, it is all right." A few moments before he died, he cried out in his delirium, "Order A. P. Hill to prepare for action! pass the infantry to the front rapidly! tell Major Hawks"—then stopped, leaving the sentence unfinished. Presently, a smile of ineffable sweetness spread itself over his pale face, and he said quietly, and with an expression, as if of relief, "Let us cross over the river, and rest under the shade of the trees;" and then, without pain, or the least struggle, his spirit passed from earth to the God who gave it.[46]

What was Jackson seeing through the shadowy mist of death and eternity? Anna suggested:

Was his soul wandering back in dreams to the river of his beloved Valley, the Shenandoah (the "river of sparkling waters"), whose verdant meads and groves he had redeemed from the invader, and across whose floods he had so often won his passage through the toils of battle? Or was he reaching forward across the River of Death, to the golden streets of the Celestial City, and the trees whose leaves are for the healing of the nations? It was to these that God was bringing him, through his last battle and victory; and under their shade he walks, with the blessed company of the redeemed.[47]

Lewis looked on as he watched Jackson's eyes close, the general's shallow breathing finally stilled, not wanting to accept that Jackson was gone. It was 3:15 p.m. Anna was weeping softly. Though he had predicted the time of death almost to the minute, Hunter McGuire stood in unbelieving silence. As reality sank in, hot tears began to flow down Jim Lewis's face. With his hat in his hands, "big-hearted" Lewis bowed his head and wept like a child. His great heart was broken, and he could not be comforted. Anna took special note of his sorrow: "Tears were shed over that dying bed by strong men who were unused to weep, and it was touching to see the genuine grief of his servant, Jim, who nursed him faithfully to the end."[48]

But Lewis had one more act of service to perform before he too would join Jackson under the shade of the trees. He would receive one of the most honored positions available at Stonewall Jackson's funeral.

7

Go Home to Thy Friends

The Funeral of Stonewall Jackson

Thinking of departed friends is to me something sweet and mellow.
—*Abraham Kuyper*

Greater love hath no man than this, that he lay down his life for his friends.
—*John 15:13*

The voice of God is a friendly voice. No one need fear to listen to it unless he has already made up his mind to resist it.
—*A. W. Tozer*

SANDIE PENDLETON AND James Power Smith dressed their commander's dead body and placed the corpse in a crude wooden coffin. They went about their task methodically; like the rest of the South, they were in shock. Monday, May 11, the coffin was loaded onto a train at Guiney Station and pulled into Richmond at four o'clock that afternoon. The body was taken to the governor's mansion, where it was embalmed and placed in a "metallic casket." The casket had a glass door over Jackson's face, and on the coffin was "a silver plate upon which was engraved the simple inscription: 'Lieutenant-General T. J. Jackson. Born January 21st, 1824; died May 10th, 1863.'"[1] Pendleton and Henry Kyd Douglas stood guard until a gloomy darkness descended upon the capital of the Confederacy.

Tuesday, May 12, dawned beautifully sunny and warm. At 10 o'clock, the military procession that would accompany Jackson's body gathered on the grounds of the Capitol. It was spring in Richmond. Just like it was in 1862 when Jackson first marched into Capitol Square with 175 VMI cadets. At eleven o'clock, Jackson's body was removed from the governor's mansion and placed in the waiting hearse.

At the head of this illustrious group was the military band of the Thirtieth Virginia Infantry. Next in line was the military escort, composed in part by George E. Pickett's division. Then came the Public Guard, the Camp Guard from Camp Lee (numbering close to one hundred men), then six pieces of artillery. Next in line was the Twenty-first Battalion Virginia Cavalry, followed by the hearse. The hearse, drawn by four white horses, was decorated with six "mourning plumes." Inside, Jackson's casket was wrapped in the Confederate flag. Behind the hearse, leading Jackson's riderless horse, Superior,[2] was Jim Lewis. Surrounding the hearse were the pallbearers. The list reads like a who's who of Confederate officers: Sandie Pendleton, James Power Smith, Hunter McGuire, Henry Kyd Douglas, James Longstreet, Richard Ewell, J. H. Winder, Arnold Elzey, George E. Pickett, Richard Garnett, W. M. Kemper, M. D. Corse, and Samuel Bassett French.[3] Marching behind this group and the hearse was "a number of the original Stonewall Brigade."[4] Following these were carriages in which rode President Jefferson Davis and Vice President Alexander H. Stephens and Jackson's family. Behind these carriages, on foot, were members of Davis's cabinet and "chief officers of the Government led by the Secretary of War." Next was the remainder of Jackson's staff, mounted on horses "with appropriate badges of mourning." Following these was Governor John Letcher, "other State officers, and the members of the City Council of Richmond."

The Thirtieth Virginia Infantry band began playing the "Psalm of David" as one of Thomas Jefferson's grandsons, George Wythe Randolph,[5] raised his sword, giving the signal for the historic procession to start toward the Capitol. Band director A. J. Bowering later wrote: "I have played to men standing against the wall awaiting the command that would send them into eternity and in hospitals I have done my best to soothe the dying hours of the men of Virginia, but never was I so impressed. The tears rolled down the faces of my men and I knew that I was weeping."[6]

After circling the Capitol, Jackson's casket was carried by the generals into the senate chamber. There it would rest until midnight, wrapped in the flag that Jackson died defending. The historic chamber filled with mourners—"shattered and emaciated veterans, noble-bowed matrons, and pale, delicate maidens gathered around that sacred bier, in the awed hush of a common sorrow, too deep for words."[7] Hour after hour, patriotic Virginians filed by the casket to get one more glimpse of their beloved Christian warrior. Many Virginia ladies paused momentarily before the fallen hero. Jackson had defended their honor, homes, firesides, and the sacred sod of Old Virginia. With tears falling from their cheeks and "for the memory of the noble chieftain" these Southern ladies "pressed their lips upon the lid of his coffin."[8] This heartbreaking scene was simply too much for one old man to suffer: "Witnessing the deep feeling of sorrow manifested by these fair daughters of Virginia, an elderly and respectable looking gentleman addressed them in tones of condolence, as follows: 'Weep not; all is for the best. Though Jackson has been taken from the head of his corps, his spirit is now pleading our cause at the bar of God.'"[9]

As the time for public viewing was coming to a close, one old veteran was told that he was too late. Adamantly refusing to be denied entrance, marshals on duty threatened him with arrest. "The old soldier hereupon lifted up the stump of his mutilated arm, and with tears streaming from his eyes, exclaimed: 'By this arm which I lost for my country, I demand the privilege of seeing my general once more.'"[10] Governor Letcher, Jackson's old friend dating back to Lyle's Bookstore, was moved by the soldier's impassioned plea and intervened on his behalf. The crippled soldier was the last person to view Jackson's body. It was a fitting conclusion to the day's events—the grief-stricken, one-armed veteran, looking upon the lifeless body of his one-armed commander.

While all the excitement was taking place at the Capitol, Anna and Julia were in private chambers nearby. Hetty was given charge of Julia, but the incessant clamoring of requests to hold "Stonewall's baby" was more than Hetty was willing to tolerate. Anna later wrote: "Hetty, finding the child growing worried at so much notice and handling, sought a refuge beyond the reach of the crowd. She ensconced herself, with her little charge, close to the wall of the house, underneath my window in the back yard, and here I heard her crooning, and bewailing that 'people would give her baby no rest.'"[11]

As the heartbreaking and historic pageantry played out, a lonely figure stood silently off to the side, largely unnoticed by the pressing crowds. Jim Lewis wiped away tears as he nursed his grieving heart and waited for the next leg of his friend's journey—home. Home to where Jackson had told Anna he wanted to be laid to rest; home to the green pastures and blue mountains of Lexington.

On May 13, 1863, Francis H. Smith was handed a communiqué from the adjutant-general's office:[12]

Sir—By command of the Governor, I have this day to perform the most painful duty of my official life, in announcing to you, and through you to the Faculty and cadets of the Virginia Military Institute, the death of the great and good, the heroic and illustrious Lieut.-Gen. T. J. Jackson, at fifteen minutes past three o'clock yesterday.

This heavy bereavement, over which every true heart in the Confederacy mourns with irrepressible sorrow, must fall, if possible, with heavier force upon that noble State institution to which he came from the battlefield of Mexico, and where he gave to his native State the first year's service of his modest and unobtrusive but public-spirited life. It would be a senseless waste of words to attempt an eulogy upon this greatest among the greatest of the sons who have immortalized Virginia. To the corps of cadets of the Virginia Military Institute, what a legacy he has left you! What an example of all that is good and great and true in the character of a Christian soldier!

The Governor directs that the highest funeral honors be paid to his memory; that the customary outward badges of mourning be worn by all the officers and cadets of the institution.

By Command,

W. H. Richardson

Even though unofficial word of Jackson's death had already reached Lexington at midnight on May 10,[13] seeing the words in print stirred Smith's emotions. With trembling hands, he slowly removed his spectacles, lowered the letter, and stared out his office window. There, on the parade grounds, cadets were drilling. To the fifty-year-old superintendent the scene seemed surreal. The parade-ground grass had turned a lush green as spring brought new life to the Shenandoah Valley. Across town, Ellen Downing was tending to her newborn son, Lylburn. In surrounding Rockbridge County, farm boys who weren't off fighting for the Confederacy were doing their spring planting. As Smith watched the cadets march, their bayonets gleaming in the bright sunlight, they suddenly appeared to him so young, so fragile.

The VMI superintendent loved those boys. Many of them could call heaven their home thanks to his efforts. So successful were Smith's efforts, he claimed, "Not one graduate (exclusive of the first graduating class, of which I cannot positively speak) has ever left the Institution, who was not, at the time of graduation, thoroughly convinced of the Divine Character of our Holy Religion."[14]

These young men were much more than students to him, and he took his duties at VMI very seriously. Smith's thoughts drifted as he was reminded of his obligations. "There is no part of the duty of the superintendent which weighs so heavily upon his mind and heart," he wrote in his 1859 annual report, "as that connected with the control . . . of the moral conduct of those committed to his charge."[15] He added: "Blessed are they for whom the confusion and disarray of their boyish life is quickened into a true life by the moving of the Spirit of God! Blessed are they for whom the beginnings also of faith and love, when the new character receives, as it is forming, the Christian seed, and the man is also a Christian."[16] He was further reminded of the words he would sometimes inscribe in the Bibles given to graduating cadets: "I have prayed for thee, that thy faith fail not."[17]

Smith remembered the dramatic revivals and conversions in 1856, the prayer meetings in his office and in Section Room no. 10, and his Sunday-evening sermon readings in his parlor with cadets.[18] He recalled correspondences with parents and agonizing over the young men's souls.

One letter in particular illustrates his sincerity in reaching the cadets with the gospel: "A most wonderful work of divine grace is in progress at this time among our young men. Among those under conviction is your son. He has been regularly attending our prayer meetings of late, and I have an appointment with him . . . on the momentous question, 'what shall I do to be saved?'"[19]

As Smith recalled that this "wonderful work of grace" was precipitated by the accidental shooting death of a Washington College student, the loud boom of artillery practice on the parade ground startled him back to the present and the unpleasant reality at hand. A gentle breeze lifted the gray smoke of the artillery fire toward the heavens. His eyes followed it upward as if to convince himself, he slowly whispered, "My God—Jackson is dead!" Smith—"Old Spex" the cadets called him—knew full well how much the VMI cadets lately revered Jackson.

Though Jackson had often been ridiculed behind his back during his tenure at the institute, his reputation among the corps of cadets had changed. No longer the odd, stiff, eccentric, dry teacher; Jackson had become a legend among the cadets. The same young men who had snickered at his eccentricities were willing to follow him into battle and eternity, if necessary.

One of Jackson's former students, Abram Fulkerson, expressed the sentiments of most cadets in writing to his wife of Jackson's death:

> The intelligence of the death of Gen. Jackson came upon us like a shock. We feel that his death is a national calamity. The poorest soldiers among us appreciated his worth—loved the man, and mourn his loss. I knew him well. He was my preceptor for more than four years and whilst during that time I did not appreciate the man, as schoolboys are not like to do, yet I always had great reverence for the man on account of his piety & uprightness of character. Among the many heroes of this revolution, none have lived so much adored, none have died so much deplored, and none have left a character as spotless as that of Stonewall Jackson. Could his life have been spared till the close of this cruel war, the unanimous voice of a grateful people would have proclaimed him chief ruler of the nation. But God has seen proper to take him from us, and what He does is right and for the best. It is [illegible] therefore that we make the sacrifice cheerfully, th'o we cannot see why our country should be deprived of his services at this her hour of greatest need.[20]

When Jackson carried the day in defending Old Virginia, the cadets pointed with pride as one of their own had led the way. He was equally proud of "the Institute." As Jackson was about to commence his brilliant victory at Chancellorsville, another officer had—

remarked on how well represented the Virginia Military Institute was on this march. Jackson himself had taught there, and so had two of his present divisional commanders, [Robert E.] Rodes and [Raleigh] Colston. Stapleton Crutchfield, Jackson's chief of artillery, was a V.M.I. graduate, as was Thomas Munford of the lead cavalry regiment. Indeed, when they were counted up, the number of brigadiers and colonels of line and staff in the column who were V.M.I. graduates came to more than twenty. At that Jackson turned to Munford and said, "Colonel, the Institute will be heard from today."[21]

Though he and Jackson were never close, Superintendent Smith and Jackson respected and admired each other's Christian character and witness. They also shared a common concern for the souls of others—including blacks—as Smith had taught a black Sunday-school class prior to Jackson.

It was now Smith's sad and dreaded duty to officially announce Jackson's death to the Institute. He looked across the parade ground one more time, then, with a sorrowful sigh, he sat at his desk to pen General Orders no. 30.[22] Though styled a military order, his words read like a sermon worthy of an Old Testament saint, betraying the unequaled esteem by which Jackson had come to be held at VMI:

General Order—No. 30.

It is the painful duty of the Superintendent to announce to the Officers and Cadets of this Institution the death of their late associate and Professor Lieut. General Thomas J. Jackson. He died at Guinea's Station, Caroline Co. Va on the 10th inst of Pneumonia, after a short but violent illness, supervening upon the severe wound received in the battle of Chancellorsville. A nation mourns the loss of Genl. Jackson. First in the heart of the brave men he has so often led to victory, there is not a home in the Confederacy that will not feel the loss and lament it as a great national calamity. But our loss is distinctive. He was peculiarly our own. He came to us in 1851, a Lieutenant and Brevet Major of Artillery from the army of the late United States, upon the unanimous appointment of the Board of Visitors as Professor of Natural and Experimental Philosophy, and Instructor of Artillery. Here he laboured with scrupulous fidelity for 10 years, in the duties of these important offices. Here he became a soldier of the Cross and as an humble conscientious and useful Christian man he established the character which has developed into the world renowned Christian Hero.

On the 21st of April 1861 upon the order of his Excellency Governor Letcher, he left the Institute, in command of the Corps of Cadets for Camp Lee, Richmond, for service in the defense of his state and country and he has never known a day of rest—until called by Divine command to cease from his labors.

The military career of Genl. Jackson fills the most brilliant and momentous page in the history of our country and on the achievements of our arms, and he stands forth a colossal figure in this war for our Independence. His country now returns him to us—not as he was when he left us—his spirit has gone to God who gave it—his mutilated body comes back to us—to his home—to be laid by us in the tomb. Reverently and affectionately we will discharge this last solemn duty—and

> "though his early sun has set
> Its light shall linger round us yet
> Bright—radiant—blest."

Young Gentlemen of the Corps of Cadets—The memory of General Jackson is very precious to you. You know how faithfully—how conscientiously he discharged every duty—You know that he was emphatically a man of God, and that Christian principle impressed every act of his life. You know he sustained the honor of our arms when he commanded at Harper's Ferry—How gallantly he repulsed [Robert] Patterson at Hainesville; the invincible stand he made with his Stonewall Brigade at Manassas; you know the brilliant series of successes and victories which immortalized his Valley Campaign, for many of you were under his standard at McDowell, and pursued and discomfited [Robert] Milroy and [Robert] Schenck at Franklin. You know his rapid march to the Chickahominy; how he turned the flank of [George B.] McClellan at Gaines Mill; his subsequent victory over [John] Pope at Cedar Mountain; the part he bore in the great victory at Second Manassas; his investment and capture of Harper's Ferry; his rapid march and great conflict at Sharpsburg; and when his last conflict was passed, the tribute of the magnanimous Lee, who would gladly have suffered in his own person, could he by that sacrifice have saved General Jackson, and to whom alone, under God, he gave the whole glory of the great victory at Chancellorsville. Surely the Virginia Military Institute has a precious inheritance in the memory of General Jackson. His work is finished. God gave him to us, and to his country. He fitted him for his work, and when his work was done He called him to Himself. Submissive to the will of his heavenly Father, it may be said of him, that while in every heart there may be some murmuring, his will was to do and suffer the will of God.

Reverence the memory of such a man as General Jackson. Imitate his virtues, and here, over his lifeless remains, reverently dedicate your service, and your life, if need be, in defense of the cause so dear to his heart; the cause for which he fought and bled, the cause in which he died.

Let the Cadet Battery, which he so long commanded, honor his memory by half-hour guns tomorrow from sunrise to sunset, under the direction of the commandant of cadets. Let his lecture room be draped in mourning for the period of six months.

Let the officers and cadets of the Institute wear the usual badge of mourning for the period of thirty days; and it is respectfully recommended to the alumni of the institution to unite in this last tribute of respect to the memory of their late professor.

All duties will be suspended tomorrow.

> By Command of Major-General Smith.
> A. Govan Hill,
> Acting Adjutant, V.M.I.

The next day, General Orders no. 31 was issued,[23] announcing Jackson's funeral:

The funeral of Lt. Gen. Jackson will take place tomorrow. Maj. Scott Ship Commandant of Cadets will command the Military Escort and direct the procession.

The body will move from the Institute at 11 o'clock A.M.

Half hour guns will be fired from sunrise until the procession moves.

The Flags of the State & Confederacy will be displayed at half mast during the day.

Jackson's funeral train departed Richmond on May 13 for Lynchburg. All along the way, grief-stricken Virginians paid their last respects as they tearfully lined the tracks, the train winding its way through the hamlets and villages of Virginia's war-ravaged countryside. Inside the train, in addition to Jackson's immediate family, rode Sandie Pendleton, Hunter McGuire, Governor John Letcher, James Power Smith, Senator G. A. Henry of Tennessee, and the ever-present Jim Lewis. Arriving at Lynchburg at six-thirty that same evening, the funeral party met other dignitaries and made their way to the wharf on the James River. Here, Jackson's casket was loaded onto the packet boat *The Marshall,* which arrived at Lexington the next day, Thursday, May 14, as the sun was setting below the Allegheny Mountains. The vessel was met by the corps of cadets, and the young men bore their professor back to the institute. His body was placed in his old lecture room, where it laid in state throughout the remainder of the night. Just as it had in Richmond, sadness gripped the hearts of all present. One man observed, "It was a touching scene and brought tears to many eyes. When the body was deposited just in front of the favourite chair from which the lectures were delivered, professors, students, visitors, all, were deeply moved by the sad, solemn occasion, and gazed in mute sorrow . . . an air of gloom was visible on every face."[24]

Throughout the night an honor guard of two cadets stood vigil in one-hour shifts. Late into the night, locals packed the lecture room, piling flowers "high upon the casket until it was hidden from view."[25]

On Friday morning, at ten o'clock, the funeral procession began at the VMI grounds and ended at the Presbyterian Church. The *Lexington Gazette* later described the procession:

The procession moved from the Institute on Friday morning at 10 A.M. The Funeral escort was commanded by Maj. S. Ship, Commandant of Cadets, a former pupil of Gen. Jackson and a gallant officer who had served with him in his Valley Campaign, as Major of the 21st Va. Regt.

The Escort was composed as follows:

1. Cadet Battalion
2. Battery of Artillery of 4 pieces, the same battery he had for ten years commanded as Instructor of Artillery and which had also served with him at 1st Manassas, in [the] Stonewall Brigade.

3. A company of the original Stonewall Brigade, composed of members of different companies of the Brigade, and commanded by Capt. A. Hamilton, bearing the flag of the "Liberty Hall Volunteers."

4. A company of convalescent officers and soldiers of the army.

5. A Squadron of cavalry was all that was needed to complete the escort prescribed by the Army Regulations. This squadron opportunely made its appearance before the procession moved from the church. The Squadron was a part of Sweeny's battalion of Jenkins's command, and many of its members were from the General's native North-western Virginia.

6. The Clergy.

7. The Body enveloped in the Confederate Flag and covered with flowers, was borne on a caisson of the Cadet Battery, draped in mourning.

   The pall bearers were as follows:

   > Wm. White ; Professor J. L. Campbell—representing the Elders of the Lexington Presbyterian Church.
   > Wm. C. Lewis; Col. S. McD. Reid—County Magistrates.
   > Prof. J. J. White; Prof. C. J. Harris—Washington College.
   > S. McD. Moore; John W. Fuller—Franklin Society.
   > George W. Adams; Robt. I. White—Town Council.
   > Judge J. W. Brockenbrough; Joseph G. Steel—Confederate District Court.
   > Dr. H. H. McGuire; Capt. F. W. Henderson—C. S. Army.
   > Rev. W. McElwee; John Hamilton—Bible Society of Rockbridge.

8. The Family and Personal Staff of the deceased.

9. The Governor of Va., Confederate States Senator Henry of Tenn. The Sergeant-at-Arms of C. S. Senate, and a member of the City of Richmond Council.

10. Faculty and Officers of Va. Mil. Institute.

11. Elders and Deacons of Lexington Presbyterian Church of which church Gen. Jackson was a Deacon.

12. Professors and Students of Washington College.

13. Franklin Society.

14. Citizens.[26]

Three ministers officiated at the Lexington funeral. James Beverlin Ramsey of Lynchburg "offered a prayer of wonderful pathos."[27] William F. Junkin, Jackson's brother-in-law by his first marriage, eulogized Jackson and added "beautiful prayers." The congregation sang "How Blest the Righteous, When He Dies" and then, Jackson's spiritual commander, William S. White, preached from 1 Corinthians 15:26: "The last enemy that shall be destroyed is death."

As in Richmond, all who were present knew they had lost a great hero, a great Christian, and a great friend. A daughter of Jackson's close friend John Preston later explained why so many experienced the outpouring of grief: "We were not in any sense spectators, we were heartbroken mourners, a clan bereft of its chieftain; a country in peril, from whom its defender had been snatched."[28]

Leaving the church, the mourners proceeded up Main Street toward the Presbyterian cemetery. In the hundreds of mourners, Jim Lewis was one of the most noticeable. As was the case in Richmond, he was given the distinct honor of leading the riderless horse. This time the horse was Jackson's favorite, Little Sorrel. The two who had spent more time with Jackson over the last two years than anyone—Jim Lewis and Little Sorrel—shared this last march with Jackson. As they progressed, Lewis shouted to the crowd, "I never knew a piouser gentleman!"[29] His was not the only black face in the grieving multitude. Scores of Jackson's Sunday-school students, including Lylburn Downing's parents, mourned their teacher's death. Margaret Junkin Preston noted, "There were not many more sincere mourners at his grave than these very people, whom he had done so much to teach the way of life."[30]

The ceremony at the graveside was not long. Grief, travel, and the burden of what the South's future might hold without Jackson had sapped the strength of all. He was laid to rest in his family plot, beside his first daughter and close to his first wife, Ellie, and the son who had been stillborn.

After the funeral, Jim Lewis joined Sandie Pendleton as his field servant. After Gettysburg, both would join Jackson in heaven. Willie Preston would be there too, along with John Lyle and so many others. No more tears, no more war, no more sad partings.

EPILOGUE

He Calleth Together His Friends

With all our mistakes before us, we can but look up humbly to His providence. Let us follow what seems to be the path of duty, even walking amid uncertainties.

—*John Preston*

But many that are first shall be last; and the last shall be first.

—*Matthew 19:30*

Academic historians seem to think the facts are the story; the facts are only the bare bones of the story.

—*Shelby Foote*

THOMAS JONATHAN "STONEWALL" JACKSON is an enigma, or so it would seem to our shallow culture—a culture that attempts to pigeonhole everyone into predetermined categories of religion, race, social status, and politics. But Jackson does not fit neatly into modernity's superficial type-casting. Tom Jackson was the poor, orphaned young mountain boy who would, by sheer determination, graduate from West Point; the shy, backward, stammering young man who would become an influential speaker, educator, and leader in Lexington; the strict Calvinist deacon who questioned predestination; the fearless Confederate general who would weep over one of his slaves' deaths; the slave owner who would risk criminal prosecution and societal ridicule by teaching slaves and free blacks to read and to seek the same Savior who had redeemed his own soul.

These seeming contradictions in Jackson's life defy labeling by modern standards of political correctness. His relationship with his black brethren was, in many ways, illustrative of Southern Christians' bond with one another—regardless of race. James Webb wrote eloquently of what so many from outside the South fail to understand:

> On a personal level there was then, and there still remains today, an evolved compatibility between whites and blacks in the South that is purer and more honest than in any other region of the country, and this closeness grew most profoundly after slavery ended. As Wilbur Cash pointed out, "Negro entered into white man as profoundly as white man entered into Negro—subtly influencing every gesture, every word, every emotion and idea, every attitude." And as I mentioned to a gathering of Confederate descendants in a speech at the Confederate War Memorial in 1990, "Americans of African ancestry are the people with whom our history most closely intertwines, whose struggles in an odd but compelling way most resemble our own, and whose rights as full citizens we above all should celebrate and insist upon."[1]

Ironically, a recent ten-year survey showed that Southern blacks, even more so than whites, readily identified themselves with their Southern pride. "Twice-yearly polls from 1991 through 2001 that were analyzed by the University of North Carolina found 78 percent of blacks in the region claimed the label 'Southerner,' compared to 75 percent of whites. The results punched a hole in the long-held assumption that only whites are proud to be from the South."[2]

This bittersweet bond, though tainted with the legacy of slavery, cruel injustices, and prejudices, has been tempered by a mutual love for the Son of God, the Savior, who is the one person who has the power to set us all free and make us all friends to each other and friends of God.

The fruits and eternal consequences of friendships run like a golden thread through the generations—Jackson and Joe Lightburn, Francis Taylor, John B. Lyle, John Preston, Jim Lewis, Lylburn Downing, James and Raddy Jackson—all these men's lives touched each other in profound ways that are still impacting history today.

Seemingly insignificant people interacted with one another, exchanged acts of kindness, words of counsel, and shared the love of God. In doing so they overcame obstacles and moved beyond their own prejudgments. The influence of the Jackson family slaves, along with the friendship and counsel of young Lightburn, Taylor, and Lyle, all led Jackson down paths that converged with his black Sunday-school class. From this class came Christian ministers, educators, businessman, doctors, and others whose impressions linger to the present. Jackson's obedience to God's call, along with the life-transforming power of the gospel and the Africans' perseverance against overwhelming odds, combined to yield a bountiful harvest of righteousness.

This should encourage us to be better friends and to reach out to those who most need our friendship—as John Jasper did to the wounded Confederate soldiers of Richmond and as Thomas Jackson did to the blacks of Lexington. A slave ministering to Confederate soldiers? A slave owner ministering to slaves? Yes—if Christ is the model. Christ ministered to those in His day who were rejected and to those to whom it was taboo to even speak to or touch—Samaritans, lepers, publicans, sinners. If we are to join Christ, loved ones, and friends who have gathered before, we must follow Christ's example as Jackson did and as he taught his "Colored Sabbath-school" to do. Only by turning from that which displeases God to that which pleases Him—putting our faith in the risen Son of God—can we expect to "cross over the river."

They're all gathering there now, they have been for centuries, these friends of God. One by one, each crosses that eternal river—the river that John Jasper crossed, where, on the far bank, he found my great-great-grandfather had been waiting for thirty-six years. Thomas Jackson crossed this river where he was reunited with his former slave Amy and his dear friends John Lyle and Jim Lewis. There they all greeted one another and sat at the feet of the blessed Son of God. Christ brought them all there. He too is their friend, that friend who "sticketh closer than a brother."

Let Us Cross Over the River

Robin and Linda Williams

Let us cross over the river and rest in the shade of the trees
I will abide where angels glide with glorious ease
From misery and temptation I'll be forever free
Let us cross over the river and rest in the shade of the trees

I know the end is coming the shell returns to sand
The time has come to cross over and take my Savior's hand
I have no fears I am not sad for God has blessed me
And opened wide the doors to my eternal destiny

In pure delight I will repose 'neath balmy winds of peace
And sufferings of friends and foes I'll no longer see
I leave this world surrounded by friends and kindred dear
I leave this world in victory with the sound of the battle near

Let us cross over the river and rest in the shade of the trees
I will abide where angels glide with glorious ease
From misery and temptation I'll be forever free
Let us cross over the river and rest in the shade of the trees.[3]

ACKNOWLEDGMENTS
APPENDIXES
NOTES
BIBLIOGRAPHY
INDEX

ACKNOWLEDGMENTS

THIS BOOK WOULD NOT be complete without thanking the many individuals who assisted me both in research and moral support over the last four years. Megan Haley Newman, former curator of the Stonewall Jackson House in Lexington, Virginia, was always enthusiastic and obliging in my seemingly endless requests for information. Megan's work on Jackson and his relationship with nineteenth-century African Americans helped immensely in my research and in directing me to other resources. The current curator, Lindy Dosher, has also been very helpful and every bit as obliging. These two wonderful ladies allowed me unfettered access to the marvelous collection at the Stonewall Jackson House. Jackson's Lexington home remains in excellent care under current executive director, Michael Lynn.

Vaughan Stanley and his most able assistant, Lisa McCown, were unfailing in their cheerful support. These two individuals labor day after day in the basement of the Leyburn Library's Special Collection on the campus of Washington and Lee University. Any author or historian researching anything connected to Lexington will eventually be referred to their extraordinary inner sanctum. Their charge is a history lover's dream! Also, George Warren of the Rockbridge Historical Society provided valuable documents about nineteenth-century Lexington. Thanks also go to Wayne Sparkman of the Presbyterian Church in America Historical Society for providing copies of several articles by John Preston. Waite Rawls of the Museum of the Confederacy pointed me to Robert Lamb, Dave George, and Ellen Robertson, and all provided useful information about the old R. E. Lee Veteran's Camp in Richmond. Thanks to

Dr. Paula Skreslet of the William Smith Morton Library at Union Theological Seminary in Richmond for a copy of a letter from Daniel Harvey Hill to Robert Lewis Dabney. Thanks also to Dorsey Surveying of Lexington, Virginia, for assistance regarding Lexington history.

Lila Rogers of the Lexington Presbyterian Church supplied me with two copies of Robert Hunter's history of the church. This gracious and kind Southern lady allowed me the delight of thumbing through the dusty church session notes and minutes dating from Jackson's days at the church. She also granted me access to the church's Stonewall Jackson Memorial Museum.

Col. Keith Gibson, executive director of the Virginia Military Institute Museum, was extremely helpful in my research regarding Francis H. Smith and Little Sorrel. Col. Diane Jacob, head of VMI's Archives at the Preston Library, was also most helpful in granting permission for the use of various photographs and documents from the archives. Harry Crocker III of Regnery Publishing offered words of encouragement and introduced me to Jane Gardner, who contributed valuable editorial advice and criticism in assisting me in preparing the manuscript. Speaking of my publisher, much gratitude goes to Ron Pitkin and all the fine folks at Cumberland House who contributed to this effort, including my very able editor, Ed Curtis. It was a delight to work with Ed.

In writing the foreword, Dr. James I. Robertson Jr. bestowed instant credibility to the book. My appreciation for his kindness cannot be expressed in words. Professor Robertson is a true Virginia gentleman. Anyone who wants to know Jackson will find his defining biography to be indispensable. It is the final word on Stonewall Jackson. Lexington historian Royster Lyle Jr. aided me with his research on his legendary ancestor, John B. Lyle. Robin and Linda Williams were most generous in allowing me to use the beautiful lyrics to their song, "Let Us Cross Over the River." Civil War author Clint Johnson offered valuable input. And my friend Benjamin Ross, church historian at historic Sixth Mount Zion Baptist Church in Richmond, graciously reviewed the manuscript, offering his perspective and endorsement.

To all those kind and wonderful persons who granted me interviews, shared family oral history, old photographs, friendships, articles, and hospitality—Raddy Jackson, Margaret Jenkins, Mr. and Mrs. Jerry Roane,

Gladys Watson, Ralph Shepperson, Dr. Lewis Downing, Gloria Downing Pope, and those unnamed—thank you, thank you, thank you! Of course, thanks to my precious wife, Diane and my two daughters still at home, Mollie and Olivia, for their patience while Dad spent countless hours in Lexington and in his basement office surrounded by stacks of books and files, often muttering to himself into the wee hours of the morning and frequently exclaiming, "Fascinating!" Finally, and most of all, thanks to my God and my Savior, that friend who "sticketh closer than a brother." *Laus Deo.*

AUTHOR'S NOTE: A portion of the proceeds from the sale of this book will go toward establishing a suitable memorial to Jim Lewis and to the other African Americans whose bodies were never moved from the original black cemetery in Lexington and to supporting gospel and literacy efforts upon the continent of Africa.

For further information contact:

Friends Memorial
P.O. Box 752
Stuarts Draft, VA 24477

APPENDIX 1

Steadfast unto the End

The Death and Funeral of Little Sorrel

The horses that were alive at the close of the war were, for the most part, tenderly cared for, and have long ago joined their comrades on the other side. I hope they are all grazing together in the green fields of Eden.

—*Luther W. Hopkins*

A righteous man regardeth the life of his beast: but the tender mercies of the wicked are cruel.

—*Proverbs 12:10*

Always take care of the poor horses.

—*Robert E. Lee*

OTHER THAN ROBERT E. LEE'S horse, Traveller, the most recognizable military horse's name in American history is that of Jackson's trusty steed, Little Sorrel.[1] Without question, no other horse in the War Between the States witnessed such fierce battle scenes—and survived—as did this horse: First and Second Manassas, Kernstown, McDowell, Front Royal, Winchester, Cross Keys, Port Republic, Cedar Mountain, Harpers Ferry, Sharpsburg, Fredericksburg, the Seven Days' battles, and that fateful final ride at Chancellorsville.

Jackson came by his favorite mount when Confederates captured a number of horses at Harpers Ferry in 1861. After his troops had seized an eastbound Baltimore and Ohio train, they found that four cars contained cattle and a fifth carried horses. The general officially claimed the property for the Confederate government and dutifully paid for the horses he chose to use personally.

Originally, Jackson, with the assistance of his quartermaster, John Harmon, chose two horses: Big Sorrel for himself and Fancy for his wife. But within a couple of days, he learned that the larger horse's skittish disposition was unsuitable for the battlefield. Big Sorrel also had an uneven and rough gait, which would have made Jackson's long hours in the saddle impossible. He noticed that the smaller gelding was easier to handle and "showed a smooth pace and even temper." The name Fancy was changed to Little Sorrel, and the smaller horse became Jackson's mount. So smooth in pace was Little Sorrel that Jackson was known to fall asleep in the saddle while on long marches. The general kept both horses but allowed chaplain Beverly Tucker Lacy to use Big Sorrel.

The relationship between rider and horse in those days is often overlooked by modern students of warfare. Soldiers' lives often depended upon their horses' instincts and mutual trust. Jackson and Little Sorrel had such trust and understanding. James I. Robertson wrote of one example of this understanding: "By that stage of the war, Little Sorrel had learned its master's embarrassment at the cheers from the soldiers. Whenever Confederates raised loud and friendly noise, the horse would break into a gallop and carry its rider speedily away."[2]

Such instinctive understanding was immeasurable in battle. A slight miscue by horse or rider could mean death for either or both. And if blessed by providence and experience, their great hearts became one. Horses often performed heroic feats and remained steadfast under horrific conditions. Such stories of equine bravery often go unnoticed today, but the loving memory of these faithful animals has been recalled by more than one old veteran:

Ah! the horses—the blacks and bays, the roans and grays, the sorrels and chestnuts that pulled Lee's army from the Rappahannock to Gettysburg and back, and all the other horses that pulled and tugged at the wagons, at the batteries of artillery; the horses that carried the men, the unstabled horses and the half-fed horses. Let my right hand forget its cunning if I forget to pay proper tribute to those noble animals that suffered so much for their masters. How often my mind goes back to that horse that I saw com-

ing across the field from the front at Bull Run with his sides all dripping
with blood. He was a hero, for he had been out "where the fields were shot,
sown and bladed thick with steel," and was coming back to die.[3]

Little Sorrel was a Morgan horse and descended from the original
Justin Morgan horse born in Springfield, Massachusetts, in 1789. Morgan
horses had the distinguishing characteristic of being smaller than thoroughbreds and were not known for their beauty. Jackson and Little Sorrel
shared the mutual characteristic of not being physically impressive—
until the fighting began.

Morgans have sturdy but shorter legs than thoroughbreds and a
somewhat stocky body. They also possess the very important characteristic of remaining calm in the midst of chaos; another characteristic Little
Sorrel shared with Jackson. Morgans became the favorites of the U.S.
Cavalry during the War Between the States and the favorite horse for
Southern soldiers to commandeer whenever possible. Known for being
quick and agile, they were also popular among cowboys in the West for
their excellent abilities in working cattle. Morgans are also known for
their endurance, requiring less feed and having fewer foot and leg
problems—a truly low-maintenance horse.

Henry Kyd Douglas described Little Sorrel as "a remarkable little
horse. Such endurance I have never seen in horse flesh. We had no horse
at Headquarters that could match him. I never saw him show a sign of
fatigue." He added that the horse could "eat a ton of hay or live on cobs."

Little Sorrel was believed to be eleven years old when Jackson acquired him. He was gingerbread in color with no white markings. Standing only fifteen hands high (five feet at the shoulder), he was not much
to look at. But the horse made up in disposition and spirit what he
lacked in appearance. He could easily carry Jackson forty miles a day. His
calm spirit suited him perfectly for battle, and he was rarely overexcited
by rifle or artillery fire. But one notable exception to this was the accidental wounding of Jackson at Chancellorsville. There, Little Sorrel
bolted and carried his rider into some underbrush, where Jackson's face
struck an oak limb.

After Jackson's funeral in Lexington, Little Sorrel was dispatched by
Governor John Letcher to North Carolina to Anna's family farm. While

there, the horse gained a reputation for being a "rascal." Little Sorrel could untie latches and ropes, unlatch stable doors, and remove rails from a fence so he could jump into another pasture. He was also known to release other horses from a barn or field and lead them to "more pleasant pastures."

Anna Jackson's resources were not adequate for stabling and caring for Little Sorrel. So, for a few years after the war, Little Sorrel lived at VMI in Lexington, where he was free to graze on the lush parade ground. Though arthritic and stiff in his final years, the old fellow never lost his love of battle. Whenever the cadets conducted artillery practice, the sound of the booming guns would cause the horse's ears to stand up, his nostrils to flare, and he would canter around the field, as if looking for his old master to once again engage the Yankee invaders. Cadet parades or band performances also excited the horse and caused him to prance around to impress spectators.

Appearing frequently at county fairs and veterans' reunions, Jackson's old horse never failed to draw a crowd. Cadets often had to stand guard around Little Sorrel to prevent onlookers from plucking hairs from the horse's main and tail for souvenirs.[4] At an event in Hagerstown, Maryland, Kyd Douglas's nephew led Little Sorrel through the crowd when a band struck up a rousing rendition of "Dixie." The animal's ears and tail stood up, and he trotted off with a "mettlesome step," making it difficult for the young boy to keep up.

Ultimately, Little Sorrel was moved to the Confederate Soldiers Home at Richmond's Robert E. Lee Camp. There, he became the adored pet of the old men. Eventually, the horse's arthritis became so severe that he was unable to stand. The veterans in charge of the horse fashioned a sling and hoist so that the animal could be brought to his feet for curious visitors. On one such occasion, an accident caused Little Sorrel to fall, breaking his back in the process and leading to his death.

Arriving in Richmond the night before Little Sorrel died, taxidermist Frederic S. Webster wrote of Little Sorrel's accident and injuries: "One morning the girdle or band slipped too far forward, and the animal's heavy hind quarters broke the vertebral column near the pelvis, and he could no longer stand."[5] The veterans at the home were heartbroken, and one was assigned nurse's duty. Webster described the final sad scene:

"An old Confederate veteran, Tom O'Connell, stood by during the day, and at night slept beside his charge until he went over the green fields of some animal heaven to rest in peace and honour."[6] Little Sorrel died at six o'clock in the morning on March 16, 1886, at the age of thirty-six.[7]

Webster was well known. He had assisted in the mounting of two other famous horses from the war—Philip H. Sheridan's horse and Lee's horse Traveller. Webster would remove the skin and skeleton from Jackson's horse after getting accurate measurements. Only the hide was used in mounting Little Sorrel, and Webster actually received the bones of the horse as part of his fee for the mounting.[8]

The taxidermist indicated that his efforts were partly "patriotic duty": "My sole task of removing the skin and skeleton was successfully done in rapid time; but was undertaken because of the record of having carried the famous and beloved General through the heat and blast of a desperate war; *the only righteous war ever fought.*"[9]

After tanning, the hide was stretched over a framework of plaster. For a while, Webster displayed the mounted horse at his studio in Washington, D.C., and made it available for viewing "during the meeting of the Grand Army Veterans. A number of members visited the Studio, and we listened to many soul-stirring incidents of their fighting days, facing Old Sorrel. . . . The skeleton was retained by me with the consent of Colonel [E. V.] Randolph—virtually, as part payment for my service."[10]

Eventually, the stuffed horse made its way back to the Lee Camp home in Richmond, where it was displayed for many years. The home was closed after the Commonwealth of Virginia discontinued funding after the death of Sgt. Jack Blizzard, the last Confederate veteran living there, who died on January 27, 1941, at the age of ninety-seven. Demolition of many of the home's buildings began that same year.[11] Eight years later, after "inheriting" Little Sorrel, the Virginia Division of the United Daughters of the Confederacy donated the stuffed hide to VMI. Little Sorrel arrived at VMI on April 1, 1949.[12]

For almost twenty years, Little Sorrel was displayed at VMI's Preston Library. It was then moved into the basement museum of Jackson Memorial Hall, where it remains one of the main attractions at VMI. In the early days, it was common for both cadets and tourists to pluck hair from the horse's main or tail. Cadets were also known to rub the horse's withers and flank for luck prior to exams. But this caused undue wear on the hide. Little Sorrel is today behind a protective enclosure.

Webster eventually reassembled the bones and donated them to the Carnegie Institute in Pittsburgh in 1903. There they remained until, after years of efforts by patriotic Southerners, the skeleton was "loaned" to VMI, arriving on campus on August 9, 1949.[13] Carnegie Museum director Wallace Richards commented,

> Stonewall Jackson lived, taught, fought, died and is buried in the South. Most of his effects and relics are kept near his tomb, at the Virginia Military Institute. As far as the Carnegie Museum is concerned, there is no question of the skeleton's value. It is a symbol of a vital period in this country's struggle and growth. For this very reason, approval has been given to transfer it to an institution where it may be exhibited with other important relics of the period and where its emotional appeal is most personal and direct.[14]

Originally sent on indefinite loan, the bones were finally donated to the institute by Carnegie in 1960. First assembled and displayed beside the stuffed hide in the Preston Library when it arrived in 1949, it was later moved to a biology classroom, where it remained until 1989. While on display in the biology class, Little Sorrel had the habit of losing a tooth from time to time. These were usually glued back into place, but at least one tooth would not be reunited with its owner until later.

In 1989 the bones were disassembled and stored in the museum. There they would lie forgotten by the public until January 1996. At that time the president of the Virginia Division of the UDC, Juanita Allen, learned from Pat Gibson, the wife of museum director Keith Gibson, that Little Sorrel's bones were not under the stuffed hide in the museum. And so the Gibsons and Allen planned a funeral for Little Sorrel. With Colonel Gibson's recommendation, Allen submitted a request to then VMI superintendent Gen. Johiah Bunting for permission to inter the bones of Little Sorrel on the parade grounds of VMI beneath the school's life-size bronze statue of Stonewall Jackson.

Permission was granted, and initially, a small ceremony was planned for the summer of 1997. "Small" would not be a proper sendoff for the bones of Little Sorrel, however. The media learned of the ceremony, and after a couple of newspapers published stories, public interest swelled the total number of attendees to more than three hundred.

I first heard about the ceremony via e-mail. Having just read Robertson's biography of Jackson, I chose to attend the interment.

On a hot, humid Sunday, July 20, 1997, I drove a van full of my twelve-to-nineteen-year-old Sunday-school students to Lexington, about thirty miles from my home in the Shenandoah Valley. Men and women in period dress, a bagpiper, reenactors, and a cavalry unit added to the historic atmosphere. James I. Robertson was the keynote speaker. Other participants included:

- the Reverend William Klein, pastor of the Lexington Presbyterian Church
- ladies of the Virginia Division of the UDC who had visited every Virginia battlefield where Jackson and Little Sorrel had fought and there gathered dirt with which to cover the casket
- Cadet Adam Pool of VMI
- Professor Wayne Neal of VMI's Bagpipe Band
- the Virginia Grays Fife and Drum Band
- George Moor, president of the U.S. Cavalry Association, who appeared as Stonewall Jackson for the event
- the Second Virginia Cavalry reenactors
- the Fincastle Rifles Camp of the Sons of Confederate Veterans
- the Harry Gilmour Camp of Sons of Confederate Veterans
- the staffs of the VMI Museum and Grounds Department

The funeral procession exited from the front entrance of Jackson Memorial Hall. With women dressed in black mourning attire and Confederate battle flags flapping in the breeze, the solemn assembly made its way to the four-foot-deep grave in front of Jackson's statue on the parade ground. There, Cadet Pool placed an eighteen-inch-tall walnut casket—containing thirty-five pounds of cremated bones belonging to Little Sorrel (along with the long-lost tooth)—on the ground.

Just days before the funeral, a retired biology professor dutifully returned one of Little Sorrel's incisors to Colonel Gibson. Since the bones had already been cremated, Gibson placed the wayward tooth in the casket with the cremated remains.

The forty-five-minute ceremony consisted of remarks by Colonel Gibson, Klein, Allen, and Robertson. Then four reenactors lowered the casket into the grave. Attendees were invited to take a handful of dirt from the various Virginia battlefields and toss it in on the casket while the band played "Dixie." The crowd was dismissed after a closing prayer, and a lone bagpiper played a haunting rendition of "Amazing Grace."

After the ceremony, I noticed one of the reenactors with the rope that had been used to lower the casket into the grave. He was cutting it into six-inch pieces. My son asked the man for one of the lengths. At first the reenactor said that the pieces were keepsakes for the other reenactors, but later he gave my son one of the small lengths. I then cut it in half so I too would have a keepsake from this event.

On July 18, 2000, a fire caused extensive damage to the Lexington Presbyterian Church, where Jackson worshiped and served. The roof and steeple were consumed, causing an 850-pound bell to drop through the floor of the second-story gallery. Water severely damaged the church's nineteenth-century pews. Most of the structure was saved, and the steeple clock was painstakingly restored—down to the intricate hand carvings on the clock's four faces. The steeple itself was reconstructed from timbers salvaged from the interior of the church. The members also secured replicas of the damaged pews.

When I heard of the fire, I took my family to Lexington to view the damage. When I saw much of the rubble—pieces of brick and stone and charred timbers—in front of a large green trash dumpster, I collected some of the pieces. Later, I made a shadow box with the church rubble, my souvenirs from Little Sorrel's interment ceremony, and a photograph of James I. Robertson during the ceremony. This shadow box today occupies a place of honor in my home and serves as a constant reminder of Jackson's legacy.

APPENDIX 2

Stonewall Jackson's Colored Sunday School

MARGARET JUNKIN PRESTON

Margaret Preston's article appeared in the *Sunday School Times* on December 3, 1887, and is useful in the study of Jackson's gospel and literary efforts in Lexington on behalf of African Americans in the community. Though Preston's views are typical of nineteenth-century whites regarding the educational limitations of blacks, Jackson's efforts reveal that he believed blacks should have just as many opportunities as whites to respond to the gospel. He also trusted that, by becoming Christians, their prospects for advancement would be enhanced. Thus it is interesting to note that Preston's attitude seems to evolve from questioning the "comprehension of the Negro" near the beginning of the piece to stating near the end of the article that the black pupils were just as capable of "comprehensive biblical knowledge" as whites.

SOME THREE or four years before the opening of the Civil War, two persons were conversing together as to what could be done for the better religious instruction of the Negroes around them. They lived in the heart of Virginia, where there was no carrying out of the stringent laws against any instruction of the slaves which their white owners were willing to give them. Portions of all the churches, in the town of which I speak, were set apart for their use, and large numbers of them belonged to the different denominations. Still it was apparent that the Sunday services, intended for the whites were largely above the comprehension of the ordinary Negro. Sunday schools had been gotten up for them at various times, but they had not been a success in the region of which I speak.

"Major," said the young lady to her friend, (the young man had been educated at West Point, and had distinguished himself greatly in the Mexican War, but had left the army under the influence of Christian principle, and was at this time a professor at the Military College)— "Major, I have a great notion to announce among the servants of our neighbors that I will have a Bible class for them in my father's study every Sunday afternoon. I think I have somewhat of a gift for simplifying Bible teaching, and I believe I can interest these people enough to bring as many together as I could teach. What do you think of my plan?"

He mused a little while before returning any answer.

"Since you propose the thing," he then said, "I think I can hit upon a better plan; which is that, instead of collecting merely the servants of your neighbors in your father's study, we should get up, in our church lecture-room, a regular Sunday school, for the servants at large."

"But that has been tried," was the rejoinder. "You know our friends T— and R— gave such a school their best endeavors, and it dwindled away."

"But it shall succeed if I undertake it, because I make it a point to weigh all circumstances before I act; and if the thing is feasible, and I am right, then I make it succeed, if that is possible. Now this is the plan I would adopt: So that no fault could be found with my action, I will go around to the principal householders in the town, and ask their permission to gather their servants into an afternoon Sunday school. Then, after I have so gathered them, for two or three Sundays, I will undertake them myself."

"And not let me give you any help?" interposed the young lady.

"Yes, I shall be glad of your help in due time, especially as the first suggestion has come from you; but let me try my own powers of organization first, and let me test the manageability of the Negroes. If I find that they are docile, and willing to receive instruction, then I'll open the lecture-room doors to you, and to as many other teachers as are willing to assist."

Accordingly, during the ensuing week the Major went round to the principal owners of servants in the place, and stated his plan. There being four or five churches of as many different denominations in the town, of course these slaveholders belonged to all these different denominations. There was not a single objection made to the plan proposed. Indeed, the masters and mistresses universally hailed it with pleasure. The Major then addressed himself to some of the most influential men and women among the slave population whom he knew, and found them willing to send their children or come themselves to the school.

The first Sunday they were collected together,—and he was surprised at the goodly number that presented themselves,—he had simple prayer and singing, he himself conducting the music. For he knew well that a Negro meeting of any sort without singing was not to be thought of, singing constituting so large a part of their worship. He then explained to them, in a very familiar style, the need we all have of being taught the way of salvation; and he asked them if they did not think a colored Sunday school would be a good thing to help them find that way.

"Yes, [sir]!, Yes [sir]! a half-hundred voices called out. "[That's] right, Mars' Major! [Give] us a Sunday school!"

"Well," he went on to say, "I've been to see your masters and mistresses, and they are all glad to have something done in this way for you; but they are not going to make you come to the school. They want you to come, but they can't make Christians of you unless you are willing to be taught yourselves. Now I won't undertake to start a school unless you all promise me that you will try and come regularly to it. If you come one Sunday, and stay away the next, that won't do; you must be willing of your own accord to come regularly, and be regular members of a class. If you promise this, there are plenty of young white men and young white women who would be glad to teach, and who will come every Sunday to do it. Whoever wishes to become a regular member of the school, let him come forward and give me his name."

There was a forward movement at once among the audience; men and women, gray-headed, some of them, half-grown girls and boys, and toddling children, began to proclaim their names.

"Put down [my] name, Mars' Major," and "[I'm] comin'," [I'm] comin'," "Me too," was heard on all sides; and before the three-quarters of an hour, to which the Major had limited the service, was over, he had the names of fifty Negroes on his roll.

The next Sunday, the aspect of the school was very encouraging; the number was augmented, and there was an evident interest taken in the exercises.

This continued for two or three Sundays, when, according to the Major's plan; he invited various young ladies and gentlemen of the town to his assistance, and divided off the school into regular classes.

The young superintendent's interest grew with his work; the organization became systematic, even to a rigid degree, but the attendance only increased. The instruction was almost wholly orally, as only a few of the older servants had been taught to read. Brown's Child's Catechism, which most of the Sunday school teachers of thirty years ago will remember, was taught, and in a surprisingly short period many of the larger pupils learned it by heart. The mistresses at home often taught the lesson to their servants, and thus they would come prepared to answer the questions.

There was no end of the trouble which the Major took with his school. It began to be the very apple of his eye. If any of the regular pupils were absent, he would invariably visit the master or mistress to make inquiries as to the reason of their non-attendance. More than this; he had slips printed with the name of every pupil, on which he made out monthly reports, carrying them himself, every fourth Saturday, to the owners of the pupils, that they might know the truth in regard to their attendance. He cultivated the acquaintance of every scholar in the school, from the old "gran'dad" down to the little [child]. Often, as I have been walking in the streets with him, have I been touched by the courtesy of their politeness to "Mars' Major." None of them did he ever pass without lifting his cap to them; and not a child passed him without giving him a pull at his frizzly forelock, or curtsying till her apron touched the ground.

Thus the school continued to grow and flourish, and its fine effect was everywhere apparent among the Negro population. They were more orderly, they kept the Sabbath day better, and from the Sunday school many of them passed into church membership. This continued up to the opening of the war, when the demand came for officers and men to form the Confederate Army. The Major was summoned from his post, at first to become a drill-master for the raw recruits that were ordered by the Governor to collect at Harper's Ferry. There was nothing except his home from which the Major tore himself away with such keen regret and reluctance as from his beloved colored Sunday school; and his pupils parted with him we cannot say with how many tears. Little did they or we imagine how wide a sphere of action their young superintendent was to have, as compared with his duties in the Military College, or his unremitting labors in the Sunday school; for this young Major of whom we speak became afterward one of the most renowned leaders of armies,—the "Stonewall Jackson" of the Civil War.

But the school did not stop operations for one single Sunday, notwithstanding the absence of the superintendent. A fellow-professor in the Military College (afterwards one of Stonewall Jackson's staff) took up the work the Major dropped into his hands, and conducted the school with the same orderly system. Even during the absence of this second superintendent, in the camp or on the battlefield, pains were always taken to have his place supplied by someone willing to take up the work. And when the Major had become a general, and was sweeping back and forth through his native Virginia at the head of his army, he rarely wrote a letter home in which something was not said about his well-beloved Sunday school.

Success or defeat, anxiety or suffering, glory or grief,—nothing made him forget it, or cease to be interested in its welfare.

I believe it is a matter of fact that never during the four years of war were the services of the school intermitted, unless on some Sunday when the town was in possession of the Federal troops, or some terrible battle had occurred that spread consternation over the entire community. And when the dead General was brought back to his home, wrapped in the flag for which he had died, there were not many more sincere mourners at his grave than these very people, whom he had done so much to teach the way of life.

After the close of the war, it was a question with the second superintendent, into whose hands the charge of the school fell, whether the

Negroes, now so suddenly freed, would be willing to attend the school, as such attendance was entirely optional, and not only so, but as there was probability that the old slaves would separate themselves, as far as all religious teaching was concerned, from the whites. But the result was otherwise. There was no diminution in the attendance upon the school; indeed, it became larger, until it attained to three times its original number. Every effort was made to teach the children to read. Sunday school papers were introduced for distribution, an organ was got for the school, and one of the most brilliant musicians in the town conducted the music every Sunday. The system of lessons was widened; series on the life of our Lord, on the parables, on the miracles, on Old Testament history, on the Commandments, on the Lord's Prayer, on the Creed, were regularly taken up, and no pains were spared to make the teaching as thorough as the mind of the pupils could take in. And well were the superintendent and teachers rewarded for their labors. When the secession of the school came to a final close, it would not have been easy to find anywhere a white Sunday school in which the pupils gave greater evidence of comprehensive biblical knowledge. The music of the school was particularly fine, and many a visitor had been thrilled by it, and had listened in wonder to answer which displayed the clearest understanding of what might be called systematic theology.

"There is scarcely any height to which you cannot conduct your pupils, if you will make the step short enough," was the favorite axiom of the second superintendent. (It must be remembered that the school, which was in operation over thirty years, never had but two superintendents.) He made the step short, and it will not be possible for these pupils ever to forget the system of gospel truth so taught.

Three Negro churches were formed in the town, and multitudes of the pupils became members of these churches. In many instances, young men went abroad from the school for further instruction, and became preachers to their own people.

This state of things has continued up to the present year, the superintendent remaining the same, and many of the teachers in the school being those who first took up the work. No white school in the town was ever taught with more assiduity or unfailing interest; and the result of these labors, from beginning to end, has been of the most gratifying kind.

The most harmonious feeling has existed between the other colored Sunday schools and this one, although these others were wholly taught by colored people. But within the last year or two, it has been thought well to let these colored schools absorb the Negro children, because it seemed too much to expect them to attend two schools every Sunday. So, a few months ago, it was concluded that the labors of the white school might well now come to a close. It had been in operation over thirty years; it had done an inestimable work in its day; the necessity for its existence was no longer such as it had been. And so, within the year that is passing, the labors of the Major's schools were brought to a close.

"That day for which all other days were made" can only reveal the good that this school has done; and we have sometimes wondered if the Major was not doing a grander work, in the eyes of God, in leading his little battalion of colored people into the paths of peace, than when, at the head of his enthusiastic army, he was making a name which has since echoed over the world.

NOTES

Full bibliographical data can be found in the bibliography.

INTRODUCTION

1. Monsell, *Young Stonewall.*

2. During the three years I attended the school, a large wooden sign—approximately five feet square—was prominently displayed in the cafeteria with a simple prayer of thanksgiving, reminding students from where their blessings came. The sign was left over from the black high school. I never saw anything like it in any other school I attended.

3. Ironically, McLaughlin was involved in a legal threat against Jackson for his ministry to blacks—allegedly "an unlawful assembly."

4. Robertson, *Stonewall Jackson,* x.

5. Grant and Grant, *Best Friends,* 11.

6. Jackson, *Life and Letters of Stonewall Jackson,* 142–43.

7. Galli, "Defeating the Conspiracy," 17.

8. Webb, *Born Fighting,* 207–8.

9. Washington-Williams, *Dear Senator,* 222.

10. Robertson, *Stonewall Jackson,* x.

CHRONOLOGY

1. The author realizes that the term *Civil War* is not considered by purists to be the most historically accurate description of the war that occurred between the North and South from 1861–65. It is, however, the name by which most Americans know the war. It is also a term that even Robert E. Lee used on numerous occasions, both before and after the conflict. The author uses the term more favored in the South, *War Between the States* (WBTS).

CHAPTER 1: LET THE OPPRESSED GO FREE

1. Wyeth, "Horrors of Camp Morton," 328–33.

2. It wasn't until May 2005, after reading an article I had written for the *Washington Times* Civil War Page about John Jasper and my great-great-grandfather that my family discovered the whereabouts of my ancestors' grave. A gentleman had read the article and e-mailed to tell me he was

working on the restoration project of the Confederate Oakwood Cemetery in Richmond. He had recalled the name Crutchfield in the records and, after further research, confirmed that John Crutchfield was indeed buried in a common grave in Oakwood with two other Confederate soldiers. It was the first time in 140 years that any family member knew where he was buried.

3. Hatcher, *John Jasper,* 97–98.

4. Day, *Rhapsody in Black,* 58–59.

5. Ibid., 79.

6. Ibid., 116.

7. Many years later, when William E. Hatcher lay dying on his bed in Fork Union, Virginia, he is said to have whispered to friends and family gathered, "John Jasper, we're brothers now, and we'll live forever round the throne of God!"

8. From an article titled *God Struck Me Dead,* 15–18, as cited in Raboteau, *Slave Religion,* 317.

9. Raboteau, *Slave Religion,* 317.

10. Derry, *Story of the Confederate States,* 21. The first commercial American slave ship, the *Desire,* was built at Marblehead, Massachusetts, in 1636.

11. Farrow, Lang, Frank, *Complicity,* xxix.

12. Ibid., 4.

13. Ibid., 23.

14. Hemphill, Schlegel, and Engelbert, *Cavalier Commonwealth,* 119.

15. *Slavery's Legacy in West Africa,* April 12, 2004, http://www.npr.org /programs/re/archivesdate/2004/apr/slavery (accessed May 16, 2004).

16. The British Parliament did not pass a prohibition on the slave trade until 1807; the U.S. Congress followed suit in 1808.

17. McKim, *A Soldier's Recollections,* 318.

18. Ibid.

19. Ibid.

20. According to McKim, "In the year 1826, there were 143 emancipation societies in the whole country; and of this number 103 were established in the South" (ibid., 318).

21. Walsh, *Notices of Brazil in 1828 and 1829,* cited at "Aboard a Slave Ship, 1829," Eyewitness to History, www.eyewitnesstohistory.com (2000).

22. Falconbridge, *Black Voyage,* quoted in "Alexander Falconbridge's Account of the Slave Trade," www.pbs.org .

23. Excerpt from a December 27, 1856, letter written by Robert E. Lee in response to a speech by President Franklin Pierce.

24. Slavery still exists in parts of the world today, most notably in Sudan. This has been well documented by Christian Solidarity International, a group that seeks to purchase and free Sudanese slaves. See www .csi-int.org.

25. Blacks, Hispanics, Jews, and Native Americans fought for the South but in much smaller numbers than whites.

26. Perry, *Lady of Arlington*, 41.

27. Noted British novelist Charles Dickens observed, "The Northern onslaught upon slavery was no more than a piece of specious humbug designed to conceal its desire for economic control of the Southern states."

28. Robertson, *Stonewall Jackson*, 191.

29. Pryor, *The Mother of Washington and Her Times*, 166.

30. Jordan, *Black Confederates and Afro-Yankees in Civil War Virginia*, 308.

31. Mansfield, *Then Darkness Fled*, 217.

32. Ibid., 36.

33. From the Federal Writers Project, "Ninety-Two-Year-Old Negro Tells of Early Life as Slave," 4.

34. Jordan, *Black Confederates and Afro-Yankees in Civil War Virginia*, 106.

35. Galli, "Defeating the Conspiracy," 2.

36. Raboteau, *Slave Religion*, 320.

37. From *American Missionary* 6, no. 2 (February 1862): 33, cited by ibid., 320.

38. Hemphill, Schlegel, and Engelbert, *Cavalier Commonwealth*, 224.

39. Woodson was himself a black and the son of a slave born in Virginia. He is also considered the father of black history and is credited for initiating Black History Month.

40. Woodson, *The Education of the Negro Prior to 1861*, 2.

41. Ibid., 220–21.

42. Ibid., iii.

43. Ibid., iv.

44. White, *The African Preachers*, 40, 56. According to White, ninety-year-old Uncle Jack was known to walk as much as four miles to attend church on the Lord's Day, such was his zeal for Christ. Uncle Jack was once arrested by "lewd fellows" for preaching the gospel, and they threatened to punish him by whipping. The accused replied, "I have never had the honor of even one stripe for my master. You can lay it on when it pleases you." Uncle Jack's accusers were so impressed with his sincerity that they let him go. White commented that the distribution of the biography of Uncle Jack

"among the freedmen of the South could not fail to produce the happiest results." See White, *Rev. William S. White, D.D., and His Times,* 61.

45. "The Fruit of Freedom" by Mark Sidwell, *Christian History,* Issue 62 (vol. 18, no. 2), 38. Sidwell writes that Phillis Wheatley "was born in Gambia, West Africa, stolen from her parents at age 7, enslaved, and brought to America."

46. Hatcher, *John Jasper,* 44. Hatcher (1834–1912) was a Baptist pastor and theologian and a friend of Charles H. Spurgeon. He wrote numerous books, including the biography of John Jasper. Hatcher also founded Fork Union Military Academy in Fluvanna County, Virginia.

47. Pitts, Chaplains in Gray, 49. This information was taken from an article in the (Richmond) Religious Herald, September 10, 1863. The following is from an unedited microfiche of the original article: "To the Confederate army goes the distinction of having the first black to minister to white troops—'A correspondent of the SOLDIER'S FRIEND mentions a Tennessee regiment which has no chaplain; but an old negro, 'Uncle Lewis,' preaches two or three times a week at night. He is heard with respectful attention—and for earnestness, zeal and sincerity, can be surpassed by none. Two or three revivals have followed his preaching in the regiment. What will the wise Christian patriots out of the army, who denounce those who wish to see competent negroes allowed to teach, as tainted with anti-slaveryism, say with regard to the true Southern feeling of that regiment, which has fought unflinchingly from Shiloh to Murfreesboro?'"

48. Jordan, *Black Confederates and Afro-Yankees in Civil War Virginia,* 106.

CHAPTER 2: THE FATHERLESS FINDETH MERCY

1. Robertson, *Stonewall Jackson,* 169.

2. Cook, *Thomas J. Jackson,* 30.

3. Weston is the county seat of Lewis County, West Virginia, and about four miles southeast of Jackson's Mill, where Jackson spent his childhood. During Jackson's youth, this area was still part of the Commonwealth of Virginia.

4. Cook, *The Family and Early Life of Stonewall Jackson,* 62.

5. Cook, *Thomas J. Jackson,* 31.

6. According to Jackson's nephew, Thomas Jackson Arnold, Jackson's Uncle Cummins "was one of the largest slaveholders in the county of Lewis." See Arnold, *Early Life and Letters of General Thomas J. Jackson,* 55.

7. Cook, *The Family and Early Life of Stonewall Jackson,* 63.

8. Jackson and Meyers, *Colonel Edward Jackson*, 86.

9. Cook, *The Family and Early Life of Stonewall Jackson*, 64.

10. Jackson and Meyers, *Colonel Edward Jackson*, 87.

11. Arnold, *Early Life and Letters of General Thomas J. Jackson*, 29.

12. Ibid., 64. In a letter to his sister, Jackson wrote, referring to one of the family slaves, "Give my respects to Seely, if you should see her, and tell her that there is not a day that passes by without my thinking of her, and that I expect to see her in less than five months."

13. Cook, *The Family and Early Life of Stonewall Jackson*, 64.

14. Sweeney, "Ruth Lightburn Bailer Recalls General J.A.J Lightburn."

15. Cook, *The Family and Early Life of Stonewall Jackson*, 80.

16. Ibid., 64.

17. Cook, *Thomas J. Jackson*, 21.

18. Cook, *The Family and Early Life of Stonewall Jackson*, 64–65.

19. Ibid., 56.

20. Ibid., 56–57.

21. Ibid., 53.

22. Ibid., 69. Many of Jackson's early biographers referred to the negative influence of Cummins Jackson and Thomas's tendency to pick up his uncle's bad habits. But there is nothing to substantiate this.

23. Ibid., 49.

24. Ibid.

25. Morton, *A History of Rockbridge County*, 233.

26. Robertson, *Stonewall Jackson*, 20–21.

27. Robertson, *Stonewall Jackson's Book of Maxims*, 12.

28. Ibid.

29. Ibid., 13, 19, 36.

30. Jackson, *Life and Letters of Stonewall Jackson*, 48.

31. Dabney, *Life and Campaigns of Lt. General Thomas J. Jackson*, 55.

32. Ibid.

33. Robertson, Stonewall Jackson, 73.

34. Ibid.; Dabney, *Life and Campaigns of Lt. General Thomas J. Jackson*, 56–57.

35. Dabney, *Life and Campaigns of Lt. General Thomas J. Jackson*, 57.

36. Ibid.

37. Ibid., 59.

38. Ibid., 60.

39. Jackson, *Life and Letters of Stonewall Jackson*, 49, also Robertson,

Stonewall Jackson, 89. Scofield mistakenly assumed that Jackson's middle initial stood for "Jefferson." Also on the same church records was recorded the name of Robert E. Lee, who had served as a vestryman in 1842.

40. Robertson, *Stonewall Jackson,* 89.

41. Jackson, *Life and Letters of Stonewall Jackson,* 50.

42. Dabney, *Life and Campaigns of Lieutenant General Thomas J. Jackson,* 83.

43. Hill was Jackson's brother-in-law through Jackson's marriage to Mary Anna Morrison. Anna was the daughter of Robert H. Morrison, president of Davidson College, and the younger sister of Isabella Morrison Hill, wife of Daniel Harvey Hill. D. H. Hill was professor of mathematics at Washington College and a member of the Lexington Presbyterian Church, where he taught a Sunday-school class.

44. Jackson, *Life and Letters of Stonewall Jackson,* 53.

45. Ibid., 54.

46. Robertson, *Stonewall Jackson,* 103.

47. Ibid., 104.

48. Dabney, *Life and Campaigns of Lieutenant General Thomas J. Jackson,* 83.

49. Smith, *History of the Virginia Military Institute,* 7.

50. The Franklin Society can trace its roots in Lexington to 1796. According to author Henry Boley, the Franklin Society was "primarily a debating society, with literary and scientific emphases, no question of local, state or national importance, secular or religious, escaped the thoughtful and scholarly consideration of this group of illustrious men" (Boley, *Lexington in Old Virginia,* 81). In addition to being a forum for debate, it at one time boasted the largest library west of the Blue Ridge Mountains. Historian Charles Turner ("The Franklin Society," *Virginia Magazine of History and Biography* 66, no. 4 [October 1958]) quoted another writer from the society's period, Eugene P. Link, as saying that the organization was one "in which the people met, discussed the designs of their enemies, contrived the means of defeating them, encouraged each other in the good fight of liberty, directed and concentrated public opinion so as to make it more effectual. This society was a mighty engine in the politics of that gloomy period." Members included Robert E. Lee, John Preston, William Nelson Pendleton, John Letcher, and Thomas J. Jackson. Some of the diverse topics debated included secession, slavery, emancipation, dancing, banking, political parties, tariffs, inflation, immigration, and the possible annexation of Mexico. After a debate on May

11, 1816, on the question "Ought the Virginia legislature pass laws for gradual emancipation?" those members present voted overwhelmingly in the affirmative, seven to one. On November 23, 1850, the society debated the question, "Is the existence of slavery indispensable to the southern states?" The vote was almost two to one in the negative, nine to five.

51. Boley, *Lexington in Old Virginia*, 28.

52. Wise, *Drawing Out the Man*, 9.

53. Boley, *Lexington in Old Virginia*, 28.

54. Ibid., 34

55. Wise, *Drawing Out the Man*, 9.

56. One of these board members and its first president was Claudius Crozet. A Frenchman, Crozet was a former West Point professor, had fought under Napoleon, and served as Virginia's chief engineer. He also built a railroad tunnel through the Blue Ridge Mountains at Afton, Virginia. Completed in 1858, this tunnel was an engineering marvel in its day and was used by the Chesapeake and Ohio Railway until 1943. Plans were recently announced to refurbish and reopen the tunnel as a scenic bike path. The nearby town of Crozet was named after the Frenchman.

57. Wise, *Sunrise of the Virginia Military Institute*, 314.

58. Preston quoted in Eidsmoe, *Warrior, Statesman, Jurist for the South*, 32.

59. In Jackson's day, the Maury River was known as the North River. The name was changed to honor Confederate Gen. Matthew Fontaine Maury, known as the "Pathfinder of the Seas," and also a VMI professor.

60. Wise, *Drawing Out the Man*, 13.

61. Robertson, *Stonewall Jackson*, 114 (and verified by Col. Keith Gibson, VMI Museum, April 22, 2003).

62. Smith, *History of the Virginia Military Institute*, 258.

63. White, *Rev. William S. White*, 153.

64. Hunter, *Lexington Presbyterian Church*, 68–69. The original letter is in the VMI archives.

65. "Religious Feeling," *Lexington Gazette and Advertiser*, April 24, 1856, courtesy of the Washington and Lee Leyburn Library Special Collections.

66. Jackson lived in Lexington for ten years.

67. *Lexington Gazette*, September 25, 1856, cited by Pearson, "Thy Kingdom Come."

68. Pearson, "Thy Kingdom Come," 9–10.

69. Readers should not confuse nineteenth-century "ecumenical" efforts

with the modern movement. Most Southern churches in the nineteenth century agreed on the fundamental doctrines of the Christian faith and had not yet been tainted with twentieth-century modernism or those who deny such basic tenets of the faith as creation, the inerrancy of Scripture, and the divinity and bodily resurrection of Christ.

70. A person who distributes religious literature.

71. Pearson, "Thy Kingdom Come," 10.

72. Jackson came to love Lexington and shared his sentiments with his second wife, Anna: "Here was spent my happiest days; and it is still to me the most sacred of all places, as here the mountains keep watch and guard around the home and the tombs of those who were dearest to me on earth." Anna referred to Lexington as "this little gem of a place."

73. Dabney, *Life and Campaigns of Lieutenant General Thomas J. Jackson,* 83.

74. John Blair Lyle should not be confused with Lt. John Newton Lyle, of the Fourth Virginia, who fought under Jackson's command.

75. Lyle's father was Capt. William Lyle, a veteran of the Revolution, a trustee of Washington College, and an elder in Timber Ridge (Presbyterian) Church. Lyle's father also became one of the first high sheriffs of Rockbridge County. The Lyles of Rockbridge County had emigrated from Ireland, and many of the clan became missionaries and pastors.

76. White, *Rev. William S. White,* 142.

77. Boley, *Lexington in Old Virginia,* 96.

78. Letcher was, prior to Virginia's vote for secession, a staunch Unionist. But Lincoln's request for Virginia to supply troops "to subjugate the Southern States" pushed him into the secessionist camp.

79. Ruffner was Lyle's nephew. He should be credited with starting the first black Presbyterian Sunday school in Lexington. From 1849–51 he served as chaplain at the University of Virginia. His father, Henry Ruffner, was a Presbyterian clergyman and onetime president of Washington College.

80. Lyle, "John Blair of Lexington and His 'Automatic Bookstore,'" 23.

81. Grant and Grant, *Best Friends,* 38.

82. Lyle, "John Blair of Lexington and His 'Automatic Bookstore,'" 20.

83. Jackson, *Life and Letters of Stonewall Jackson,* 79.

84. Lyle, "John Blair of Lexington and His 'Automatic Bookstore,'" 20.

85. White, *Rev. William S. White,* 140.

86. Ibid., 140.

87. Ibid. Capt. Hugh A. White, the fifth son of Pastor White, was a mem-

ber of the Liberty Hall Volunteers and the Stonewall Brigade. Before the war, he taught in Jackson's Sunday-school class. He was killed at the battle of Second Manassas and, according to Jackson, "fell, sword in hand, gallantly cheering on his men."

88. Hunter, *Lexington Presbyterian Church*, 133.

89. Grant and Grant, *Letters Home*, 45.

90. White, *Rev. William S. White*, 141.

91. Ibid., 142.

92. Lyle, "John Blair of Lexington and His 'Automatic Bookstore,'" 23.

93. Grant and Grant, *Shelf Life*, 148.

94. White, *Rev. William S. White*, 157. White notes six other new members that day, but the records of the presbytery of Lexington, as quoted in Robertson, *Stonewall Jackson*, 810, indicate there were only three members inducted the day Jackson joined.

95. Dabney, *Life and Campaigns of Lieutenant General Thomas J. Jackson*, 84.

96. Jackson, *Life and Letters of Stonewall Jackson*, 58.

97. Ibid.

98. Dabney, *Life and Campaigns of Lieutenant General Thomas J. Jackson*, 84–85.

99. Ibid., 85. There is some disagreement as to who this friend was. Some historians have concluded it was Harvey Hill while others believe it was John Lyle. But the comment does not sound like Lyle; its tone is much more like Hill's.

100. Ibid.

101. Daniel Harvey Hill to Robert Lewis Dabney, July 11, 1864, Dabney Papers, Union Theological Seminary.

102. Hill, "The Real Stonewall Jackson."

103. A distinction should be made here between *providence* and *predestination*. Jackson was unarguably a devout believer in the providence of God in history. His questions about predestination were specifically over human beings having a choice of believing or rejecting the gospel.

104. Jones, *Christ in the Camp*, 94.

105. White, *Rev. William S. White*, 138.

106. Hunter, *Lexington Presbyterian Church*, 63.

107. Ibid., 77.

108. Allan, *The Life and Letters of Margaret Junkin Preston*, 81.

109. Grant and Grant, *Best Friends*, 109.

110. Jackson, *Life and Letters of Stonewall Jackson*, 80.

111. White, *Rev. William S. White,* 142.

112. Lyle, "John Blair of Lexington and His 'Automatic Bookstore,'" 27.

113. Today, this cemetery is known as the Stonewall Jackson Memorial Cemetery.

114. Lyle, "John Blair of Lexington and His 'Automatic Bookstore,'" 27.

115. Jackson, *Life and Letters of Stonewall Jackson,* 79.

116. Boley, *Lexington in Old Virginia,* 159.

CHAPTER 3: HE THAT IS GREATEST AMONG YOU

1. Newman, "The African-American Experience in Thomas 'Stonewall' Jackson's Lexington," 7.

2. Robertson, *Stonewall Jackson,* 191.

3. Pearson, "Thy Kingdom Come," 7.

4. Robertson, *Stonewall Jackson,* 2. See also Cook, *The Family and Early Life of Stonewall Jackson,* 8–9.

5. From an article appearing in the *Clarksburg Exponent,* September 24, 1911.

6. Arnold, *Early Life and Letters of General Thomas J. Jackson,* 28.

7. Cook, *The Family and Early Life of Stonewall Jackson,* 51. Jackson also referred to "Uncle Robinson" and another slave—"Aunt Nancy"—in a letter to his sister in July 1850, noting that both of them had died. See Arnold, *Early Life and Letters of General Thomas J. Jackson,* 162.

8. Some records mention a female slave named Ann and indicate that Jackson sold her in 1859. Little else is known about her.

9. Newman, "The African-American Experience in Thomas 'Stonewall' Jackson's Lexington," 21–22.

10. Jackson, *Life and Letters of Stonewall Jackson,* 119.

11. Ibid.

12. Newman, "The African-American Experience in Thomas 'Stonewall' Jackson's Lexington," 22.

13. Jackson, *Life and Letters of Stonewall Jackson,* 114.

14. Ibid.

15. Ibid., 115.

16. Ibid.

17. Robertson, *Stonewall Jackson,* 192.

18. Allan, *The Life and Letters of Margaret Junkin Preston,* 129.

19. Jackson, *Life and Letters of Stonewall Jackson,* 115.

20. Ibid., 115–116

21. Coulling, *Margaret Junkin Preston,* 122.

22. Jackson, *Life and Letters of Stonewall Jackson,* 116.

23. Ibid., 117.

24. Ibid.

25. Ibid., 135.

26. Ibid., 118.

27. Jackson, *Julia Jackson Christian,* 9–10, as quoted by Newman, "The African-American Experience in Thomas 'Stonewall' Jackson's Lexington," 79.

28. Ibid.

29. Jackson, *Life and Letters of Stonewall Jackson,* 118.

30. Ibid.

31. Jackson, *Life and Letters of Stonewall Jackson,* 207–8.

32. Newman, "The African-American Experience in Thomas 'Stonewall' Jackson's Lexington," 20.

33. "Re-enactors Plan May Encampment," *Lexington News-Gazette,* February 3, 1988.

34. I had never heard this before and was somewhat skeptical, thinking that Jackson might be confusing the entombment of Lee's daughter Annie at Lee Chapel in the 1990s. Annie had died in North Carolina during the war, and her body was reinterred in Lexington. I contacted Patricia Hobbs, director of the Lee Chapel and Museum in Lexington, to confirm his story. A few days later I received a packet from her with news stories published in the *Richmond Times-Dispatch* as well as Washington and Lee's college paper regarding Robert E. Lee III. He had died on September 7, 1922, and his body was entombed in the family crypt at Lee Chapel "temporarily." His wife brought a "friendly suit" against Washington and Lee to have his body moved to Charleston, South Carolina. The Richmond article, dated July 18, 1939, noted that Mrs. Lee had "promised Colonel Lee that I would not have his body placed in the university chapel" and that she "also had promised her first husband, Gustavus Pinckney of Charleston, that she would be buried beside him in Magnolia Cemetery. The removal of Colonel Lee's body from Virginia to Magnolia will enable Mrs. Lee to be buried between her two husbands, she explained." Thus, Jackson's recollection was correct, and he had indeed participated in the removal of one of Robert E. Lee's grandsons from the family crypt some sixty-five years ago.

35. Withrow Scrapbook, Volume 12, courtesy of the Stonewall Jackson House, Lexington, Virginia. James Jackson is listed as one of the founding

fathers in a 125th anniversary commemorative booklet published by the church in 1992. The booklet quotes an April 16, 1886, article published by the *Rockbridge County News:* "On last Sunday, about 75 converts of the First Baptist Church (colored) were baptized in the North River. It took one hour and was witnessed by at least 1000 people." The church is known today as the First Baptist Church.

36. Boley, *Lexington in Old Virginia,* 204.

37. Ibid., 205.

38. 1870 census records, Rockbridge County, lists the following individuals in the same household: James Jackson, age thirty-one, M/M (male/mulatto), Kysanna Jackson, age twenty-nine, F/M, and Thomas Jackson, age ten, M/M.

39. Newman, "The African-American Experience in Thomas 'Stonewall' Jackson's Lexington," 25.

40. The 1988 *News-Gazette* article states that the son's name was Thomas J. Jackson.

41. Withrow Scrapbook, Volume 12, Courtesy of the Stonewall Jackson House, Lexington, Virginia.

CHAPTER 4: EXCEPT SOME MAN SHOULD GUIDE ME

1. Originally constructed in 1835, the lecture room was demolished in 1906. No known photographs exist of the inside of this structure, but it was described as "one large room, with no separate class rooms." See Rockbridge Historical Society proceedings, vol. 8, 33. "Fairs," organized by the ladies of the church, met in the lecture room as did other civic groups. The Rockbridge Bible Society also met in this building "the first Saturday of every month at 11 a.m."

2. The Lexington Presbytery was taken from the Hanover Presbytery of central Virginia, arguably one of the most influential Christian organizations and regions of any in America's Christian history. Founded by the Reverend Samuel Davies (known as "the Apostle of Virginia") in 1753, Hanover was the mother presbytery of the Presbyterian Church in the South. The Lexington Presbytery inherited a rich heritage from Hanover—that of teaching blacks to read so they could be evangelized and converted to Christ. According to one scholar, "No white person in colonial America was as successful as Davies in stimulating literacy among slaves in the South." Davies's purpose in teaching blacks to read was more than utilitarian. "Davies as a Presbyterian believed that the attainment of true religion by anyone, bond or free,

black or white, required extensive knowledge that came from not only hearing the word of God but also reading it." Davies's work among blacks "was the first sustained and successful program by a white clergyman in the South to stimulate large numbers of Africans and African Americans to read in English." Davies, unlike many of his colonial contemporaries believed in the "full humanity of the African people." In a 1757 sermon to slave owners, he proclaimed: "His immortality gives him a kind of infinite value. Let him be white or black, bond or free, a native or a foreigner, it is of no moment in this view: he is to live forever!" Davies laid the responsibility for the slaves' condition squarely at the feet of their masters: "Your Negroes may be ignorant and stupid as to divine things not for want of capacity, but for want of instruction; not through perverseness, but through your negligence. . . . They are generally as capable of instruction, as the white people." Davies's comments regarding slaves being "capable of instruction as the white people" put him at odds with many whites, particularly Northern slave traders and Southern slave holders. So successful were his efforts that James Davenport noted them in a letter to Jonathan Edwards, telling "of a remarkable work of conviction and conversion among whites and negroes, at Hanover in Virginia, under the ministry of Mr. Davies." One hundred years later, Davies's mantle of success among blacks passed to Thomas J. Jackson. For a thorough treatment of Davies's efforts, see Jeffrey H. Richards, "Samuel Davies and the Transatlantic Campaign for Slave Literacy in Virginia," *Virginia Magazine of History and Biography* 111, no. 4 (2003).

3. William Henry Ruffner graduated from Washington College and studied at the University of Virginia under Dr. William Holmes McGuffey, author of the famous *McGuffey Readers*. Ruffner's father, the Reverend Henry Ruffner, served as president of Washington College. There are conflicting statements in various sources regarding the dates of this class and which Ruffner actually taught the class—the son or the father. My research mentions William Henry Ruffner as the one who assisted Lacy, but some also refer to him as president of Washington College (the father occupied that office, however). William Spottswood White wrote that he had secured the services of a "younger minister" about this same time to teach blacks on Saturday afternoons. Henry Ruffner would have been sixty years old in 1845, so White's comment suggests the son was involved in this ministry. Moreover, Lacy and William Henry Ruffner were close to the same age, and it would seem likely that they would have worked together. Two extensive biographical articles about the elder Ruffner, one by his son, do not mention

that Henry Ruffner taught a black Sunday-school class or instructed blacks at all. All of these facts lead one to conclude it was the son, William Henry Ruffner, who taught the class in the 1840s, though it is possible that both the son and the father were involved to some extent.

4. This is the same Beverly Lacy who served as a "missionary chaplain" on Jackson's staff and became the unofficial chaplain of the Second Corps. Late one cold night in December 1862, Jackson and Lacy discussed the importance of religion in the life of the Confederate army. The conversation led Jackson to offer the chaplain position to Lacy. Jackson invited Lacy to share his quarters for the evening, and before going to bed, the two men prayed. Lacy baptized Jackson's daughter, Julia, on April 23, 1863, just days before Jackson was wounded at Chancellorsville. Lacy would accompany Anna Jackson on the funeral train to Richmond.

5. See Brown, "Stonewall Jackson in Lexington," 200, n. 11.

6. Pearson, "Thy Kingdom Come," 35.

7. Hunter, *Lexington Presbyterian Church*, 109.

8. Ibid., *26*.

9. There are conflicting reports as to the year in which Jackson started his class. Dabney and Anna Jackson both indicate it was 1855 (see Dabney, *Life and Campaigns of Lieutenant General Thomas J. Jackson*, 93; Jackson, *Life and Letters of Stonewall Jackson*, 77). Plus, Ann Jackson, the general's great-granddaughter, wrote that the class began in 1855 (however, she erroneously adds that the class ended at "the outbreak of the war"; see Newman, "The African-American Experience in Thomas 'Stonewall' Jackson's Lexington," 18, 64.) But William Spottswood White indicated that the class began in 1856 (White, *William S. White*, 157). It is presumed that, as pastor of the church (and because Jackson sought his permission for the Sunday school), White would be the most reliable source on the inauguration of the class. Unfortunately, church session records do not note when Jackson's black Sunday-school class began and only briefly offer any information on the class. But a May 31, 1856, letter from Jackson to Margaret Junkin closes with Jackson's sharing a prayer request with her: "Our afternoon Sunday school Our Lord blessed very much last Sunday. I had about one hundred Students. Pray much for it" (Preston Papers, #1543, University of North Carolina; cited in Robertson, *Stonewall Jackson*, 170. See also Coulling, *Margaret Junkin Preston*, 79).

10. Hemphill, Schlegel, and Engelbert, *Cavalier Commonwealth*, 229.

11. Washington, *Up from Slavery*, 17–18.

12. Hemphill, Schlegel, and Engelbert, *Cavalier Commonwealth*, 279.

13. Farwell, *Stonewall*, 124.

14. Pearson, "Thy Kingdom Come," 53.

15. Code of Virginia, 2nd edition, including legislation to the year 1860. It was with this statute that several prominent Lexington attorneys threatened to prosecute Jackson.

16. Woodson, *The Education of the Negro Prior to 1861*, 10–11.

17. Ibid, 220–21.

18. Hunter, *Lexington Presbyterian Church*, 30.

19. Smith, *Climbing Jacob's Ladder*, 88.

20. Cook, *The Family and Early Life of Stonewall Jackson*, 79–80.

21. Ibid., 50.

22. Ibid., 56.

23. Robertson, *Stonewall Jackson*, 168.

24. DeLaney, "Aspects of Black Religious and Educational Development in Lexington," 143.

25. Jackson, *Life and Letters of Stonewall Jackson*, 118.

26. Robertson, *Stonewall Jackson*, 190.

27. Some historians, including Robertson, are not convinced that Jackson taught blacks to read, although Robertson admits, "Jackson was . . . on the perimeter of the law by leading a service on Sunday afternoons" (Robertson, *Stonewall Jackson*, 168).

28. Reid was a fellow church member of Jackson's and would serve as one of the general's pall bearers.

29. McLaughlin nominated Jackson for membership in the prestigious debating society known as The Franklin Society. He would eventually become a judge and served as a colonel for the Confederacy. McLaughlin delivered a speech at the unveiling of the bronze statue over Jackson's grave. Ironically, the first contribution for this statue came from members of Jackson's black Sunday-school class.

30. This description of the event first appeared in the August 16, 1876, *Lexington Gazette* under the caption "Stonewall Jackson and his Negro Sund. School." It was reprinted in a booklet by J. D. Davidson titled *A Curiosity in Chancery and Rhyme and Prose*, which was probably published in 1878. It is cited here through the courtesy of the Stonewall Jackson House, Lexington, Virginia.

31. The date cited for the "organizing" of the Sunday-school class is incorrect. By 1858, Jackson's class had been in operation for two years.

32. Grant and Grant, *Best Friends,* 65.

33. "The Colored Sunday School," *Lexington Gazette,* November 8, 1860, courtesy of Washington and Lee Leyburn Library Special Collections.

34. White, *Rev. William S. White,* 157.

35. Pearson, "Thy Kingdom Come," 14.

36. Deacon records of the Lexington Presbyterian Church, January 2, 1858, cited in ibid., 41–42.

37. Ibid., 42.

38. White, *Rev. William S. White,* 138.

39. Lexington Presbyterian Church Session notes, vol. 1, sess. 345, July 7, 1859, courtesy of the Lexington Presbyterian Church, Lexington, Virginia.

40. Hunter, *Lexington Presbyterian Church,* 93.

41. William "Willie" C. Preston, son of John Preston and stepson of Margaret Junkin Preston, along with Hugh A. White, son of Jackson's pastor, William S. White, were among the young boys Jackson taught in his regular Sunday-school class. Both were killed at Second Manassas.

42. Doyle, "Some Recollections of Stonewall Jackson by One of His Sunday School Pupils," courtesy of the Stonewall Jackson House, Lexington, Virginia.

43. Jones, *Christ in the Camp,* 85.

44. Robertson, *Stonewall Jackson,* 168.

45. Lenoir Chambers held the same view on the subject as Dabney; see Chambers, *Stonewall Jackson,* 1:271.

46. Dabney, *Life and Campaigns of Lieutenant General Thomas J. Jackson,* 94.

47. Brown, "Stonewall Jackson in Lexington," 4. See also, Jackson, *Life and Letters of Stonewall Jackson,* 72.

48. Sidwell, "Stonewall Jackson's Black Sunday School," 92.

49. Robertson, *Stonewall Jackson,* 143. Jackson was also a "life member" of the organization.

50. White, *Rev. William S. White,* 143.

51. Dabney, *Life and Campaigns of Lieutenant General Thomas J. Jackson,* 98.

52. Robertson, *Stonewall Jackson,* 17.

53. Margaret Preston's "Stonewall Jackson's Colored Sunday School Class" has been republished in its entirety as a nine-page appendix to Jackson, *Life and Letters of Stonewall Jackson* in the reprint edition by Sprinkle Publications. All citations are to this edition.

54. At that time in the South, it was considered improper for a lady's name to appear in print, thus the likely reason for the anonymity.

55. Preston, "Stonewall Jackson's Colored Sunday School Class," 1–2.

56. Ibid.

57. Ibid, 3

58. Ibid, 4.

59. Courtesy of the Virginia Military Institute Archives.

60. Preston, "Stonewall Jackson's Colored Sunday School Class," 4.

61. DeLaney, "Aspects of Black Religious and Educational Development in Lexington," 142.

62. Jackson served both as teacher and superintendent of the black Sunday school.

63. Robertson, *Stonewall Jackson,* 168.

64. Jackson, *Life and Letters of Stonewall Jackson,* 78.

65. Ibid.

66. Preston, "Stonewall Jackson's Colored Sunday School Class," 5.

67. White, *Rev. Williams S. White,*158.

68. Preston, "Stonewall Jackson's Colored Sunday School Class," 5.

69. Ibid, 6

70. Jackson, *Life and Letters of Stonewall Jackson,* 182. Robertson notes that White never told this story himself, but it was repeated by J. William Jones, and the Reverend Moses D. Hoge spoke of it publicly.

71. Jones, *Christ in the Camp,* 87.

72. Ibid.

73. Cable, "The Gentler Side of Two Great Southerners," 292–94.

74. *Southern Historical Society Papers* 9 (January 1881): 44.

75. Preston, "Stonewall Jackson's Colored Sunday School Class," 9.

76. Ibid, 8.

77. Newman, "The African-American Experience in Thomas 'Stonewall' Jackson's Lexington," 20.

78. J. A. Holmes is mentioned in a list of "preachers from Rockbridge County" in an article titled, "Brief History of Randolph Street Colored Methodist Church of Lexington, Virginia," October 18, 1924, Withrow Scrapbook, vol. 13, 50, Special Collections, Leyburn Library, Washington and Lee University, Lexington, Virginia. Theodore C. DeLaney noted that Holmes "joined the Methodist Episcopal Church and became a prominent minister" (DeLaney, "Aspects of Black Religious and Educational Development in Lexington," 143).

79. From an article in the *Baltimore Sun,* September 8, 1963, courtesy of the Stonewall Jackson House. There is a handwritten note attached to the

article signed by H. A. Preston making mention of the connection with the Sunday-school class.

80. Moore was a U.S. congressman representing the Rockbridge County area from 1833 to 1835.

81. From Withrow Scrapbook, vol. 18, 123–24 (file notes of June 28, 1931), Special Collections, Leyburn Library, Washington and Lee University, Lexington, Virginia.

82. Ibid.

83. Ibid.

84. Ibid.

85. Ibid.

86. Ibid.

87. Ibid.

88. Ibid.

89. Ibid.

90. Ibid.

91. Ibid.

92. From an address by J. William Jones in an article in the *Southern Historical Society Papers* 35 (January–December 1907): 97. Jones was present for the unveiling of the Jackson statue, and according to a July 23, 1891, *Rockbridge County News* article, Jones "delivered his admirable lecture on the Christian Character of Stonewall Jackson in the Presbyterian Church on Sunday night [prior to the unveiling] to a large congregation." This first contribution is also noted in an undated article by Isabel Arnold—"Stonewall Jackson—He being dead yet speaketh," courtesy of the West Virginia State Archives. Arnold stated, "We know that the first gifts for his monument in Lexington came from the negroes." She was a distant cousin of Jackson's.

93. Jones, *Christ in the Camp*, 88.

94. Many African Americans today still acknowledge Jackson's efforts in educating and evangelizing the slaves of Lexington. DeLaney, an associate professor of history at Washington and Lee University, stated, "A particularly religious man, [Jackson] . . . worked hard to evangelize slaves in the Lexington area" and that this effort involved "dedicated teachers who helped make it a success" (DeLaney, "Aspects of Black Religious and Educational Development in Lexington." 140). While DeLaney admits some good resulted from Jackson's efforts, he adds, "Unfortunately, the Sabbath school existed as a paternalistic institution that conveyed values which whites hoped to instill in the black participants" (ibid., 151).

95. Bean, *The Liberty Hall Volunteers,* 13.

96. Ibid., ix.

97. Bean, *Stonewall's Man,* 44.

98. Coulling, *Margaret Junkin Preston,* 91.

99. Ibid., 92.

100. Bean, *Stonewall's Man,* 44.

101. Coulling, 91.

102. Ibid.

103. Ibid., 92.

104. Hunter, *Lexington Presbyterian Church,* 99–100.

105. Smith, *History of the Virginia Military Institute* 169.

106. Hunter, *Lexington Presbyterian Church,* 100.

107. Margaret Preston asserted that the school ceased around 1887. Chambers also wrote that the school existed "to the middle 1880's."

108. Preston, "Religious Education of the Colored People of the South," 307.

109. Ibid., 314.

110. Ibid., 315.

111. Ibid., 323.

112. Bean, *The Liberty Hall Volunteers,* 131.

113. Ibid., 132n.

114. Coulling, *Margaret Junkin Preston,* 127.

115. Preston fathered ten children that survived childbirth: eight by his first wife, Sally Caruthers Preston, and two by his second wife, Margaret Junkin Preston. One son from Preston's first marriage, Thomas Lewis Preston, accepted the pastorate of Lexington Presbyterian Church in September 1883. At the University of Virginia, he studied under William McGuffey, author of the popular *McGuffey Readers.*

116. Hunter, *Lexington Presbyterian Church,* 81.

117. Ibid., 99.

118. Riley, *Stonewall Jackson,* 139, cited in Newman, "The African-American Experience in Thomas 'Stonewall' Jackson's Lexington," 98.

119. "Stonewall Jackson's Cook Still Loyal to Lost Cause," November 3, 1901, Withrow Scrapbook, vol. 16, p. 57, Special Collections, Leyburn Library, Washington and Lee University, Lexington, Virginia.

120. Newman, "The African-American Experience in Thomas 'Stonewall' Jackson's Lexington," 98.

121. Boley, *Lexington in Old Virginia,* 204.

122. "Stonewall Jackson's Cook Still Loyal to Lost Cause," November 3, 1901.

123. Boley, *Lexington in Old Virginia,* 204

124. Lewis Gravely Pedigo, untitled article, courtesy of the Stonewall Jackson House, Lexington, Virginia.

125. Boley, *Lexington in Old Virginia,* 204.

126. Newman, "The African-American Experience in Thomas 'Stonewall' Jackson's Lexington," 39.

127. William Spottswood White performed Jefferson and Mary's wedding ceremony.

CHAPTER 5: BY THEIR FRUITS YE SHALL KNOW THEM

1. Robertson, *Stonewall Jackson,* 722.

2. Ibid.

3. Ibid.

4. Shelor, "A Memorial to Stonewall Jackson." The article also appeared in the *Roanoke World-News.* See also "Dr. L. L. Downing, Colored Pastor Honors Stonewall Jackson," Stonewall Jackson House, Lexington, Virginia, which states, "Dr. Downing heard the praises of the great General from the lips of the people, both white and colored, throughout the community. . . . He came to regard 'Stonewall' Jackson . . . as one of the best friends the colored race ever had."

5. See Jackson, *Life and Letters of Stonewall Jackson,* 182.

6. This school opened on September 12, 1927, with Lylburn preaching a "dedication sermon" the previous day. Enrollment was comprised of 182 students who attended grades one through nine. The school was "a center for black education, leadership, and community service."

7. From "Moments in Fifth Avenue History," presumably from a church bulletin of the Fifth Avenue Presbyterian Church, Roanoke, date and author unknown, which refers to Jackson as a "great man" and confirms that Downing's visits to the cemetery where Jackson was buried, along with his reverence for Jackson, made him "determined to erect a monument to the distinguished General who was so beloved by the people of Lexington."

8. Ibid.

9. DeLaney, "Aspects of Black Religious and Educational Development in Lexington," 148.

10. "History of the Negro Baptist Church in Lexington, VA 1867–1980," 125th Anniversary booklet, First Baptist Church, Lexington, 1992.

11. "Moments in Fifth Avenue History," Roanoke.

12. From a Fifth Avenue Presbyterian Church history booklet that included a foreword by Downing, published at the time of the church's twenty-fifth anniversary. The article was reprinted in the church's commemorative one-hundredth-anniversary booklet in 1992.

13. U.S. Department of the Interior, National Park Service, National Register of Historic Places, Lylburn Downing School, Lexington, Virginia.

14. Fifth Avenue Presbyterian Church history booklet.

15. Fifth Avenue Presbyterian Church, one-hundredth-anniversary booklet.

16. This was the first African American church in America to honor a Confederate hero. The gesture attracted nationwide attention.

17. In 1906, the lecture room in Lexington—which had been built in 1835 and had housed the black Sunday school for all its years of operation—was torn down.

18. Shelor, "A Memorial to Stonewall Jackson."

19. Ibid.

20. Courtesy of the Stonewall Jackson House, Lexington, Virginia. Used with permission of Gloria Downing Pope and Lewis C. Downing.

21. Downing was one of five founders of the Burrell Memorial Hospital in Roanoke. The hospital was built because black doctors could not, at that time, treat their patients in other Roanoke hospitals. Downing's obituary noted that he was the first African American physician to be named a member of the American College of Hospital Administrators and that he served as a first lieutenant during World War I. He died in May 1965.

22. The Stonewall Jackson Memorial, Inc. is today known as the Lee-Jackson Foundation. According to their Web site: "The Lee-Jackson Foundation of Charlottesville was founded in 1953 by the late Jay W. Johns, a successful Pennsylvania industrialist transplanted to Virginia, who became a great admirer of Generals Robert E. Lee and Thomas J. 'Stonewall' Jackson. He believed that both these Americans possessed distinguished traits of character that should be emulated by future generations. Since both these Virginians were involved in education, the Foundation honors them by working to increase educational opportunities for Virginia's youth. The Foundation has traditionally focused on scholarships as the best vehicle to encourage high school students to continue their education, and sponsors an annual essay competition to make its awards" (www.Lee-Jackson.org).

23. Edited for brevity, courtesy of the Stonewall Jackson House, Lexington, Virginia. Used with permission of Gloria Downing Pope and Lewis C. Downing.

24. "Dr. L.L. Downing, Colored Pastor, Honors Stonewall Jackson," courtesy of the Stonewall Jackson House, Lexington, VA. For a number of years, Jackson's home in Lexington was used as a hospital.

25. *Norfolk Journal and Guide*, February 27, 1937.

26. Bill Reinhold, "Living with Jackson—A Sermon of John 4:3–42," Fifth Avenue Presbyterian Church, Roanoke, VA.

27. Ibid.

28. Ibid.

29. Ibid.

30. Ibid.

31. From an article in the *Roanoke Times and World-News*, January 18, 1993.

Chapter 6: A Brother Beloved

1. Robertson, *Stonewall Jackson*, 290–91. See also Newman, "The African-American Experience in Thomas 'Stonewall' Jackson's Lexington," 37.

2. Robertson, *Stonewall Jackson*, 290.

3. Douglas, *I Rode with Stonewall*, 154.

4. Ibid., 154–55.

5. Robertson, *Stonewall Jackson*, 224.

6. From Couper, *One Hundred Years at VMI*, 4:79, as quoted by Robertson, *Stonewall Jackson*, 291.

7. From Smith, "Stonewall Jackson," 98, quoted by Newman, "The African-American Experience in Thomas 'Stonewall' Jackson's Lexington," 94. Smith, the son of a minister, was a divinity student on Jackson's staff.

8. Vandiver, *Mighty Stonewall*, 293.

9. Ibid., 457.

10. After the war, McGuire, a native of Winchester, became the chair of surgery in the Medical College of Virginia. He also became president of the American Medical Association in 1896.

11. Quoted from *Southern Historical Society Papers* 19 (1891): 311.

12. Douglas, *I Rode with Stonewall*, 155.

13. Jackson, *Life and Letters of Stonewall Jackson*, 288.

14. Vandiver, *Mighty Stonewall*, 321, 348, 353.

15. Jackson, *Memoirs of Stonewall Jackson*, 402.

16. Ibid., 370.

17. John Preston to Maggie Preston, December 5, 1861, in Allan, *The Life and Letters of Margaret Junkin Preston,* 122.

18. Jackson, *Memoirs of Stonewall Jackson,* 473.

19. Vandiver, *Mighty Stonewall,* 325

20. Alexander Swift Pendleton was the son of Brig. Gen. William Nelson Pendleton, rector of the Episcopalian Church in Lexington—the church founded by Francis Henney Smith and where Lee served as vestryman.

21. Bean, *Stonewall's Man,* 69.

22. Vandiver, *Mighty Stonewall,* 325.

23. Sandie Pendleton to Nancy Pendleton, October 26, 1862, as quoted in Bean, *Stonewall's Man,* 81.

24. Bean, *Stonewall's Man,* 213.

25. Ibid.

26. Ibid., 217.

27. Douglas, *I Rode with Stonewall,* 155.

28. *Lexington Gazette and Citizen,* December 17, 1875.

29. Robertson, *Stonewall Jackson,* 923.

30. An 1896 newspaper article in the Washington and Lee University's Leyburn Library's Special Collection notes that the neglect of the new cemetery was still a concern: "The colored citizens of Lexington are exercised about the neglected condition of their cemetery." See Withrow Scrapbook, vol. 13, 51–52.

31. Megan Haley Newman, curator of the Stonewall Jackson House, believes that the contractor who did some of the excavating and who was hired to move the remains was not thorough in his work and that many, if not most, of the remains were likely left in their original graves and homes were built over them. In an e-mail exchange on April 4, 2005, Washington & Lee history professor Theodore C. DeLaney agreed and wrote, "My family always said that a few shovels full of earth were taken from each grave to the new cemetery, it is doubtful that any skeletal remains were moved." DeLaney is an African American and a native of Lexington.

32. Vandiver, *Mighty Stonewall,* 369.

33. Ibid.

34. McGuire, "Death of Stonewall Jackson."

35. Robertson, *Stonewall Jackson,* 741.

36. Ibid., 742.

37. Anna Jackson's brother.

38. Robertson, *Stonewall Jackson*, 745.

39. Ibid., 746.

40. Ibid. Some physicians have recently examined the accounts of Hunter, Dabney, and Anna Jackson and have concluded that the cause of Jackson's death was not pneumonia but more likely a serious secondary infection—sepsis. One study concludes, "The organism responsible for Jackson's death was probably Group A *Streptococcus*" (Rozear and Greenfield, "Let Us Cross Over the River").

41. Jackson, *Life and Letters of Stonewall Jackson*, 467.

42. Robertson, *Stonewall Jackson*, 751.

43. Jackson, *Life and Letters of Stonewall Jackson*, 470.

44. Bean, *Stonewall's Man*, 118.

45. Sears, *Chancellorsville*, 448.

46. McGuire, "Last Wound of the Late Gen. Jackson (Stonewall)," 403–12, as quoted in Rozear and Greenfield, "Let Us Cross Over the River," 29–46.

47. Jackson, *Life and Letters of Stonewall Jackson*, 471.

48. Ibid., 470.

CHAPTER 7: GO HOME TO THEY FRIENDS

1. "Funeral Procession in Honor of Lieut. Gen. Thos. J. Jackson," *Richmond Daily Dispatch*, May 13, 1863.

2. This was the last horse acquired by Jackson, but his favorite remained Little Sorrel.

3. Bean, *Stonewall's Man*, 121.

4. "Funeral Procession in Honor of Lieut. Gen. Thos. J. Jackson," *Richmond Daily Dispatch*.

5. Randolph served briefly as the Confederate secretary of war; he was born at Thomas Jefferson's Monticello in Charlottesville. At the time of Jackson's death, he was a brigadier general in the army.

6. Bean, *Stonewall's Man*, 122.

7. Ibid,, 123.

8. "Funeral Procession in Honor of Lieut. Gen. Thos. J. Jackson," *Richmond Daily Dispatch*.

9. Ibid.

10. Jackson, *Life and Letters of Stonewall Jackson*, 475–76.

11. Ibid., 477.

12. Smith, *History of the Virginia Military Institute*, 140–41.

13. From the diary of cadet Charles T. Haigh, May 11, 1863, Manuscript #016, VMI archives, Lexington, VA.

14. Virginia Military Institute. *Register of the Officers and Cadets,* 7.

15. Dooley, "Gilt Buttons and the Collegiate Way," 33.

16. Eidsmoe, *Warrior, Statesman, Jurist for the South,* 35.

17. Dooley, "Gilt Buttons and the Collegiate Way," 34.

18. Smith, *History of the Virginia Military Institute,* 256.

19. Francis H. Smith to the mother of Cadet John J. Smith, March 1, 1856, VMI Archives, Lexington, VA.

20. Abram Fulkerson to Selina Fulkerson, May 18, 1863, Manuscript #0363, Fulkerson Family Papers, VMI Archives, Lexington, VA.

21. Sears, *Chancellorsville,* 242.

22. Smith, *History of the Virginia Military Institute,* 141–44.

23. VMI Archives.

24. Robertson, *Stonewall Jackson,* 761.

25. Ibid.

26. *Lexington Gazette,* May 20, 1863.

27. Bean, *Stonewall's Man,* 126.

28. Robertson, *Stonewall Jackson,* 761.

29. Ibid. See also Allan, *The Life and Letters of Margaret Junkin Preston,* 166.

30. Preston, "Stonewall Jackson's Colored Sunday School," 7.

Epilogue

1. Webb, *Born Fighting,* 246.

2. Reeves, "Many Blacks Take Pride in Southern Roots."

3. "Let Us Cross Over the River." Words and music by Robin and Linda Williams (New Music Times, Inc./Lime Kiln Arts, BMI).

Appendix 1: Steadfast unto the End

1. Sorrel means light brown or chestnut color. Little Sorrel was also known as Old Sorrel.

2. Robertson, *Stonewall Jackson,* 628.

3. Hopkins, *From Bull Run to Appomattox,* 208–9.

4. Robertson, *Stonewall Jackson,* page 922.

5. From a letter of Frederic Webster dated July 15, 1939, courtesy of the Virginia Military Institute (VMI) Museum and Archives. Webster died in 1946.

6. Ibid.

7. Some sources say Little Sorrel was thirty-seven when he died. Luther Hopkins suggested that he was possibly as old as thirty-nine, the same age as Jackson when he died.

8. Webster gives some detail as to how he came to possess Little Sorrel's bones: "The chief point of interest seems to be centered on how I came into possession of the skeleton. It was by the sweat of my brow—literally—and the kindly commission from a well-known southern gentleman, Colonel E. V. Randolph of Richmond, Va. He came to my studio on Pennsylvania Ave Washington, D.C., when the horse was still living and made all [the] arrangements for me to go to Richmond when the horse should surrender. A telegram was to advise me of the event. There were no telephones at that time—in 1886, if memory serves me correctly. Shortly thereafter, the expected event happened, and I arrived in Richmond the night before the thirty-six year old champion of years, died."

9. Webster, letter, July 15, 1939.

10. Ibid.

11. The Virginia Museum of Fine Arts is one of the buildings now occupying this site along with the National Headquarters of the United Daughters of the Confederacy, the Confederate Memorial Chapel, and the Virginia Historical Society. The chapel was one of only three of the original camp buildings left standing.

12. From a memorandum to VMI's board of visitors by VMI superintendent R. J. Marshall, May 3, 1949, courtesy of the VMI Museum and Archives. All evidence suggests that Little Sorrel's stuffed hide had remained in storage at the R. E. Lee Camp property until 1949.

13. Bill of lading, Dillner Transfer Co., Pittsburgh, PA, courtesy of the VMI Museum and Archives.

14. From a news release by the Carnegie Institute, Pittsburgh, PA, August 7, 1949, courtesy of the VMI Museum and Archives.

BIBLIOGRAPHY

Allan, Elizabeth Preston. *The Life and Letters of Margaret Junkin Preston.* Boston: Houghton Mifflin, 1903.

Arnold, Thomas Jackson. *Early Life and Letters of General Thomas J. Jackson, "Stonewall" Jackson, by His Nephew.* New York: Revell, 1916.

Bean, W. G. *The Liberty Hall Volunteers: Stonewall's College Boys.* Charlottesville: University Press of Virginia, 1964.

———. *Stonewall's Man: Sandie Pendleton.* Chapel Hill: University of North Carolina Press, 1959.

Boley, Henry. *Lexington in Old Virginia.* 1936. Reprint, Lexington, VA: Liberty Hall Press, 1974.

Brown, Katherine L. "Stonewall Jackson in Lexington." *Proceedings of the Rockbridge Historical Society* 9 (1982): 197–210.

Cable, G. W. "The Gentler Side of Two Great Southerners." *Century* 47, no. 2 (December 1893): 292–94.

Chambers, Lenoir. *Stonewall Jackson: The Legend and the Man.* 1959. 2 vols. Reprint, Wilmington, NC: Broadfoot, 1988.

Cook, Roy Bird. *The Family and Early Life of Stonewall Jackson.* 4th ed. Charleston, WV: Education Foundation, 1963.

Cook, Roy Bird. *Thomas J. Jackson: A God-fearing Soldier of the CSA.* Cincinnati: C. J. Krehbiel, 1961.

Coulling, Mary Price. *Margaret Junkin Preston: A Biography.* Winston-Salem, NC: John F. Blair, 1993.

Couper, William. *One Hundred Years at VMI.* 4 vols. Richmond: Garrett and Massie, 1939.

Dabney, Robert Lewis. *Life and Campaigns of Lieutenant General Thomas J. Jackson.* 1866. Reprint, Harrisonburg, VA: Sprinkle, 1983.

Day, Richard Ellsworth. *Rhapsody in Black: The Life Store of John Jasper.* Philadelphia: Judson Press, 1953.

DeLaney, Theodore C. "Aspects of Black Religious and Educational Development in Lexington, Virginia, 1840–1928." *Proceedings of the Rockbridge Historical Society* 10 (1983): 139–51.

Derry, Joseph T. *The Story of the Confederate States.* Richmond: Johnson Publishing, 1895.

Dooley, Edwin L. "Gilt Buttons and the Collegiate Way: Francis H. Smith as Antebellum Schoolmaster." *Virginia Cavalcade* 36 (Summer 1986): 33.

Douglas, Henry Kyd. *I Rode with Stonewall.* Chapel Hill: University of North Carolina Press, 1940.

Doyle, Thomas S. "Some Recollections of Stonewall Jackson by One of His Sunday School Pupils." *Columbia (S.C.) State,* n.d., courtesy of the Stonewall Jackson House, Lexington, Virginia.

Eidsmoe, John. *Warrior, Statesman, Jurist for the South: The Life, Legacy, and Law of Thomas Good Jones.* Harrisonburg, VA: Sprinkle Publications, 2003.

Falconbridge, Alexander. *An Account of the Slave Trade on the Coast of Africa.* London: Phillips, 1788.

Farrow, Anne, Joel Lang, and Jenifer Frank. *Complicity: How the North Promoted, Prolonged, and Profited from Slavery.* New York: Ballantine Books, 2005.

Farwell, Byron. *Stonewall: A Biography of General Thomas J. Jackson.* New York: Norton, 1992.

Federal Writers Project. "Ninety-Two-Year-Old Negro Tells of Early Life as Slave." In South Carolina Narratives, vol. 14, pt. 2. Born in Slavery: Slave Narratives from the Federal Writers' Project, 1936–1938. Washington, DC: Library of Congress, 2001–.

Galli, Mark. "Defeating the Conspiracy." *Christian History* 18, no. 2 (1999): 12–17.

Grant, George, and Karen Grant. *Best Friends: The Ordinary Relationships of Extraordinary People.* Nashville, TN: Cumberland House, 1998.

———. *Letters Home: Advice from the Wisest Men and Women of the Ages to Their Friends and Loved Ones.* Nashville, TN: Cumberland House, 1997.

———. *Shelf Life: How Books Have Changed the Destinies and Desires of Men and Nations.* Nashville, TN: Cumberland House, 1999.

Hatcher, William E. *John Jasper: The Unmatched Negro Philosopher and Preacher.* New York: Revell, 1908.

Hemphill, William Edwin, Marvin Wilson Schlegel, and Sadie Ether Engelbert. *Cavalier Commonwealth: History and Government of Virginia.* New York: McGraw-Hill, 1957.

Hill, Daniel H. "The Real Stonewall Jackson." *Century Magazine* 47 (February 1894).

Hopkins, Luther W. *From Bull Run to Appomattox.* 1908. Reprint, Stuarts Draft, VA: Virginia Gentleman Books, 2001.

Hunter, Robert F. *Lexington Presbyterian Church, 1789–1989.* Lexington: Lexington Presbyterian Church, 1991.

Jackson, Mary Anna. *Julia Jackson Christian.* Charlotte, NC: Stone & Barringer, 1910.

———. *Life and Letters of Stonewall Jackson—By His Wife.* 1892. Reprint, Harrisonburg, VA: Sprinkle, 1995.

———. *Memoirs of Stonewall Jackson by His Widow.* Louisville, KY: Prentice Press, 1895.

Jackson, Nancy Ann, and Linda Brake Meyers, comps. *Colonel Edward Jackson, 1759–1828, Revolutionary Soldier.* Franklin, NC: Genealogy Publishing Service, 1995.

Jones, J. William. *Christ in the Camp, or Religion in Lee's Army.* Richmond: B. F. Johnson, 1887.

Jordan, Ervin L., Jr. *Black Confederates and Afro-Yankees in Civil War Virginia.* Charlottesville: University Press of Virginia, 1995.

Lyle, Roster, Jr. "John Blair Lyle of Lexington and His 'Automatic Bookstore.'" *Virginia Cavalcade* 21 (Autumn 1971).

Mansfield, Stephen. *Then Darkness Fled: The Liberating Wisdom of Booker T. Washington.* Nashville, TN: Cumberland House, 1999.

McGuire, Hunter Holmes. "Death of Stonewall Jackson." *Southern Historical Society Papers* 14 (1886).

———. "Last Wound of the Late Gen. Jackson (Stonewall)—The Amputation of the Arm—His Last Moments and Death." *Richmond Medical Journal* (1866): 403–12.

McKim, Randolph H. *A Soldier's Recollections: Leaves from the Diary of a Young Confederate.* 1910. Reprint, Harrisonburg, VA: Sprinkle 1996.

Monsell, Helen Albee. *Young Stonewall: Tom Jackson.* Indianapolis: Bobbs-Merrill, 1953.

Morton, Oren F. *A History of Rockbridge County, Virginia.* 1920. Reprint, Baltimore: Regional Publishing Company, 1980.

Newman, Megan Haley. "The African-American Experience in Thomas 'Stonewall' Jackson's Lexington." The Stonewall Jackson House, Lexington, VA, 1994.

Pearson, E. Lynn. "Thy Kingdom Come: The Evangelical Stewards of

Antebellum Lexington, 1851–1861." Stonewall Jackson House, Lexington, VA, 1989.

Perry, John. *Lady of Arlington: The Life of Mrs. Robert E. Lee*. Sisters, OR: Multnomah, 2001.

Pitts, Charles F. Chaplains in Gray: The Confederate Chaplains' Story. 1957. Reprint, Concord, VA: Reenactors Missions for Jesus Christ, 2003.

Preston, John Thomas Lewis. "Religious Education of the Colored People of the South," *Southern Presbyterian Review*, April 1885, 305–23, which was republished from the *New Englander*, 1878.

Preston, Margaret Junkin. "Stonewall Jackson's Colored Sunday School Class." *Sunday School Times*, December 3, 1887. The article has been republished in its entirety as a nine-page appendix to Mary Anna Jackson, *Life and Letters of Stonewall Jackson—By His Wife*, 1892, repr., Harrisonburg, VA: Sprinkle, 1995.

Pryor, Sara Agnes Rice (Mrs. Roger A.). *The Mother of Washington and Her Times*. New York: Macmillan, 1903.

Raboteau, Albert J. *Slave Religion: The "Invisible Institution" in the Antebellum South*. New York: Oxford University Press, 1978.

Reeves, Jay. "Many Blacks Take Pride in Southern Roots." Associated Press. November 25, 2005.

Riley, Elihu S. *Stonewall Jackson: A Thesaurus of Anecdotes of and Incidents in the Life of Lieut.-General Thomas Jonathan Jackson, CSA*. Annapolis, MD: Riley's Historic Series, 1920.

Robertson, James I., Jr. *Stonewall Jackson: The Man, the Soldier, the Legend*. New York: Macmillan, 1997.

———. *Stonewall Jackson's Book of Maxims*. Nashville, TN: Cumberland House, 2002.

Rozear, Marvin P., and Joseph C. Greenfield Jr. "Let Us Cross Over the River: The Final Illness of Stonewall Jackson." *Virginia Magazine of History and Biography* (January 1995): 29–46.

Sears, Stephen W. *Chancellorsville*. Boston: Houghton Mifflin, 1996.

Shelor, Kathleen. "A Memorial to Stonewall Jackson—Stained Glass Window in Roanoke Church, Depicting Hero's Last Words, Recalls Tragedy of 73 Years Ago Today." *Richmond Times-Dispatch*, May 10, 1936.

Sidwell, Mark. "Stonewall Jackson's Black Sunday School and the Religious Instruction of Slaves." *Biblical Viewpoint* 28, no. 2 (1994): 88–97

Smith, Edward D. *Climbing Jacob's Ladder: The Rise of Black Churches in Eastern American Cities*. Washington, DC: Smithsonian Institution Press, 1988.

Smith, Francis H. *History of the Virginia Military Institute*. Lynchburg, VA: J. P. Bell, 1912.

Smith, James Power. "Stonewall Jackson." *Southern Historical Society Papers* (August 1920): 98.

Sweeney, Edwin. "Ruth Lightburn Bailer Recalls General J. A. J Lightburn as Century Mark Approaches." *Clarksburg Exponent-Telegram*, December 1, 1991.

Vandiver, Frank E. *Mighty Stonewall*. 1957. Reprint, College Station: Texas A&M University Press, 1974.

Virginia Military Institute. *Register of the Officers and Cadets of the Virginia Military Institute, Lexington, Va., July 1863*. Richmond: Macfarlane & Fergusson, 1963.

Walsh, Robert. *Notices of Brazil in 1828 and 1829*. 2 volumes. Boston: Richardson, Lord & Holbrook, 1831.

Washington, Booker T. *Up from Slavery: An Autobiography*. New York: Doubleday & Company, Inc., 1901.

Washington-Williams, Essie Mae. *Dear Senator: A Memoir by the Daughter of Strom Thurmond*. New York: ReganBooks, 2005

Webb, James. *Born Fighting: How the Scots-Irish Shaped America*. New York: Broadway Books, 2004.

White, William Spottswood. *The African Preachers*. 1849. Reprint, Harrisonburg, VA: Sprinkle, 1998.

———. *Rev. William S. White, D.D., and His Times (1800–1873): An Autobiography*. Richmond, VA: Presbyterian Committee of Publication, 1891.

Wise, Henry A. *Drawing Out the Man: The VMI Story*. Charlottesville: University Press of Virginia, 1978.

Wise, Jennings C. *Sunrise of the Virginia Military Institute as a School of Arms*. Lexington, VA: n.p., 1958.

Woodson, Carter G. *The Education of the Negro Prior to 1861*. Washington, DC: Associated Publishers, 1919.

Wyeth, John A. "Horrors of Camp Morton." *Southern Historical Society Papers* 18 (1890): 328–33.

INDEX